GW00542091

EDWARD J. BYRNE

Thomas J. Morrissey SJ

Edward J. Byrne, 1872-1941

THE FORGOTTEN ARCHBISHOP OF DUBLIN

the columba press

First published in 2010 by
the columba press
55A Spruce Avenue, Stillorgan Industrial Park,
Blackrock, Co Dublin

Cover by Bill Bolger
Origination by The Columba Press
Printed in Ireland by ColourBooks Ltd, Dublin

ISBN 978 1 85607 703 3

Contents

Preface

by
Archbishop Diarmuid Martin

Edward Byrne became Archbishop of Dublin at a difficult moment in Irish society and in Irish political life. From the outset of his episcopacy he was deeply saddened by the civil war and his inability to bring both sides together to prevent it.

Unlike his immediate predecessor, Archbishop Byrne could not be described as a political prelate. His entries into the political arena were most often inspired by his sense of pastoral care for individuals, especially those condemned to death, and for promoting harmony after the bitterness of the civil war.

His appointment while still a young priest as Vice-Rector of the Irish College in Rome was, however, an indication that he was considered a man of sound political judgement. At that time, the Irish College was not just a seminary but played a significant role in representing in Rome the political interests of the Irish church and indeed of the people of Ireland

Edward Byrne was above all a pastor. He had worked as a curate in the Pro-Cathedral Parish in Dublin's inner city at a time when poverty was rampant. He was greatly loved by the people of the parish. His interest in fostering the plans for Our Lady's Children's Hospital in Crumlin was typical of his very concrete concern for the poor, in this case hoping that the children of the newly developing areas in the south of a growing Dublin would get quality health care.

He was the pastor of a growing church. The churches which were built during his time as Archbishop are all of great character and warmth and, interestingly, have adapted well to the needs of liturgical renewal.

He was a reconciler. He attempted to bring the various sides in the civil war together in order to avoid bloodshed. An often overlooked dimension of the 1932 Eucharistic Congress was that it was one of the first major national events to bring together people of all sides just years after the civil war.

Sadly, Archbishop Byrne's health was to suffer greatly right from the earliest years of his episcopacy. He continued his ministry in so far as possible, even though his activity was accompanied by long suffering.

Edward Byrne was a reserved man. He did not seek the limelight. He was, however, a man of independent judgement and intellectual honesty. He kept his own political views to himself and the archives produce very little concrete evidence about what he himself actually felt about political issues. Fr Morrissey has done a wonderful job in capturing the reality of the life and the humanity of this reserved yet generous pastor of the church in Dublin.

Introduction

Edward Joseph Byrne lived in exciting times and knew many of the leading personalities but, apart from brief diary entries in his youth, he left scarcely any observations and very few letters.

He was born in 1872 and his early years were spent between a family farm in Co Wicklow and his mother's apartment in Dublin. He acquired a love of nature from his years in Wicklow that remained with him. A quiet, gentle boy, he was popular with both contemporaries and older people, while retaining something of the reserve of the only child, used to his own space and, in his case, to reading and drawing. Following education in Belvedere College and in Holy Cross College, Clonliffe, the diocesan seminary, he completed his studies for the priesthood in Rome as a student of the Pontifical Irish College. After ordination, he served for brief period in a number of parishes before being appointed vice-rector of the Irish College Rome by Archbishop Walsh. Already, he was being spoken of as a future bishop. After a little more than two years, he was appointed to the archbishop's parish, centred on the Pro-Cathedral, Marlborough Street. He served there for sixteen years: a period that included the great strike/lock-out of 1913 and the 1916 Rising. He shunned the spotlight and worked quietly in the background, known mainly for the quality of his sermons and for devotion to and empathy with the poor of Dublin. In 1920 he was consecrated bishop by Archbishop Walsh, and succeeded him a year later as the country moved towards civil war. His was a widely acclaimed appointment, not least among the poor of the city. Six feet in height and straight-shouldered, it was noted that he carried the mantle of authority with dignity and ease.

One of Edward Byrne's first challenging tasks was to join with the Lord Mayor, Laurence O'Neill, in convening a meeting

of the leaders of the pro-Treaty and anti-Treaty sides. Their efforts towards conciliation failed. Following a general election
which supported the Treaty, the archbishop, reluctantly, joined
Cardinal Logue and the other bishops in denouncing the armed
resistance of the anti-Treaty supporters. In spite of that, he appealed, whenever requested, on behalf of republican prisoners
in special need, and challenged William Cosgrave at times on
the action and policy of government.

His episcopate was noted for the number of churches and
schools he opened to meet the needs of the expanding population of Dublin. But before long, it became evident that he was
suffering from a form of motor neuron disease. Despite that, he
continued in office and supervised two of the great events of the
first half of the twentieth century – the celebration of the Centenary
of Catholic Emancipation in 1929, and the International Eucharistic
Congress in 1932 with its co-celebration of 1500 years of
Christianity in Ireland. Not a dynamic man of action, Edward
Byrne had the gift of moulding and inspiring people to work together, and of keeping to the forefront the spiritual significance
of the events. The combination of lay planning and organisation,
the zeal of the Dublin clergy, and the co-operation of the other
bishops resulted, first, in the outstanding co-ordination and dignity of the Centenary Celebrations – described by Cosgrave as
the proudest day of his life – and then in the devotion, organisation and involvement of the entire Catholic population in the
Eucharistic Congress, which involved all classes and, more than
any other factor, contributed to easing the divisions of the Civil
War.

In the 1930s, the archbishop continued to give active support
to the key lay bodies, the Catholic Truth Society, the Society of St
Vincent de Paul, the Catholic Young Men's Society, and An
Ríoghacht in its proclamation of Catholic social teaching. These
were the years of the communist threat, the Economic War, the
divisions associated with the Spanish Civil War, and the new
Irish Constitution. Dr Byrne continued to attend public functions for as long as he could, despite the pain and humiliation of
his physical decline. In his final years, he could no longer perform
public ceremonies and was largely confined to his residence. He
remained, however, cheerful, patient, and mentally alert and,

indeed, played an important role in approving De Valera's Constitution. At his death there were remarkable expressions of appreciation of the man and of the bishop. All sections mourned his passing, and the poor of Dublin wept in the streets.

Acknowledgements
In researching this book, I have been encouraged by the support and interest of the present Archbishop of Dublin, Dr Diarmuid Martin, who has also kindly written the Preface. I am also deeply indebted to the following: Noelle Dowling of the Dublin Diocesan Archives; Albert McDonnell, vice-rector of the Irish College Rome, and archivist, Martin Fagan, of the Irish College Rome; Fergus O'Donoghue SJ, and Damien Bourke of the Irish Jesuit Archive; the archivists of University College Dublin ; the staff of the National Archives of Ireland, and of the Archives of the National Library of Ireland; the archivists of Killaloe Diocesan Archives and of the Armagh Diocesan Archives, the McRory papers; the archivist of the Kildare and Leighlin Archives; the staff of the Limerick Diocesan Archives; and Fr Marcel Chappin SJ, archivist of the Archives of the Secretariat of State, the Vatican. Other Sources are mentioned in the Notes.

The book also owes much to the assistance of the late Monsignor Michael Nolan, who gave me the benefit of his long acquaintance with Dublin diocesan history, and I was helped by the advice of Fr Seán Farragher, Blackrock College, and Mgr Christy O'Dwyer, Cashel. I have also enjoyed the assistance of the staff of Maynooth College Library and, on many occasions, of the librarians of Milltown Park Library.

It remains to thank the rector and members of the Jesuit community at Manresa Centre of Spirituality for their on-going support; to thank Eileen Toomey and Valerie Corrigan for their generosity in copying so many manuscripts, and Joseph Murray for his ready remedying of computer problems. Finally, a heart-felt expression of gratitude to my three patient and selfless readers – Sr Maria Mullen, and historians Fr Fergal O'Donoghue SJ, and Dr Dáire Keogh. Needless to say, any mistakes in the text are of my own making. A pleasant feature in writing this book has been the attention and enthusiasm of Seán O Boyle of The Columba Press and the expertise of his staff.

ABBREVIATIONS AND SOURCES:

ADA   Armagh Diocesan Archives, O'Fiaich Memorial
       Library: Cardinal Logue, Cardinal O'Donnell, and
       Cardinal MacRory papers.
DDA   Dublin Diocesan Archives: Abp Byrne, and Mgr
       Cronin papers.
KDA   Killaloe Diocesan Archives: Bp Fogarty papers.
LDA   Limerick Diocesan Archives: Bp Hallinan and Bp Keane
       papers.
ICRA   Irish College Rome Archives: Tobias Kirby papers,
       William Murphy papers, and especially John Hagan
       papers.
IJA   Irish Jesuit Archives: Frs John Fahy and Michael
       Browne papers.
NAI   National Archives of Ireland: Taoiseach's Dept. The
       Dept of Foreign Affairs.
NLI   National Library of Ireland: Shane Leslie papers. Hanna
       Sheehy-Skeffington papers, letters to.
UCDA   University College Dublin Archives: De Valera papers,
       MacSwiney papers, Patrick McGilligan papers,
       FitzGerald papers, Mulcahy papers.
ICD   *Irish Catholic Directory.*

THE PRELUDE

The Years Before the Archbishopric 1872-1921

CHAPTER ONE

1872-1895

Early Years. Education – Belvedere, Clonliffe, Rome.
Political Interests. Ordination

On 28 October 1920, Edward J. Byrne, a curate, was consecrated bishop in Dublin. He had spent most of his life as a priest in the overcrowded parish of Marlboro Street; 'no better training ground', in the opinion of the *Freeman's Journal*, for a future bishop in Dublin. 'He knows its life and the difficulties and dangers and needs of that life through and through.' For the Catholics of Dublin, 'he is all their own, a Dubliner of the Dubliners, graced by the culture of old Rome. Their good wishes and prayers will accompany him in his labours ... Politically, his Lordship's episcopate starts in dark and evil days whatever be the harvest of the future. God knows we are sowing it in tears of blood ...'

* * *

Edward was born in Dublin on 10 May 1872, the only child of Edward and Ellen Byrne. His father had a farm on Lord Carysfort's estate at Killahurler, Co Wicklow, about six miles from the town of Arklow. His mother was formerly Ellen Maguire of Ballytegue, Co Wexford.[1] To judge by their respective correspondence, she was better educated than her husband and was ambitious to succeed in business. More at home in the city than on the farm, she devoted much of her time and energy to working in a millinery establishment in Dublin and, in 1889, to establishing her own business in women's fashionable clothes at No 16 Nassau Street,[2] and travelling seasonally to London to buy stock in keeping with the latest fashion. She lived much of the year in accommodation in Dublin. Both parents loved and cared for their only child, without spoiling him. They passed on to him their strong religious faith.

Edward's diary, one of the few sources for his early years, indicates that he grew up on the farm and returned there at school holidays. His entries demonstrate no sign of hard work on the land or with stock. His parents' hopes for him extended beyond the subsistence provided by his father's holding. He had happy memories of his early years and holidays at Killahurler. He wrote of finding birds eggs, of 'counting sheep and cattle with Papa', going to the hayfield and the bog, and fishing in the river. He learned to ride a pony, and generally acquired a love of nature and the countryside. It would later be recalled that as archbishop he 'knew the names of every flower by the wayside from Dublin to Wicklow'.[3]

As an only child, he learned to occupy himself and be relatively self-sufficient. He admitted being very lonely on one occasion, but a few days later was happy in his own company: 'After Mass in Johnstown, drove to Arklow, sat on the strand, calm sea, a very fine day'.[4] He never had to fight his corner in the hurly-burley of a large family, and turned out a gentle and reflective, yet lively and cheerful boy, most at ease in the company of a few chosen friends yet generally popular. The companions of his schooldays spoke of his 'unfailing high spirits and good comradeship'.[5]

Schooling
It is not clear where Edward's early schooling took place. It was certainly with the Sisters of Mercy, and was probably in Arklow or Dublin. He appears to have been a lively, even mischievous pupil.[6] In 1883, at the age of eleven, he went to Belvedere College Dublin for his secondary education. He stayed at his mother's accommodation. He did well at school, though he was punished from time to time. Some of the punishment he thought unfair, and he felt that generally there was too much physical punishment.[7] From his diary it is evident that outside of the classroom he 'practised music', did some sketching and painting – for which he had an aptitude – and played chess, draughts, whist, marbles, collected stamps, and read *Boys Own* paper, and *Robinson Crusoe*. In addition he played some cricket, tennis, and football, watched the races at Mountjoy Square while military bands played, and with his mother visited the Zoo, had dinner, and listened to the band of the 1st Cornwall Regiment. All in all, a normal enough boyhood for a middle-class pupil at Belvedere.

Edward was at the college during the rectorship of the celebrated Fr Tom Finlay, who generated an atmosphere of work and competition in the school.[8] Edward adapted well. Despite several weeks' absence from school, due to an unexplained illness in the autumn of 1886, he proved very successful the following year when he sat the Junior Intermediate Examination. He had the distinction of winning one of the few first class exhibitions accorded in those days by the Intermediate Board for all Ireland. Not surprisingly, it was an occasion for pride and congratulations from his family, relatives and friends.[9]

At the end of his time in Belvedere, Edward had mixed feelings. He was an exhibitioner and prize winner at school, and yet, as mentioned, had been punished from time to time and sometimes unfairly, in his view. His sense of grievance, however, seems to have been balanced by the overall kindness and training he had received, the knowledge imparted to him, the camaraderie, and the friendliness and dedication of his teachers despite the occasional too vigorous exactions of some. As a result, he later readily acknowledged his debt to his old school and old masters, and became president of the Belvedere College Union, 1922-1925, and vice-president from 1925-1939.[10] Moreover, as archbishop, from 1922-1940, he subscribed to and was president of the Belvedere Social Club, later the Belvedere Newsboys' Club, which catered for young boys selling newspapers on the streets of Dublin and provided them with material and spiritual assistance, basic education and opportunities for games and relaxation.[11] He also imbibed something of the Jesuit spirituality, in terms of detachment or inner freedom and including devotion to the Sacred Heart, and seems to have availed of Jesuits as spiritual advisers during much of his life.

The Years in Clonliffe College

That September, 1887, aged 15 years, Edward entered Holy Cross College Clonliffe, a seminary for aspirants to the priesthood in the Dublin archdiocese. Strangely, he was accompanied to the college, not by his parents, but by a family friend, William MacMullen. At his new college, Edward continued his secondary schooling and sat the matriculation examination for entry to the Royal University of Ireland, an examining body of which Clonliffe was a recognised college. By the standards of a later age, fifteen was too young to enter a seminary and to make a life-long commitment. At the time, however, it was not unusual to accept fifteen-year-olds who seemed well-motivated and had an aptitude for study.

Holy Cross College was a boarding school with regulations unfamiliar to Edward: early rising, fixed spiritual duties, fixed times for meals and study as well as classes, all regulated by a bell. In addition, there was only limited contact with relatives and friends, and no newspapers. Radios did not yet exist. It was a secluded world with somewhat Spartan conditions. He suffered from chilblains, sore throat, and 'bilious attacks', and missed family and friends, Italian opera and other cultural outlets.[12] Yet, in a letter to William Mac Mullen he announced that he was 'well and happy in Clonliffe' and not upset by early rising. Mac Mullen counselled: 'Persevere, my boy, with God's assistance, in the glorious calling in which you have entered.' He concluded with the observation that it must be a great day for him, 'the visit of Monsignor Persico and the bishops who have been invited to meet his Excellency'.[13] He asked Edward to write him a long letter about it.

Monsignor Ignatius Persico was a member of the Capuchin order, who had arrived in Dublin on 7 July as Papal Envoy to Ireland. Three days after McMullen's letter, on 21 October, Edward's father informed him of a great demonstration at Arklow for the visit, as he expressed it, of 'The Archbishop Walsh and Cardinal Prescoe'.[14] Both references presupposed Edward's interest in socio-political matters.

Political interests
That interest was borne out by entries in his diary. On 7 April 1886, he had recorded: 'Great excitement through the city inconsequence of Mr Gladstone proposing his great Home Rule Bill in the House of Commons.' His interest survived the defeat of the Bill. On Easter Sunday, 10 April 1887, he attended a 'Plan of Campaign' meeting at Coolgreny, Co Wicklow. The 'Campaign' was very much part of Irish life during his years at Clonliffe. It was an agrarian movement that had seized the public imagination in many parts of the country. Aimed at protecting tenants unable to pay their rents, it did so by having the tenants in a landlord's estate bargain collectively. Where a landlord refused to lower his demands, the combined tenants were to offer him reduced rents. If he declined to accept these, the tenants were to pay no rents, and the money they were prepared to pay became an 'estate fund' for the maintenance and protection of the tenants likely to be evicted for their action. In the case of someone

bidding for the land where an eviction occurred, he was to be boycotted, shunned by his neighbours, in Parnell's words, 'as if he were a leper of old'. Archbishop Walsh of Dublin caused something of a sensation by refusing to condemn the Plan of Campaign and declaring that there was right on both sides and that 'the maintenance of social order' required that 'rent-fixing' be 'dealt with by some authority independent of both'.[15]

The arrival of Monsignor Persico heralded Rome's investigation of complaints against the operation of the Plan of Campaign. Anxiety was felt among some of the Irish bishops, not least Dr Walsh of Dublin, about the outcome of the envoy's investigation. The interest of the seminarians was likely to have been stimulated by the Envoy's arrival and by the sense of uncertainty about his report to Rome.

Daily life goes on
Irrespective of the Papal Envoy's mission, life continued as usual at the seminary. Edward's diary made reference to his studies, which included philosophy, his companions, walks undertaken together, games, and to his reading poetry by Shakespeare and the Irish novelist, dramatist and poet, Gerald Griffin (1803-1840). On Sundays and special church feasts, the seminarians in their black suits made their way to the Pro-Cathedral in Marlboro Street to attend Mass and other ceremonies. Edward's mother made an effort to attend whenever her son was present. Occasionally she apologised for not attending, and her apologies conveyed something of the religious atmosphere in which Edward was brought up. In November 1887 she could not attend because she was attending the mission being given by the Redemptorist Fathers, who were 'splendid preachers'. His father attended 'twice a day'. She was still attending the mission in December. The following spring she was not present because it coincided with her 'sodality morning'. She had been at 7 o'clock Mass, and did not feel up to going out again.[16]

In April 1888, writing from her new address, 2 Monders Building, Cullenswood Avenue, in the suburb of Ranelagh, she told of the illnesses of some of their relatives and added unsympathetically: 'I am in as bad health myself as any of them, and at the same time I'm obliged to be on my feet all day and have a deal of anxiety on my mind.' Her business interests probably occasioned part of her anxiety, but there was also the matter of

Edward's boarding fees and additional costs. Extant bills for April and July 1888 mention a pension of £30, and charges for further items: Medicine, 2 shillings and 2 pence (2/2), Doctor 11/-, (these, perhaps related to his 'bilious attacks'), barber 3/-, Washing 30/-, Intermediate Certificate 10/-. She tried to cut down on excessive expenditure. When Edward spoke of £2.10.0 for a new coat, she considered it too expensive and told him that when he was home at Christmas his father would get a tailor to look after him. She also reminded him to bring home any clothes that needed mending.

In her letter in which she referred to her health and anxiety, she added succinctly: 'I enclose all the scraps I can lay my hands on about the Pope and the Plan of Campaign. The world will be on fire about it.' Although the seminarians were not allowed read newspapers, a blind eye was turned to cuttings sent in the post. Her remarks referred to the Pope's condemnation of the Plan of Campaign following Monsignor Persico's report and the anger it roused. The situation necessarily excited attention and concern among the clergy, a concern felt by Edward and his fellow seminarians.

Reaction to the Papal condemnation
On 23 April 1888, the Holy Office decreed, with the approval of Pope Leo XIII, that 'a rent fixed by mutual consent cannot, without violation of contract, be reduced to the arbitrary will of the tenant alone', and that boycotting 'was altogether foreign to natural justice and Christian charity', a 'new form of persecution and proscription' against persons (who) agreed to pay rent to their landlords or persons who exercised 'their right to vacant farms'.

There was some appreciation of Rome's objections to boycotting, but intense anger at the reference to 'rent fixed by mutual consent' which assumed the tenant was an equal and free partner and showed a misunderstanding of the Irish situation. The extent of the public anger was graphically conveyed by Archbishop Croke of Cashel, in a letter to Monsignor Tobias Kirby, rector of the Irish College Rome, on 6 June 1888: 'The Pope is cursed in every mood and tense from Donegal to Baltimore; and wherein his picture was found in private houses, it has been either displaced simply or torn to bits.'[17] Archbishops Walsh and Croke endeavoured to put the best possible construction on the Roman decision in order to assuage the bitter hostility. The public reaction was a further reminder to bishops, priests and seminarians that obedience to Rome did not apply when it came to serious political and economic issues. It was a reminder that Edward Byrne tried to keep in mind during his career.

Scarcely had the public mood quietened when another issue captured attention. In 1889 the *Times* produced letters accusing Parnell of complicity in the Phoenix Park murders, seven years previously, of the Chief Secretary, Frederick Cavendish, and his Under Secretary, Thomas Burke. A commission was appointed to investigate the allegation. A star witness, who helped to prove the letters were forgeries and to identify the forger, was Edward's archbishop, Dr William Walsh. Edward's father wrote to him on 9 May 1889, 'I know you will like to see the evidence of the Archbishop ... I will send you the whole of his evidence as soon as it comes out.' He added that they had moved house again. They had taken 'a very nice apartment in Sandymount, 11 Leahy Terrace, right besides the Star of the Sea Catholic church'. He anticipated that they would have 'a jolly time' when Edward arrived. They could have any amount of sea bathing and they were 'convenient to all amusement'.

Meantime, and until 1891, Edward worked hard for a B.A. in philosophy. His mother worried that he was working too hard; but, on 9 May 1990, the eve of his birthday, she reminisced happily, 'I must not forget this night and tomorrow morning 18 years ago, the first day you saw the light of day. I thank God he has favoured me with a good and dutiful child.' She was sending him a 'parcel of goodies' and his father would visit him and tell him all the news

Some of the news had to concern Charles Stewart Parnell, for whom Wicklow people had a special regard. His family was greatly respected as good landlords and employers.[18] Parnell's relationship with Mrs O'Shea led to a split in the Irish Parliamentary Party, as a result of which the majority of the party, supported by the Catholic bishops, opposed Parnell's leadership. The country was deeply divided. The Catholic clergy were strongly critical of Parnell, except for a small number, especially in Wicklow and Wexford, who stood by him. Anti-clericalism came to the forefront as priests were hooted in the streets of Cork, an assault was attempted on the bishop, and a shot was fired at John Healy, Bishop of Clonfert.[19] For all his

seclusion and the single-mindedness of his preparation for the
BA examination, Edward had some awareness of the depths of
division. In February 1890, his father sent him a newspaper account of William O'Brien's speech in parliament, which he described as worth reading. As the struggle continued into 1891,
Edward became anxious to learn the state of public opinion. His
mother, in reply, sadly informed him on 13 March 1891: 'I fear
poor Parnell is losing ground' and, fearful perhaps of the impact
on her son, she continued, 'Whatever will happen I hope it will
be for the best – the bishops and priests ought to know better
than we do – there has been a large meeting of clergy in Dublin
all condemning Parnell as leader.' As regards herself, she was
feeling much better since her visit to the doctor in London.[20]

The Graduate
In the early summer of 1891, Edward sat his BA examinations in
philosophy. The results were announced towards the end of
July. He did well but not brilliantly. His results were: Logic,
55%; Metaphysics, 72%; Ethics, 60%; History of Philosophy,
63%. Congratulations came from his parents and various relatives and friends.[21] He and his mother took a holiday in Wales.

Death of Parnell
Early in October 1891, the news broke that Parnell had died. The
sense of shock and grief was palpable in the capital city. It was
something that Edward and his companions were unlikely to
forget. All sides mourned the loss and, despite the discourage-
ment of the clergy, thousands of mourners followed Parnell's remains to his burial place in Glasnevin cemetery: a further reminder
of O'Connell's dictum – the people 'take their religion from
Rome but their politics from home'.

Looking ahead
In the final part of the year, Edward's major concerns were related to
his first year of theology studies and to his fracturing his wrist in a
serious accident. By the following summer the fracture was well
healed, and he learned that he and his fellow-student, Michael
Cronin, were to continue their theological studies at the Irish
College Rome. Cronin was considered a brilliant student, and the
fact that Edward was chosen to go with him indicated that he was
viewed as academically above average, and as having other qualities that would make him acceptable in the Irish College.

A student in Rome

For Edward's parents, who had moved to another address, this time in the Dublin suburb of Rathmines, his departure was deeply felt, especially by his father whose health had become fragile. Despite the developments in rail and sea travel, Rome seemed to him a great distance away. As Edward journeyed to mainland Europe, he was twenty years of age, a handsome young man, six feet in height, and with blue eyes.[22] He and Michael Cronin had received bursaries from their archbishop. The Dublin diocesan bursary accounts noted that the yearly pension for Byrne and Cronin was £45 each for the years 1893-1895.[23]

Edward left no account of his first impressions of Rome and of the Irish College. He could have had no doubts about the significance of the college for the Irish church. An Irish college was established in Rome as far back as 1628, and served both as a seminary and as the focus of Irish Catholic interests in Rome until Ireland formed diplomatic relations with the Holy See. At the time of Edward's arrival, however, the college was in something of a decline. Its student capacity was 70 students, but attendance had fallen to less than 35. Many of the Irish bishops were not sending students. The Irish College was seen as expensive compared to home-based seminaries, Rome's climate was thought to be deleterious and, moreover, academic performance and discipline had declined in recent decades. Irish students, indeed, had a reputation of being difficult to manage, especially in Propaganda College where they took their lectures. The rector of the Irish College, Michael Kelly, who was appointed in 1891 as heir to the aging and long established Tobias Kirby, endeavoured to attract greater numbers and to raise academic and disciplinary standards. He had been a student at the college, spoke Italian fluently, and was determined to make a success of his rectorship. He had been reminded by Bishop Abraham Brownrigg, of Ossory, who had been instrumental in his appointment, that he faced 'a difficult and perhaps unpleasant duty'. One of his ways of fulfilling that duty was to run a strict and authoritarian regime. As a result, he was not the most approachable of rectors.[24]

He experienced no difficulties, however, with his two Dublin students. At the end of Edward's first year in the college, his rector described as *Bene* (good, satisfactory) his piety, his work in Latin, Greek, Italian, English, his theological studies, and his general discipline. The theology followed was that of Thomas Aquinas, but without the narrowness that was to prevail under Pope Leo XIII's successor. In Edward's second year, *Bene* continued; but the academic reports from the College of Propaganda Fide, which had students from across the world, declared him among the top students in ecclesiastical history, doing very well in dogmatic, sacramental, and moral theology – scoring 18-20 out of 20, but not so well in sacred scripture – 15 out of 20. In his third year in the college, and his fourth year of theology, his rector raised *Bene* to *Optime*, and, scoring out of 10 in his academic studies, he received 9½, 10, 10, and 8½ for, respectively, dogmatic, sacramental, moral theology, and sacred scripture.[25]

He featured among those receiving special recognition from the Pontifical College of Propaganda Fide in 1894. He could not reach the standard of his fellow Irish student, Michael Cronin, who was in the top place in all subjects, but in 1894, showing some divergence from the scores above, he was among those who came close to the top three or four outstanding scholars in sacred scripture, an indication, perhaps, of how he had attended to that subject in that year, and in sacramental theology, while meriting only *Laudate*, or a pass mark, in dogmatic theology.[26]

At the end of his time as a student at the Irish College, Fr Michael Kelly announced, on 16 June 1895: 'Rev D. Edward J. Byrne was a student of the college from October 1892 to June 1895 inclusive, (and) undertook theological studies in that period *maxime cum laude*' (with high praise, or honours).[27]

At a later stage it was remarked that, during his time in Rome, Edward was keenly interested in the city's pagan and Christian history. He could not fail to be impressed by the ruins, architecture, engineering and sculptures of Imperial Rome as well, of course, by current Rome's institutional pomp and ceremony, its vast store of Christian art and literature, its splendid basilicas and churches. His diaries and notebooks, however, make scant reference to such features, though they do provide an insight into his studies, his more general reading, and his facility in drawing.

A black copy book, dated November 1892, contains lectures on the sacraments in Latin, and material on moral theology, but he brightened the pages with drawings and the words of the ballad *Shan Van Vocht*.[28] A further notebook has, in English, 'Instruction on Scandal' and notes in Latin, but it also has a number of quite skilful drawings of heads, many with prominent Roman noses.[29] Yet another copybook contains notes on moral theology, but also a quotation entitled 'St Theresa's bookmark', which may represent something of his spiritual aspirations and need at the time:

> Let nothing disturb thee, nothing affright thee, all things are passing,
> God never changeth. Patient endurance attaineth to all things. Who
> God possesseth in nothing is wanting, alone God sufficeth.

Inside the back cover he had quite a life-like sketch of a bishop or other church dignitary in full regalia.[30]

Further notebooks are concerned with lectures and material in Latin or Italian, except for a stout, brown-backed copybook devoted to Memorabilia, quotations from poets and others about personalities, places, national views, causes and events. It contains entries from his student days until 1938, but it is not easy to distinguish what comes from an earlier rather than a later period. There is evidence, irrespective of period, of a habit of wide reading. Among those quoted are Shakespeare, Byron, Coleridge, Tennyson, George Eliot, Mathew Arnold, Jonathan Swift, and Darcy McGee. A strong sense of national identity and patriotism runs through many of the quotations and some have the pathos of an exile. He quotes Darcy McGee:

> A shell from the shores of Ireland would be dearer far to me
> Than all the wines of the Rhineland or the art of Italie

He goes to Swift's *Drapier Letters* for 'Ireland's Rights'; and he quotes James Clarence Mangan's 'Irish National Hymn' with all the idealism of a young man. Under the heading 'Ireland's Vocation', he draws on Mangan:

> Oh Ireland! be it thy high duty
> To teach the world the might of moral beauty
> And stamp God's image truly on the struggling soul.

Again, perhaps a young man's concern, he notes concerning 'taste in art' that 'taste is defined as intuition plus experience'. Finally, in those years and later, there almost had to be quotations referring to the 'old enemy'. Hence, it is not surprising to find attributed to Daniel O'Connell, with whom the Irish

College had a long association: 'The Englishman has all the qualities of a poker except its occasional warmth.'[31]

A letter from Capri on 2 April, no year given, suggests moments of relaxation away from Rome. He was feeling alone, but he was enjoying the sun and studying. He mentioned that he had written to Dr Donnelly, Auxiliary Bishop of Dublin, to tell him where he was. It is not clear when he met Bishop Donnelly, but the latter took a personal interest in Edward's progress and well-being.[32]

A Letter Home

At some time while Edward was in Rome, his father was virtually disabled by an accident, or some other cause, to one of his feet. This circumstance, plus the fact that Edward was due to be ordained deacon later that year[33] probably accounted for the sale of the family land and premises in Co Wicklow on 1 June 1894. The first extant letter from Edward to his father was dated March 1895. Edward senior had been concerned at news that his son was unwell. Edward's rather ordinary reply of 26 March conveys his relaxed manner of writing to his parents. As so few of his letters have survived from these years, this is given in full.

> My dear Father,
> I received Mother's letter yesterday and was so sorry that you were so anxious about me. I was a little weak for a week or so but after that got all right again. I am now, thank God, as well as ever again. The hot weather is just beginning with us here and I need not tell you how glad I am to have the cold weather over. I sincerely hope that your foot is improving. I am sure you must find it very trying to be in the house for such a long time. I have not forgotten to remember you in my prayers. I trust you will very soon be able to be about again as usual.
>
> It is not necessary for me to tell you that I am looking forward anxiously to the time I shall see you all again. Say a prayer for me sometimes that I may be worthy of the last great grace that the good God is so soon to bestow upon me.
>
> I received with many thanks the shamrocks dear Mother sent me on St Patrick's Day. I was delighted to get a sprig of our national emblem. I suppose Mother started for London yesterday. I hope she will have a pleasant journey and that she

will not be too much fatigued as she usually is. His Grace, the Archbishop of Dublin, arrived here yesterday evening. He is only going to stay a fortnight in Rome. I believe our old friend the Influenza is raging away in Dublin. It appears to be all over the world and is very prevalent in Rome at present, so much so that we have been dispensed from all fast and abstinence

Tell Mother when she returns that two ancient ladies by the name of Haly called on me; they told me they had promised her to give me a call. Is there any truth in the rumour that there is a pilgrimage coming out to Rome after Easter?

With kindest regards to all friends and best love to yourself and Mother,
I remain my dear Father,
Your ever affectionate Son,
Edward J. Byrne[34]

The beginning of Edward's final year in the college was marked by the death of Dr Tobias Kirby, Archbishop of Ephesus, former rector of the Irish College, in his ninety-first year. He had been the esteemed rector of the Irish College for more than forty years, from 1850-1891, and was a friend of Pope Leo XIII, who had been a classmate in their student days. The Requiem Mass was in the College Chapel of St Agatha, and it was served and organised by the Irish College, in the presence of archbishops, monsignori, and representatives of various Roman colleges. It was an occasion likely to make a deep impression on students at the college.[35]

In Edward's final year, a young Wicklow man, John Hagan, arrived at the Irish College. A friendship developed between them which eased their business relationship in later years when Edward was archbishop and John Hagan was an influential rector of the Irish College. Both were strong nationalists, but Hagan was the more radical of the two.[36]

Ordination
In his official declaration of 16 June 1895, Rector Monsignor Kelly, gave the results of Edward's theological studies, cited earlier, and added that he 'was ordained in Dublin on 8 June 1895'. Edward, clearly, came home for his ordination to the priesthood, but there are no extant letters or memorabilia celebrating

the auspicious occasion. A letter, written many years later by someone who claimed to have visited his parents around this time, told of 'tears of joy rolling down the cheeks of his father and mother'. It can certainly be assumed that for Edward, his parents, relatives and friends it was a very special time of joy, gratitude, and congratulation, and that the blessing of the new priest was sought not only in parts of Dublin but also near the home place in Wicklow.

CHAPTER TWO

1895-1911

Dublin-Rome-Dublin

In the summer of 1895, as an extension, perhaps of his ordination celebrations, Edward and his mother took an overseas holiday which mingled business with pleasure. They travelled first to London where Edward's interest in politics led to their visiting the House of Commons and attending a debate on the Land Law (Ireland) Act, which was subsequently passed on 14 August 1896. From London they journeyed to Paris and thence to Geneva. Mrs Byrne attended an exhibition there. and on their return to London spent a day buying her 'stock for the coming season'.[1]

First years as a priest
Edward received his first appointment as a priest of the diocese on 15 August. A letter from Archbishop Walsh informed him that he was appointed to a vacancy in the parish of Rush, Co Dublin, where there was need for a second priest 'owing to the enfeebled health of the parish priest', Fr O'Carroll.[2] Edward spent three years in Rush. During his time there, a number of parishioners joined in protest against a teacher, or a school pupil and his family. Edward, not wishing to trouble the parish priest about it, wrote to the archbishop for advice. The latter sent a letter to the aggrieved parties to encourage them 'to take a reasonable view of the case'. He enclosed a copy of the letter to Edward, adding that he was sure that those concerned were 'good Catholic people, meaning well in the main. Our main effort should be able to help them to keep straight.' Edward was able to inform the archbishop on 5 August 1896 that since the reception of his Grace's letter 'the movement here appears to have subsided' and he did not anticipate any further problem.[3] The incident brought him and his ministry in Rush to the archbishop's attention. Overall, he made a favourable impression on the people of Rush; so much so that many years later when his episcopal appointment was announced he received numerous congratul-

ations from former parishioners and the town was illuminated in celebration.[4]

Edward next heard from the archbishop on 23 October 1898. As the need for an additional priest at Rush had ceased, he was to take up a curacy at Rolestown, Swords, Co Dublin. Edward left no record of his time there. While he was at Rolestown, however, he went with his father to visit old family friends. Edward Senior's health seems to have improved. He informed his wife, Ellen, on 28 June 1899, that they had a party the previous night with 'a tremendous dance' that kept up till morning. Referring to his son, he declared: 'Ned is a ... man, he danced and sang the whole night'.[5] 'Ned', as Edward was also called by many of his contemporaries, was not just the refined gentleman his mother would have nurtured, he was also able to mix with farming relatives and friends in a relaxed, sociable and entertaining way, a facility that helps explain his general popularity with his contemporaries.

Four months later, on 16 October 1899, he received notification from the archbishop that he was appointed to a vacant curacy in Howth, Co Dublin.

To his surprise, he was changed again after seven months. On 17 June 1900, he was appointed to a vacancy in the parish of Booterstown (Blackrock). It was a coveted appointment. Blackrock was a strongly middle-class, well-financed parish, more comfortable than Edward's previous curacies. He soon settled in and, as in his other appointments, got on well with his parish priest, Mgr Plunkett.

In a short space, Edward had been exposed to a variety of parishes and of pastoral experiences. In retrospect, these seemed chosen to prepare him for future advancement. From early on he had made a favourable impression by his quiet zeal, adaptability, a combination of cheerfulness, reliability and quick intelligence, and empathy for the poor and the disadvantaged. The result was that Bishop Nicholas Donnelly recommended him for the position of assistant-rector in the Irish College Rome.

Appointment to Irish College

In November 1900, Donnelly, in a confidential letter, informed Edward that while he might not welcome such a change from his pleasant parish, 'soldiers' predilections are seldom consulted when an important issue in the campaign has to be tackled'. The

Irish College was currently such an issue. It had 'just emerged from a hopeless condition of financial difficulty'. It had a present muster of 43 students, the highest number for many years. It had in its rector, Dr William Murphy, a new man to the situation, not one of its former *alumni* but an exemplary pious priest who was also a cultured gentleman. Its prospects, as a result, looked flourishing. He, Dr Donnelly, had nominated Edward because he was convinced that he was 'pre-eminently the man for the post'. The archbishop and the body of bishops agreed and he was sure that Dr Murphy too would agree. He ingenuously reminded Edward that in Rome 'no one is in exile. It is our Father's house' and that 'with your quick appreciative intelligence you are to make good use of your time there'.[6] The bishop saw the appointment as a stepping-stone to advancement in Edward's ecclesiastical career. His letter was 'confidential' because the matter was not yet public. In fact, despite his assurances, the matter was not yet decided. The statutes of the Irish College required that the rector choose the vice-rector from three names sent by the archbishops.

The other names were: J. J. Ryan, vice-president of St Patrick's College, Thurles, who Cardinal Logue considered suitable for the position because he was said to be 'a clever business man' and he had college experience; and Thomas Wall, Limerick, a student at the college, who did not want the position. 'I don't know Fr Byrne CC,' the cardinal continued, 'but the archbishop (Walsh) says he is a good, sensible, solid man. He is not anxious to go, and consented merely because he thought the archbishop wished it'.[7] Dr Donnelly, writing to Murphy on 29 November, dismissed the claims of J. J. Ryan, and assured the rector that Byrne was quite reconciled to go to Rome. 'You can readily understand how a young man in a place like Blackrock with its surroundings, its people, and its PP, would be loath to leave it, especially after such a short acquaintance, but he consulted the PP and the latter gave him such strenuous advice to go that … I feel … he will take kindly to the post and will be a valuable helper to you'.[8]

On the same date, an exasperated Archbishop of Dublin informed Murphy that he had never written 'anything approaching the same number of letters upon any subject before, or carried on any correspondence under such irritating circumstances or conditions'. His fellow archbishops kept changing their minds or not answering letters. 'However, all's well that ends well, and we have got what Dr Donnelly and I regard as an ideal man for the post. You know that he is good intellectual capacity, and in this way, as in others, sure to command the respect of the students. As for getting on well, it is his great characteristic. It is right to say that he goes with very great reluctance, and simply because he understands from me (whilst I told him that I would not think one iota less of him if he declined to go) I thought the proper course for him was to go.' 'I have told him', the archbishop continued, 'that, even in this modified way, I would not put it upon him to go permanently, or for longer than two years. By the end of a twelvemonth he will probably have made up his mind to stay, but if not, there will be plenty of time to look around, and make enquiries, at leisure, and find some other suitable man for the post. In the meantime we have the post filled and excellently filled.'[9]

Edward's reluctance to accept the position was not just because of what Donnelly termed 'his sunny berth at Blackrock', but also because of his father's decline in health and his less than happy memories of his time in Rome. The first hint of this last appeared in his response to Dr Murphy's letter welcoming him to the Irish College.

On 3 December 1901, he thanked the rector for appointing him to the vice-rectorship of his old *alma mater* and told him that his nomination by the archbishop came like a 'bolt from the blue'. He felt it hard to give up his 'nice mission' but, he assured Dr Murphy, that he had not the slightest doubt that when he got back to the Irish College 'I shall be as happy in the changed circumstances and happier than I was there in the old days ... Hoping everything will turn out for the best and we shall get on not too badly together.'[10] The last word on the appointment came in a vote of confidence from Dr Walsh to Murphy on 19 December 1901: 'I have no doubt you will find him everything that a vice-rector ought to be. All I am afraid of is that his views may change, and that when the two years that I asked him to go for, by way of experiment, are over, he will not be willing to come back to the diocese.'[11]

Edward as vice-rector
Edward was in Rome by mid-December 1901. He wrote home for Christmas, and his mother's response indicates his initial feelings: 'I am glad the weather is now in your favour and that

you like Dr Murphy so much. I am quite sure you will feel very happy after a while.'[12]

The role of the vice-rector embraced the following duties: to act in place of the rector when he was away from the College or ill; to look after the financial administration of the college (student fees, payment of bills, keeping accounts, paying staff etc); to supervise the day to day administration of the college – the work of the staff, the kitchen and so on.[13]

The New Year proved particularly busy and discordant. It was a special year in Rome. Pope Leo XIII celebrated the 25th year of his pontificate. The *Daily News*, on 4 March 1902, was stirred to marvel:

> The Grand Old Man of the Vatican, who on Sunday last completed his 92nd year, is the only Pope who has strolled along Picadilly and occupied a seat in the Distinguished Strangers' Gallery at the House of Commons, where he had the pleasure of hearing a speech by Daniel O'Connell, the Irish leader of the period. The Pope has always been fond of recalling this experience when receiving Irish pilgrimages and visitors.

On 27 April, King Edward VII visited Leo XIII for a half-hour.

For Edward the day-to-day running of the college also involved welcoming and assisting visitors to Rome, especially priests and bishops, who came to visit and perhaps to stay at the college. In June, moreover, the college experienced something of the work involved in the celebration of the centenary of the Irish Christian Brothers. Then, into his busy life, came the shock of a telegram from his mother on 11 June: 'Father Sinking Fast Come – Mother.' He returned to Ireland.

Sad Interlude
His father died on 16 June 1902 of cardiac failure. He was aged 65 years, but had suffered for five years from asthenia or a state of debility. A newspaper cutting on the 'Funeral of Mr Edward Byrne, formerly of Killahurler, Co Wicklow', reported that it 'took place ... from his residence at 41 Grosvenor Road, Rathgar', (The most recent residence of Mrs Byrne) and added:

> After the Requiem Mass at the Church of the Three Patrons, Rathgar, the remains were removed to Harcourt Street (station), conveyed by rail to Arklow, and interred in the family burial place. The esteem in which the deceased was held was shown by the large attendance of clergy and laity.[14]

Following his father's death, Edward stayed on in Ireland for some time as a support for his mother. On 7 July 1902, from St Cronan's, Bray, Dr Donnelly exhibited further marks of his patronage towards him. He was having Cardinal Moran, of Sydney, to preach next Sunday, and he invited Edward to act as assistant priest at Pontifical High Mass at 12.00, and to come 'in the evening to dinner to meet his Eminence and his Grace'. Edward attended, and made a favourable impression on the cardinal.

Return to Rome
Back in Rome, he attended to requests made to him with his customary graciousness. On 24 September 1902, Sir Thomas H. Grattan Esmonde, Lady Esmonde, and Esmonde's sister, writing from Gorey, Co Wexford, thanked him for the trouble he had taken in the matter of the silver casket, containing an address to the Holy Father, in its crossing of several frontiers. The following day, Cardinal Moran, following up their recent meeting, wrote from Archbishop's House, Dublin, announcing 'We start from Dublin on 4 October for London and Paris to Rome. Please do not forward letters except to that date'.[15]

Wanting to go home
Despite the gracious manner, the strain of responsibility and pressure, combined with the severity of the Roman winter, which he disliked and feared from his student days, rendered him quite ill with a fever towards the end of his first year at the college. In his despondency, and also, perhaps, out of concern for his mother being on her own, he wrote to Dr Donnelly desiring to be recalled from Rome. His letter is not extant, but from the bishop's reply, it would appear that he based his case on the feeble assertion that life and work in the Irish College was not to his taste. On 4 January 1903, Bishop Donnelly replied that he had received it on 21 December and 'was quite prepared for its contents'. He added:

> Of course I should not wish for a moment that you should be continued in a position that does not accord with your tastes, and whatever share I may have had in sending you into exile, I will try and balance with equal zeal in having your recalled as soon as possible.

'I regret that matter,' he continued, 'for the sake of the
College, for in the opinion of all – bishops, rector and students –
you have proved yourself the man for the post. It will be exceedingly difficult to find your successor, and it is that difficulty
which delays your recall.' He hoped that Dr Murphy had
thought out the question, and assured Edward that as soon as
any one could be found to take up the burden he would be able
to come home immediately and would be 'received with a thousand welcomes'. 'Be assured', the prelate concluded, 'of my
friendly care of your wishes ...'[16]

Continuing in Rome

By the middle of January, Edward had got over his illness and
soon seemed to have settled back into his role as vice-rector. On
2 April, he sent a long letter to his mother which told of the pressures he was experiencing. 'We have been a good deal upset
here for a long time. We have had some of the students ill, we
had all our preparations for St Patrick's Day, and to cap it all the
Rector himself got ill just at the busiest time – a fortnight before
Patrick's Day – and I may say has been ill ever since. So the
whole weight of things has been thrown on my shoulders. Of
course not one in Dublin knows Dr Murphy has been laid up
and he does not wish anyone to know. So don't breathe of it to a
soul, not even to any of the priests.' Continuing his account of
the demands on him, Edward divulged:

> You probably saw the account of our St Patrick's Day dinner
> in the *Freeman* or *Irish Catholic*, well I had to preside and the
> Rector was in bed. Of course we put in the papers that the
> Rector presided as usual. Dr Murphy is now away at the sea
> for a little to pull himself together.

'I am, thank God, quite strong', he assured his mother. 'I am
always good in an emergency to keep up.' He then asked: 'Are
you keeping all right? Is business good? Are you going to
London this season?' He saw in the papers talk of a royal visit to
Ireland. 'If the Land Bill is found to please the people the visit
would be a great success and ought to be very good for your
trade.'[17]

Conveying News and Meeting Requests

On 20 July 1903, Pope Leo XIII died. His successor, Joseph Sarto,

Patriarch of Venice, was solemnly anointed Pope Pius X on 9 August. Three days later, Bishop Donnelly thanked Edward for his thoughtful telegram conveying the result of the papal conclave and the subsequent post card with the effigy of the pontiff. He was on retreat at St Beuno's, the Jesuit retreat house in Wales, at the time, but the telegram followed him. He met Dr Murphy, of the Irish College, who was looking better.[18]

One of Edward's functions was to respond to various requests from Irish bishops. An extant example is a letter from T. J. McRedmond, Bishop of Killaloe, dated 10 September 1903, in which he passes on yet another resolution of sympathy on the death of Leo XIII and then makes a personal request: 'Chevalier Hugh Bergin was appointed at my instance Private Chamberlain to the late Pope and Knight *di Cappa e di Spada* (cloak and sword). I beg most humbly that he may be re-appointed to these dignities under His present Holiness and empower you to supplicate for them in my name ...'[19]

Further confirmation of the favourable impression he was making personally and as vice-rector was indicated by a long friendly letter from Cardinal Moran from Colombo on 16 November 1903. He was at the half-way stage in the return journey to Australia. As he had promised, he gave an account of his journey, and then added some remarks of a more political nature:

I trust that the new departure at *Secretaria di Stado* may be friendly to the College and to Ireland, though I suppose the Duke of Norfolk's influence may for a while be paramount there. I daresay an effort will be made to transfer Great Britain and Ireland as well as the United States from Propaganda to the Congregation of Ecclesiastical Affairs. In so far as Australia is concerned we won't accept any such change without having a vigorous fight in the matter. I have a great dread of English political influence being allowed any place in our Ecclesiastical administration.

He finished 'with affectionate remembrance to the Mgr Rector and all friends'.[20]

The reference to the 'Duke of Norfolk's influence' brings to focus one of the great pressures on the rector and vice-rector of the Irish College as representatives of the Irish bishops in Rome and, as it were, custodians of the interests of the Irish church.

There were cardinals and other church dignitaries ready to respond to argument and varieties of persuasion from exalted representatives of a major power like Great Britain. The adroitness and diplomacy required to forestall or counter such influences were considerable, and required, perhaps, a special psychology and temperament that Edward Byrne did not have. This is suggested by a letter of his to a successor in the Irish College, in 1920. He expressed to John Hagan his sympathy with him in the hard task he had faced during the previous years, and added: 'with my knowledge of Rome no one could realise better than I the influences that were arrayed against Irishmen on the spot'.[21] This aspect of life, it seems fair to assume, was part of what he had in mind when he asked to return home because he did not find the role of vice-rector to his 'taste and inclination'.

There was also the added burden of filling the rector's place during Fr Murphy's long absence. This involved him supervising the areas on which annual reports were made to the bishops: health and academic matters, fees and costs, the condition of the building, Irish, English and Foreign securities, and the eventual balance sheet for the year. In addition, he did some teaching and was the on-going liaison with the students. He and Dr Murphy seem to have run a happy establishment. One past student wrote to Byrne many years later from New Zealand: 'I cannot imagine students ever having such fine opportunities of seeing Rome or being so happy, and that we owed to Mgr Murphy and yourself'. He began his letter:

> You were always so kind to me in Rome that I feel I must write … I often recall with deep gratitude your example, your teaching and your goodness to the stranger from NZ and I have tried all these years to repay you by my prayers.[22]

Despite his apparent suitability for the position, Edward Byrne longed to return to a more pastoral career.

Negotiating a Return to Ireland
Towards the end of December 1903, he decided that he did not wish to stay any longer in Rome. He informed Dr Donnelly. The latter told Dr Murphy on 29 January 1904 that Fr Byrne had written to him stating that his time was up and he did not wish to remain longer in Rome. He mentioned that he was writing to the archbishop, but the latter had not heard from him so far. If

he did, it was probable that he would ask him to wait until the end of the academic year. Neither the archbishop nor himself had discovered a successor and it was unlikely that there would be anyone available 'of the same caliber as the present occupant'.[23]

On 4 February 1904, Byrne got around to writing a carefully balanced letter to Archbishop Walsh. He began by reminding his Grace that he had given him to understand, when he nominated him for the position of vice-rector, that it would not be contrary to his Grace's wishes if he, Edward, wished to return to the work of the archdiocese after two years. 'Since I took up duty here', he continued, 'I have tried to settle down permanently, thinking that a taste for college life, though in the beginning disagreeable to me, would in time be acquired.' But, 'after a very fair experience', he could state candidly that his 'taste and inclination' did not lie in this direction. Hence he asked to be allowed to return to the work of the mission where his 'inclination does naturally lie'. He hoped that his Grace would not think him ungrateful of his kindness in selecting him for the position and for many other marks of kindness in the past. Mgr Murphy was aware of his intention but he would not give him any formal notice until he had his Grace's sanction.[24]

Mgr Murphy, for his part, was concerned at losing Edward. In his annual report to the bishops for the year 1902-1903, he had written of him as vice-rector: 'An experience of now practically two years shows that a more admirable appointment could not have been made'.[25] Consequently, he wrote to Archbishop Walsh seeking to delay Edward's return for as long as possible. The archbishop replied on 14 February 1904 that he was not free to intervene because he had made a promise to Fr Byrne that he could return after two years.[26] Dr Walsh replied to Edward's letter that same day. He regretted that he had not written a few weeks earlier because then he would have had a suitable position for him. At present there was no position available. As to what was to be done, Dr Walsh did not feel free to suggest that he should remain in Rome in the interests of the college, that was a matter entirely for himself, but in the light of his position, he might do well to consider 'whether it would not be better to wait for a short while' until an opening presented itself at home. He was sure 'that for a matter of months or so, pending the selection of a vice-rector', he 'would not think of causing any embarrassment by leaving'. The time had come for Edward to 'have a free talk' with Mgr Murphy 'on the whole subject'.[27]

Edward was relieved at the archbishop's positive response, and was prepared to wait the 'matter of months' until his replacement arrived. In fact, the call home came quicker than expected. Archbishop Walsh wrote to him once more on 13 May 1904. He had endeavoured to leave him with Mgr Murphy until his successor arrived, but a vacancy became available in Marlborough Street which he thought was a suitable position for him. He had appointed him to it. It was a place that needed its full staff, so he should be at his new post 'with the least possible delay'. His position 'as regards seniority will be sufficiently satisfactory'.[28]

At the Pro-Cathedral, Marlborough Street

'Marlborough Street' (often written Marlboro) referred to Dublin's Pro-Cathedral parish, a central and busy location. The parish priest was the archbishop himself. The person in charge was known as the administrator. Edward was to spend the rest of his life closely associated with the Pro-Cathedral. He left Rome on 16 May 1904.[29] Over the next few years he became familiar with the variety of occurrences likely to happen in this central parish, with the history of the Pro-Cathedral, and the range of people the parish served.

He was scarcely settled in his new position when a papal legate, Cardinal Vannutelli, arrived in Ireland. The purpose of his visit was to attend the consecration ceremony of St Patrick's Cathedral, Armagh, on 24 July; but from the second to the seventh of August he visited various religious and charitable institutions in the Dublin region, and also the Pro-Cathedral. A month later, on 4 September, Dr Michael Fogarty was consecrated Bishop of Killaloe. It was to prove a significant appointment in the history of the time and for Edward. On 23 October, the clergy and people rejoiced with the archbishop in his announcement that the final stage in the preliminary proceedings in the promotion of the canonisation of the Irish martyrs had been reached. It was a cause to which his Grace had devoted a great deal of time and effort, and with which he would continue to work until shortly before his death.

In addition to his daily life as a curate, Edward, as Lent 1905 commenced, would have been concerned with the hierarchy's pastoral letters, which received much publicity in the press and dealt mainly with equality in university education, dangerous literature, and intemperance. Then, on 7 July, came the sobering news of the death of the rector of the Irish College, Mgr William H. Murphy. His illness during Edward's time as vice-rector was evidently more serious than Edward realised. He was succeeded, on 11 August, by the very able Reverend Michael O'Riordan, DPh, LD, of the Limerick diocese, who was to prove a major support in Rome during difficult years in Ireland. Edward's work, and the location of the Pro-Cathedral close to areas of extreme poverty, meant that he experienced what his archbishop, on 21 November, vigorously condemned as 'the abominable and sinful system of proselytism'.[30]

Problem of proselytism
Proselytism had an unpleasant history in Ireland. It was associated with trading food for religious allegiance during times of extreme poverty. It had been a preoccupation of archbishops of Dublin from Dr Troy in the beginning of the nineteenth century to Dr Walsh in the twentieth. The presence of active proselytism was one of the reasons that led Archbishop Walsh, in 1886, to open the Sacred Heart Home for boys at Drumcondra, some of whom had been 'rescued from proselytising "Birds' Nests",' as some of the establishments were called. The activity of proselytising agencies in Dublin in the years 1900-1917 is reflected in page on page of reports in the Dublin diocesan archives. The clergy's efforts to counter the agencies appear in lists of what had been done, and was being done, and in information gathered on the names and activities of proselytising institutions and schools. There were said to be some twenty-two establishments between Dublin and Kingstown (now Dún Laoghaire). Parents and children turned to these places, it was stated, because they could not get sufficient food elsewhere. 'A Report of the Saint Vincent de Paul Society on Proselytism', 11 February 1914, told of 'ragged day schools where hundreds of Catholic children received an indifferent general education, and were imbued with a spirit of hatred of the Catholic faith and teaching.' The children were drawn from homes demoralised by poverty or/and drunkenness.[31]

The aggressiveness of the Protestant campaign in Dublin impinged strongly on Catholic clergy in inner-city parishes, such as that served by the Pro-Cathedral. Edward became known for his quiet work among the poor and for his empathy for them. He also had compassion for the women involved in prostitution in the notorious red-light district near the Pro-Cathedral, which was most heavily frequented in the years of the large British garrisons. Certain necessary accommodations were reached, it appears, in the case of people taken critically ill in the local brothels. The sick person was brought to the door of the establishment and there received the 'last sacraments', as the priest could not be seen to enter such a house.[32]

The Pro-Cathedral and its associations

There were other less demanding aspects of work in St Mary's Pro-Cathedral. The administration of the sacraments, preaching, and offering Mass, was conducted in an impressive and historic building. It was opened in 1825, in the presence of most of the hierarchy and with the renowned 'J.K.L', Dr James Doyle, Bishop of Kildare and Leighlin, as preacher. Four years later, it witnessed a special Mass of thanksgiving for Catholic Emancipation. Daniel O'Connell was present on both occasions, and again in 1841 when, as the first Catholic Lord Mayor of Dublin since the Reformation, he drove in state through cheering crowds to Mass in Marlborough Street wearing his mayoral robes and chains of office. After O'Connell's death in 1847, his coffin was brought to the Pro-Cathedral. The church was draped in black, in testimony to a people's grief, as the coffin lay for four days upon a great catafalque.

Shortly before Edward came to the Pro-Cathedral, a different form of history had been set in train. In 1902, a wealthy Galway landowner and patron of the arts, Edward Martyn, had offered to endow a choir of boys and men at the Pro-Cathedral, which would specialise in singing music by the great classical composers of polyphony, most notably Palestrina. Dr Walsh, a keen musician, gladly accepted the offer. The choir was named the Palestrina Choir and Dr Vincent O'Brien was appointed the first director. In the same year, after winning the gold medal in the tenor competition at the Feis Ceol (national music festival) in Dublin, John McCormack was accepted for the choir. Vincent O'Brien, recognising the quality of his remarkable voice, gave him private tuition. For a few years he sang in the choir at Sunday Mass.[33] It is most likely that Edward Byrne, in his first years in the parish, heard and met the young man. He was certainly acquainted with, and admired by Edward Martin, [34] and he had a keen interest in music.[35] In 1907, McCormack embarked on his operatic career in *Cavalleria Rusticana* at Covent Garden. Many years later, when Edward, as archbishop, hosted the Eucharistic Congress in Dublin, one of the most enduring memories for many of those present was Count John McCormack singing to a hushed assembly of almost a million people during public Mass in the Phoenix Park.

As time passed, Fr Byrne became popular with both fellow priests and parishioners. He had an imposing presence, an easy manner, and was an eloquent preacher. Very pastoral in outlook, but shunning the limelight, he became devoted to the people of the parish, especially, as mentioned, the poor. He also took care not to neglect his own spiritual duties and prayer. Although there is scarcely anything extant on his personal spirituality, his notes provide indications of much reading on prayer and on lives of saints such as Teresa of Avila, as well as a list of 'useful books for meditation'.[36] He was a good listener and a welcoming host. A strong supporter of temperance, it is not clear that he personally abstained from alcohol. If he did, it did not limit his hospitality. In 1920, a Capuchin priest recalled meeting often 'in your hospitable room';[37] and William Brophy wrote from Wigan, on 7 September 1920:

> God be with old times when I could go to your room in
> Marlborough Street and enjoy a good hour or so and a
> good glass of whiskey ...[38]

Relevant needs and developments
Scarcely any letters or direct information about his years in the Pro-Cathedral have survived. He was necessarily concerned, however, with certain widespread abuses and developments that affected the people of the parish.

One of the first things borne in on him in his parish work was the damage being done to families by the excessive consumption of alcohol. Workers were still paid by overseers in public houses, and peer pressure made it difficult to avoid spending some of one's wages on alcohol. Organisations against the abuse of intoxicating drink developed strongly in the early years of the twentieth century, and were supported by trade union leaders such as Jim Larkin, P. T. Daly, and James Connolly. Most notable of these bodies were the Total Abstinence Association, under the auspices of the Capuchin Fathers, with which a colleague of Edward at the Pro-Cathedral, Fr Gavin, was prominently associated, and the Pioneer Total Abstinence Association of the Sacred Heart, which held its first annual meeting in October 1901 and was founded by Fr James Cullen SJ, whom Edward knew from his days in Belvedere and to whom he turned for spiritual advice from time to time.

Another major concern in episcopal and clerical ranks was what was termed 'immoral literature', associated mainly with the British popular press but also with some Irish publications taking their lead from certain British papers. The reaction to this perceived danger took the form in Limerick, in 1911, of an active lay Vigilance Committee supported by a member of the clergy. This spread to Dublin, where the priest involved was another colleague of Edward in the Pro-Cathedral, and it was taken up in a number of other Irish cities and towns, including Cork, Waterford, Clonmel, Belfast and Donegal.

And crossing over all religious, social and political differences was interest in the Irish language, which was promoted throughout the country by hundreds of people linked to the Gaelic League. The language was seen as a badge of national identity, and was promoted among the working class as actively as in the middle classes. Edward went at least once to the Gaeltacht in Carna, Co Galway, to improve his Irish.[39]

With his fondness for literature, Edward may be presumed to have taken an interest in the contemporary Irish literary renaissance. Just a block away from the Pro-Cathedral was one of the symbols of the renaissance, the Abbey Theatre, which opened in 1904, the year of Edward's return, and soon became celebrated for the quality of its acting and its plays. It is unlikely that Edward ever attended, because of the restrictions imposed by the Synod of Maynooth against priests attending theatre; but he could not but be aware of the theatre's productions from conversation with his parishioners and from newspaper reports.

Roman instructions

But to return to a more chronological presentation of events. A matter of immediate interest to Edward and the priests of St Mary's presbytery, Marlborough Street, was the issuing, in 1906, of the decree *Ne Temere* by Pope Pius X, which strongly discouraged marriages between Catholics and non-Catholics and required, when such took place, that the children be baptised and reared as Catholics. This was followed on 8 September by a condemnation of the errors of 'Modernism'. On 25 October, Cardinal Logue forwarded to his Holiness a letter from the Irish bishops congratulating him on the jubilee of his priesthood and giving thanks for his 'splendid Encyclical Letter regarding Modernism, which we have lately received'. What Fr Byrne felt about these two controversial documents is again not known, but, given his theological training in Rome, it is unlikely that he disagreed with the bishops' views.

This rather repressive attitude, however, was not reflected in his manner. Quite the contrary. The repairer of his 'piano player', following Edward's elevation to bishop, expressed the hope:

> that the Holy and Solemn position you will now occupy to Dublin's advantage, will not make you lose that cheery manner and smile that has so often cheered me on my sometimes weary way. There are so few sunny natures knocking around that we can ill afford to lose one.[40]

One suspects that his 'cheery manner and smile' played a considerable part in his popularity with parishioners and fellow clergy.

Miscellaneous events and some of their consequences

A matter of interest to Edward and his parishioners in 1908 was the passing of the Old Age Pensions Act and the Housing of the Working Classes Act. Both were to mean much to the people in the parish. The Housing Act, besides, increased the power of local authorities to build houses. Edward's concern about the people's living conditions brought him into contact with members of the local authority, especially Councillor William Cosgrave.

The next year brought occasions of celebration and stories of disaster. Edward took part in the jubilee celebrations of his *alma mater*, Holy Cross College Clonliffe, which were conducted with imposing ceremony and an address by his Grace, Dr Walsh.[41] A month later, on 13 July, a note from M. Dillon & Son, stockbrokers, to Mrs Ellen Byrne, Edward's mother, was perhaps further occasion of celebration. It certainly indicated her continuous activity as a business woman. The stockbroker informed her that he had sold for her 500 of her mining shares at the best rate possible.[42]

At the end of the year, however, Europe was shocked by news of a massive earthquake in Calabria and Sicily that caused the death of some 100,000 people. On 20 January 1910, Archbishop Walsh directed that on the following Sunday, in the Pro-Cathedral, Mass should be offered for those who had died, and that in all churches, after the Sunday Masses, a collection should be made for the suffering survivors.[43]

During that year there were two outside happenings that had a particular interest for the clergy in the Pro-Cathedral. In April, the archbishop was received by the pope, who expressed satisfaction with the state of religion in the diocese; and on 6 May, there was widespread mourning at the death of King Edward VII, whose enjoyment of life and racing and his personal interest in Ireland evoked a warm response. The archbishop sent a message of sympathy.

CHAPTER THREE

1911-1921

Hidden work during years of upheaval

During 1911, references to Edward are almost non existant, and he left scarcely any record of his work and interests. And yet much was going on that affected his life and work. There were demonstrations, for example, concerning temperance and 'immoral literature'. On 3 September the expansion of the temperance movement was marked by a large procession through the streets of the capital under the auspices of the Dublin Workmens' Temperance Association; while in November, at Maynooth College, the president, Dr Daniel Mannix, paid tribute to the great success of the Pioneer Total Abstinence Association of the Sacred Heart. The Pioneer membership had reached 200,000. On 5 November, the archbishop approved a public meeting, organised by a branch of the Catholic Young Men's Society, at which Fr Myles Ronan of the Pro-Cathedral proposed that 'the time has come for the promotion of a Dublin vigilance committee to defend our people against the insidious attempts of modern journalism to corrupt them'.[1] Meantime, in August, Edward's acquaintance, Cardinal Moran had died in Sydney. On 12 October, Edward was in a packed Pro-Cathedral as Archbishop Walsh sang a pontifical high Mass for the repose of the soul of the cardinal, and Dr Donnelly preached the sermon. In the same month, Edward with his interest in Irish history and politics, would probably have rejoiced to see unveiled at the end of Sackville Street (O'Connell Street), not a stone's throw from the cathedral, a large monument in honour of Parnell, with his words in gold lettering – 'No man has a right to set bounds to the march of a nation.' Yet, in political contrast, just three months earlier the city went *en fête* to welcome the new monarch of Britain and Ireland, George V.

Various happenings
On 26 February 1912, Edward experienced the loss of both a

physician and friend, Sir Francis Cruise. Nearly a month later, on 23 March, he wrote one of his few extant letters from these years. It indicated that his interests and contacts were wider than the poorer areas around the cathedral. The rather unusual letter sought the assistance of Monsignor John Hagan, his successor at the Irish College Rome, on behalf of a friend, Mr Portens, who 'was not a Catholic but would like to attend a papal audience'.[2] More than a week earlier, St Patrick's Day was, as usual, a celebratory occasion in the midst of Lent, and this year it was marked in many churches by prayers and a number of sermons in Irish. The Lenten pastoral letters, meantime, had tended to encourage the crusade against 'immoral literature' amongst other matters. Cardinal Logue drew attention to an anti-religion wave that was sweeping across Europe, while Dr Walsh drew attention to the forthcoming legislation on Home Rule that might influence the future of the Irish people for good or ill, and he requested prayers for guidance for the legislators.

In the midst of the unfolding political drama, there came the overwhelming news on 15 April of the sinking of the *Titanic*, with a reported loss of 1,490 lives. In the Pro-Cathedral, the archbishop presided at a solemn requiem Mass for those who perished.

As 1913 began, public interest was drawn inexorably to the political scene. The virtual certainty of Home Rule becoming law led to the formation of an Ulster Volunteer force to oppose the measure. This, in turn, gave rise to the founding of a counter force, the National Volunteers, in Dublin. For the working people of Dublin, however, there was a more immediate concern in the autumn of the year.

1913 Strike/Lock Out

From 1911-1913 there had been a succession of strikes and widespread industrial unrest, which culminated in the great strike and lock-out in 1913. It, in effect, became a personalised struggle between James Larkin, leader of the workers, and William Martin Murphy, head of the employers. Larkin had done great things for the morale and self-pride of the workers, but they and their families became pawns in the struggle between the two leaders. Archbishop Walsh empathised with the workers. He kept *au fait* with the union's arguments by reading Larkin's *Irish*

Worker, and consulting those of his priests closest to the workers and their families. Edward Byrne, being so concerned about the poorer people in the parish and the harsh circumstances of their lives, and whose judgement was valued by his Grace, was one of those most likely to have been consulted. The atrocious housing conditions in which many lived were highlighted shortly after the strike began when, on 2 September, tenement houses in Church Street collapsed, killing seven people.

Then, in October, there came the news that, through the initiative of James Larkin, the wives of unemployed working men were planning to hand over their children to be cared for in England. This immediately raised fears of proselytism and a public outcry. The archbishop condemned the 'deportation' of the children, and priests from Westland Row parish joined vigilante groups endeavouring to prevent the children embarking.[3] Feelings ran high on both sides, and workers became divided on the issue.

There is no extant evidence that Edward and the priests of the Pro-Cathedral were involved in the excessive dockland exchanges. One good effect of the whole proceedings, however, was that an increased effort was made in the Dublin archdiocese to feed the children of families in need. A special committee was formed of clergy and members of the Society of St Vincent de Paul, and some 2,450 breakfasts and 1,380 dinners were given daily in the Catholic schools in the three most affected parishes.[4] The archbishop also called for a special collection in the churches of the diocese, religious as well as diocesan, which would be used to provide food and clothing for the thousands of school-going children who, even at the best of times, were in need of such assistance.[5]

In January 1914 most of the workers endeavoured to return to work, surrendering their union membership in order to do so. Others were obliged to seek employment in Britain. The union was virtually bankrupt. Angry at the suffering experienced by so many, and all to no good effect, the archbishop publicly criticised Larkin for the first time. Byrne, and the priests of the Pro-Cathedral, meanwhile, did what they could to alleviate the plight of the impoverished families.

His Mother's death; and friends and interests
While the struggle was going on, indeed a month after the com-

mencement of the great strike/walk out, Edward's mother, Ellen Byrne, died. No details remain of the circumstances beyond the fact that she had moved accommodation once more. She was described as 'late of 21 Mountjoy Square', a location nearer to her son in the Pro-Cathedral.[6] Her death, on 27 September 1913, left Edward deeply bereaved, and on his own, without a 'home' to return to.

Despite a certain reserve, he was, fortunately, as has been seen, an affable, quietly popular man, who had a wide selection of clerical and lay friends, and enjoyed reading. A photograph from 1914 shows him and two priest friends on horseback crossing the Gap of Dunloe, Co Kerry. There is also evidence that he, and probably some priest friends, spent a number of holidays at Clonbur, Co Galway, and fished in Lough Corrib.[7]

In his pastoral role, Edward was one of the assistant priests attending the remains of the poet and patriot, T. D. Sullivan, at Glasnevin cemetery, on 2 April 1914. 'The most Rev Dr Walsh, Archbishop of Dublin, recited the prayers in the mortuary chapel and led the procession to the grave.'[8] Sullivan was to be remembered effectively the following month, when the Home Rule Bill was passed for the third and last time and a large vociferous crowd of nationalists sang his 'God Save Ireland' and 'A Nation Once Again'.[9]

Troop violence and aftermath

The following month brought a new dimension to nationalist feeling in Ireland. Rifles for the Irish Volunteers were landed at Howth, Co Dublin, on 26 July 1914. Unlike in the north of Ireland, where arms were landed without interference, police assisted by troops sought to disarm the Volunteers, but without much success. Returning to Dublin, some of the troops, jeered by a crowd at Bachelor's Walk, opened fire, killing four people and wounding thirty. There was a popular outcry and accusations of 'murder' against the army. In the Pro-Cathedral on Wednesday, 29 July, all the priests of the church were involved as requiem Mass was celebrated for three of the victims. The church was almost full. Archbishop Walsh presided, and Fr Flavin, the administrator, was the principal celebrant, assisted by Frs John Flanagan and Myles Ronan. Frs E. J. Byrne and John G. O'Reilly were masters of ceremonies. Priests from every parish in the city and surrounding townships occupied seats in the sanctuary. After the high Mass, the archbishop gave the absolution and the remains were removed for interment in Glasnevin cemetery. 'The funeral cortege was of enormous dimensions, while the entire route was lined by citizens of every class'. Significantly, a body of Irish Volunteers headed the cortege.[10]

Outbreak of World War and effect in Ireland
Some days later, on 2 August, as war clouds loomed over Europe, a letter from Pope Pius X was read in all parishes. It called on all Catholics across the world to make 'public supplication' that the whole of Europe might not be dragged 'into the vortex of a most terrible war'.[11] The following day, Germany declared war on France, and on 4 August invaded Belgium. On 20 September, John Redmond, leader of the Irish Parliamentary Party, called on the Irish Volunteers 'to serve wherever the firing line extends, in defence of right, of freedom, and of religion in this war'. An almost immediate result was a split in the Volunteers. The majority, taking the name National Volunteers, followed Redmond's call; the remainder, under Eoin McNeill, retained the name Irish Volunteers and determined that their obligation was to Ireland at home, not to fight Britain's war. A section within the Irish Volunteers, and James Connolly of the Citizen Army, were determined to avail of the world war to strike for Irish independence.

While all this was happening, Pope Pius X died and was succeeded by Cardinal Giacomo Della Chiesa, Archbishop of Bologna, who took the name Benedict XV. On 15 September, very shortly after his election, he issued an encyclical for peace. It fell on deaf ears. Exactly a month later, the Irish hierarchy reminded every diocese of the sufferings of the Belgian people in the face of the German onslaught, and encouraged subscriptions towards their relief. By then the first battles of the Marne had been fought, and Edward Byrne, like many other priests, was endeavouring to bring comfort and support to the relatives of bereaved soldiers. The archbishop, meanwhile, made it clear that he did not believe the allied propaganda that laid all the blame for the war on Germany, or that the war was being fought for the 'defence of small nations'. He refused to supply chaplains for the armed forces.

A Cathedral for Dublin

Around this time Dr Walsh wanted to purchase ground for a
site for a cathedral from Dublin Corporation. The desired location was behind the house frontage of Ormond Quay to Arran
Street . In the *Freeman's Journal* he announced that he had been
greatly struck by a remark of Cardinal Manning 'that a bishop
without a cathedral was like an admiral without a flag'. In April
1915, however, he gave up the project. The tenants in the area
would have been disturbed by the venture and they did not
want to sell, and that for him was final.[12] Edward, however, remained committed to the project of a cathedral and was to endeavour to fulfill it during his time as archbishop.

War, peace, and insurrection

Pope Benedict decreed 7 February 1915 'a day of expiation and
prayer for peace' throughout Catholic Europe. Ceremonies took
place in churches all over Ireland, and it was noted that many
soldiers attended. Seven days later, practically all the Irish bishops' Lenten pastoral letters made reference to the war and
sought renewed prayers for peace. But even as they prayed for
peace in Europe, Edward and his colleagues in the Pro-
Cathedral were conscious of an armed nationalist defiance in
Dublin. It took the form, on 1 August 1915, of a massive funeral
for the old Fenian, Jeremiah O'Donovan Rossa, which was attended by thousands of Volunteers and marked by an impas-
sioned oration by a uniformed Pádraic Pearse. Nearer home, at
Liberty Hall, a block away from the Pro-Cathedral, Edward and
his colleagues were conscious of the flagrant marches and militarism of James Connolly's Citizen Army.

Despite the displays of military intent by leaders of the Irish
Volunteers and the Citizen Army, the armed insurrection in
Dublin in Easter Week, 1916, termed the Sinn Féin Rebellion by
the government, took most of the country by surprise. The main
centre of the uprising was at the General Post Office, Sackville
(O'Connell) Street, just a block of houses and a street's width
from Marlborough Street and the Pro-Cathedral. During the
week, 'the priests of the Pro-Cathedral had to deal with a district
in which the worst ravages of fire and flame and artillery de-
structiveness were in evidence on all sides'.[13] The priests there,
and in other parishes where firing took place, won universal
praise for their courage and commitment. On the very first

evening of the revolution, Pádraic Pearse sent a request to the Pro-Cathedral for a priest. There were just three priests at the Pro-Cathedral, two being away on holidays. Fr John Flanagan answered the call at 9.00 pm and stayed in the GPO until 11.30 hearing the men's confessions. On Wednesday the British army began to close in. That morning Edward and his colleagues cele-brated Mass to the sound of shells passing over the church on their way to bombard the Citizen Army at Liberty Hall and other positions. 'Marlboro Street was swept from end to end by machine guns posted on the roof of the Theatre Royal, and Abbey Street from the Custom House.'[14]

Edward and another curate made their way to Jervis Street Hospital, which was adjacent to the General Post Office, the focal point of the insurrection, to attend the sick and especially the wounded and dying. They spent many hours in the hospital to that end, staying overnight as required. The account in the *Irish Catholic Directory* noted:

> Jervis Street Hospital, with its ever-lengthening list of wounded soldiers, insurgents and civilians, demanded the constant attention of the clergy. It provided for most of the very numerous casualties from O'Connell Street and the neighbourhood.

Spiritual help was made available to them right through the week. 'Provision to this end was made available by Very Rev Fr Bowden, Administrator, who himself remained in the hospital all day on Monday, through Monday night, Tuesday, Tuesday night, and until Wednesday morning when he left and had his place taken by Rev Fr Byrne CC, and Rev Fr McArdle CC. Rev Fr Flanagan CC, also performed very hazardous duties in connec-tion with his ministrations, and the same may indeed be said of every one of the clergy at the Pro-Cathedral. It was not until Sunday morning that the tension began to relax.' A member of the Sisters of Mercy, Sr Benedict O'Sullivan, who nursed in Jervis Street Hospital at the time, informed Fr Byrne years later that she had 'never forgotten his kindness to her the evening of the Rebellion, when the poor wounded creatures were carried into St Joseph's Ward. Even then you were regarded as our future Bishop – and Father'.[15]

A further difficulty for the priests at the Pro-Cathedral was the presence of refugees: the large body of people 'that sought shelter from burning buildings and shell and rifle fire in the cathedral and vestry'. The problem became more onerous as the week advanced. To grant the people shelter was not in itself a difficulty, but what was a quandary was how to meet their necessities'. To quote again from the *Irish Catholic Directory*, 'For three days these refugees, driven before the fires which raged all round, flocked to the vestry, their terror evident in their ... appeals and ... on their features.' Over 40 people were catered for in the vestry and 'supplied with such food as it was possible to obtain during the time'. The authorities of Marlborough House across the road made their offices available, and almost another 50 people were accommodated there.

Again, though Edward Byrne made no reference to it, matters in the Pro-Cathedral area became particularly threatening on the Thursday and Friday nights. 'For some hours there was imminent danger' that the church and vestry 'might be involved in the flames. Outbreaks extended down as far as Nagle's licensed premises, Cathedral Street, and a strong wind caused flecks of burning paper and showers of sparks over the roof of the Pro-Cathedral itself.' It was a most anxious time lest the outbreak develop further. 'The arrival of the fire brigade on the scene saved the situation ...' The fierceness of the firing in and about Marlborough Street may be gauged 'from the circumstance that no less than ten civilians were shot dead in the street'.[16] For Edward and his colleagues in the Pro-Cathedral, the events of that terrible week were, in the words of one of them, 'an awful nightmare'.[17]

The extent of the property damage was such that when the final surrender took place 'most of the buildings in O'Connell Street, Earl Street, Henry Street, Prince's Street, Eden Quay, and Lower and Middle Abbey Street were in ruins'.[18] A month later, on 2 June 1916, Rev William L. O'Farrell, who had come from Rome for his brother's wedding, remarked that O'Connell Street was still 'one mass of ruins' as were other parts of Dublin. It was 'Ypres on the Liffey'.[19]

The Aftermath

Edward Byrne's views on the Rising are not known. Among those most critical of it, however, were many of his parishioners, who viewed it as a betrayal of husbands and sons fighting the war in the British army, many of whom he knew personally.

Subsequently, however, as day after day the leaders of the insurrection were executed, and hundreds having little connection with the outbreak in Dublin were arrested and brought to prisons in England, a sense of outrage and anger turned against the British administration. Archbishop Walsh refused to co-operate with General Maxwell, who was in charge of the British forces; and Bishop Edward Thomas O'Dwyer of Limerick expressed the wrath and indignation of the general populace in a defiant public letter, which accused Maxwell of shooting young men in cold blood, an action which had 'outraged the conscience of the country', and of 'deporting by hundreds and even thousands poor young fellows without a trial of any kind'. Altogether Maxwell's regime had been 'one of the worst and blackest chapters in the history of the misgovernment of our country'.[20]

Edward's reaction to the treatment of the leaders of the Rising is probably expressed by the long poem he copied into his diary under the heading 'Easter 1916'.

The poet was Alice Furlong, and the poem concluded:

Be their's wisdom or glorious folly
They were of us; our brothers, our own –
Flesh of our flesh, bone of our very bone.
Their foeman took them, and judged them
And shot them in secret apart.
Then we heard in the terrible silence
The sob of a nation's heart.[21]

In the aftermath of the insurrection and the arrests, Archbishop Walsh and other Irish prelates, and also bishops from North America, Australia and new Zealand,[22] contributed financial aid for the dependents of Sinn Féin prisoners in British jails and the dependents of the executed leaders. It became part of the roles of priests in parishes such as that of the Pro-Cathedral to do what they could to assist such people while also continuing to comfort those families that had lost members in the holocaust that was the First World War. This must have been harrowing at times for Edward Byrne for, as would be made evident by the public response to his appointment as bishop, few priests were as close to the people as he. He was a firm believer in home visitation and was, as a result, a familiar figure to most of the residents in the parish.

During 1917 the tide of resentment against British rule continued to simmer. It found strong expression, however, on 26 September, when Sinn Féin prisoner, Thomas Ashe, while on hunger strike, died from attempts to feed him forcibly. His remains were removed from the Mater Hospital to the Pro-Cathedral with great solemnity. The procession to the packed church was attended by numerous Volunteers and 50 clergy, some of whom had travelled long distances to be present. On Sunday, 30 September, the funeral took place to Glasnevin. People came from all over the country to march in the immense cortege: ten to twelve thousand Volunteers in uniform, 30-40,000 members of the public, including women, girls and boys, and 120 priests walked in procession. The depth of national feeling was emphasised by the insistence of the ailing and elderly Dr Walsh, Archbishop of Dublin, on taking part. Unable to walk, he hired a carriage to participate in the cortege and thereby express his outrage at the government's action.

Where was Fr Byrne? Given his strong national feeling, it seems likely that he marched in procession. But there is no extant record.

Introducing Conscription

It was left to the British prime minister, Lloyd George, to unify all sectors of Irish society. He did so by announcing conscription for Ireland in April 1918. The standing committee of the Irish bishops announced on 9 April: 'With all the responsibility that attaches to our office we feel bound to warn the government against acting upon a policy so disastrous to the public interest, and to all order, public or private.' That night, Archbishop Walsh told his secretary, Michael Curran, 'of his astonishment at the ardour and almost revolutionary sentiment of some of the bishops who spoke that day'. He also mentioned that there would be a general meeting of the bishops on 18 April.[23] The Lord Mayor of Dublin, Laurence O'Neill, called a public conference at the Mansion House for the same date as the bishops' meeting. All sectors of society were coming together, and Sinn Féin had made it clear that they would fight to the death against conscription. The Mansion House conference concluded with a defiant declaration 'that the government of nations derive their just powers from the consent of the governed', that the British government had no authority to 'impose compulsory service in Ireland against the expressed will of the Irish people' and that, in consequence, 'the passing of the conscription bill by the British House of Commons must be regarded as a declaration of war on the Irish nation'. A deputation from the Mansion House Conference met the bishops at Maynooth. The bishops announced that they viewed 'conscription forced in this way upon the Irish people' to be 'an oppressive and inhuman law, which the Irish people have a right to resist by all means that are consonant with the law of God'. They instructed that Mass be offered 'in every church in Ireland to avert the scourge of conscription', and that at every public Mass on the coming Sunday an announcement should be made of a public meeting to administer a pledge 'against compulsory military service in Ireland'. Edward Byrne took the pledge like so many others. 'I was with you', Fr P. J. Lynch reminded him, 'on the platform or stage of the Banba Hall, Parnell Square, on the Sunday that we all pledged ourselves against conscription.'[24] The clergy were also instructed to announce that at an early suitable date a collection would be held outside the church gates towards supplying means to help resist the imposition of compulsive military service. In addition, Archbishop Walsh agreed to act with the Lord Mayor as trustee 'to the anti-conscription fund'. The trades unions agreed to hold a one-day general strike. The 18 April was, as Michael Curran exclaimed, 'A day of dramatic effect.' Leadership had been given, and 'there was great relief and excitement across the country'. The combination of politicians, trades unions, and a united hierarchy was a formidable alliance.[25] In the face of concerted defiance, the British war cabinet decided, at the end of June, to put off the imposition of conscription in Ireland.

Towards the end of the World War, the British prime minister, Lloyd George announced that he was postponing Home Rule. This gave a new impetus to Sinn Féin which had already gained ground by its actions against conscription. In the General Election, 1918, Sinn Féin was victorious in 24 of the 32 counties.

Edward Byrne and Episcopal response 1919-20?
Dr John Bernard, the Church of Ireland Archbishop of Dublin, observed perceptively, if a shade condescendingly, that the Catholic hierarchy were primarily influenced by three factors: nationalistic sentiment (they are 'peasants bred in the Home Rule tradition'); a desire not to forfeit influence over their people

(hence, he suggested, their approach to the Plan of Campaign and to Conscription); and a genuine 'desire to prevent bloodshed'.[26]

How to combine the second and third factors was a problem that reached critical proportions during 1919. It was rendered more acute by the enthusiasm of many of the younger clergy for Sinn Féin which, benefiting from the absence of emigration in the war years, was largely a young person's organisation.

Where was the almost invisible Edward Byrne in all these historical developments? Once again, he left no direct comment on any of them. Even in ecclesiastical affairs he is very seldom mentioned in the *Irish Catholic Directory*. He avoided publicity, judging it a form of self-advertisement.[27] And yet he was held in high regard by fellow priests and by bishops. His name topped the terna for the position of Auxiliary Bishop of Ossory to Bishop Brownrigg in 1918. His name had been sent to Rome as the outstanding candidate and then was withdrawn. At a meeting in Archbishop's House, attended, on 28 October, by Archbishop Walsh and the Bishops of Ossory, Kildare, and the Bishop-Elect of Ferns, the archbishop asked for the exclusion of Edward Byrne, despite his eminent suitability. He testified that 'he has not a sufficiently robust constitution to discharge with success the duties of coadjutorship, which are in a special degree exacting'.[28] A remarkable statement considering that Archbishop Walsh subsequently chose him as Auxiliary for Dublin!

The determination and anger generated by the threat of conscription gave added support to the militancy of Sinn Féin, and created an attitude of mind from which Edward was not immune. This is suggested by the un-ascribed quotation in his notebook, under the heading 'Ireland's Experience': 'Where did we negotiate that we were not betrayed? Where did we menace that we did not succeed?'[29]

Dáil Éireann and Martial Law

A significant part of Sinn Féin's programme was to refuse to attend Westminster Parliament and to set up an Irish parliament. On 21 January 1919, the first meeting of the Irish parliament, or Dáil Éireann, was held at the Mansion House. Thirty-seven of the elected representatives were in prison or overseas. Proceedings were conducted with conscious decorum and in Irish. It was difficult, however, to restrain the younger population. There were outbreaks of violence in different parts of the country.

Meantime, the government held the country under military rule. On 2 March, the Irish bishops, in their pastoral letters, protested strongly against the misgovernment of the country, and the contrast was noted between the words of British ministers during the war about small nations and the government's actual policy in Ireland. Archbishop Walsh, in his pastoral, observed and warned:

> Our people are now shut out by law from the employment of methods of seeking redress regarded as constitutional in the past. It would be unreasonable and indeed impossible to expect that they can long rest content with such a state of things.

The following month the archbishop fell seriously ill. By the end of April he appeared to be recovering but it was clear that he would remain an invalid. The question of an auxiliary bishop could no longer be deferred.

'Bishop-Making' and Edward Byrne

Writing to Fr John Hagan, vice-rector of the Irish College, Dr Walsh's secretary, Fr Michael J. Curran, had information which will come as a surprise to readers who find it difficult to get any clear picture of the very retiring Fr Byrne. 'I need not say', Curran commented, 'that the first published news (of Dr Walsh's illness) set everyone bishop-making. The general result is definite and interesting. Your predecessor holds the field with an undoubted majority and with the assumed, and I believe rightly assumed, support of Cardinal Logue behind him.' The second and third names mentioned were Dr Hickey (president of Clonliffe College) and Mgr Dunne, but the latter seemed rule out by reason of poor health. 'Fr Byrne', Curran continued, 'not only has a majority of the electors, but commands general support among regulars as well as ourselves. Fr Hickey will get some votes. As far as I can see Dr Donnelly and all the heads will support Fr Byrne. It speaks volumes when even a man like Canon Waters is considering abandoning Mgr Dunne and voting for Fr Byrne ... I believe the archbishop would welcome Fr Byrne, but as long as Dr Donnelly is alive his hands are tied.'[30]

There had to be something very special about this modest, self-effacing curate to have received such remarkable support. In later times it would be recalled that in the view of his contemporaries he was a gracious 'gentleman' with 'an extraordinary

personal, unaffected, charm' and sound judgement. He was also
a 'Godly man' and, as a priest, was noted 'for his energy and
zeal, for his preaching, his sodality work, and the careful visiting of the people in their homes. It was there that he came to
value the virtues and depth of faith there was among many of
the Dublin poor.'[31] There was also, as noted, his cheerful disposition and his openness to people.

Hagan received further letters over the summer and autumn
that confirmed Byrne's position as the likely successor. On 1
May, Fr E. R. Morrissey, sometimes writing under the pseudonym 'the Brewer', remarked that in speculations on the possible
successor 'Ned Byrne is most spoken of'. Mgr Dunne seemed
not available; Hickey had some admirers, 'but Mannix has few
supporters'.[32] On 6 July, Fr John Ryan, St Mary's, Foxrock, Co
Dublin, reported 'that the archbishop is better; in rumours about
his putative successor Edward Byrne usually emerges as
favourite'.[33] On 14 September, Michael J. Curran wrote again
from Archbishop's House. He noted that Byrne was mentioned
as a possible successor to 'Canea' (Dr Donnelly), who was very
ill, and that Hagan had heard Byrne mentioned with regard to
Ossory. Curran added confidently: 'Byrne will receive two-
thirds of the vote, Dr Hickey one-third, and [neither is keen on
the post]'.[34]

Meantime, an American delegation from the Irish Race
Convention at Philadelphia came to Dublin on the way to plead the
Irish case for independence before the World Peace Conference.
They obtained a hearing with the ailing archbishop and, as a let-
ter to Hagan on 5 May reported, 'the Irish-American delegates
were welcomed at the Pro-Cathedral by Fr John Flanagan and Fr
Bowden'.[35] Once again, Fr Byrne avoided all self-advertisement.

Contrasting emphasis
Fr Curran's letter to Hagan on 14 September conveyed something of the turmoil of life in Ireland. He told of the current atmosphere of raids, arrests, proclamations, court-martials. But,
he added, 'believe me there are two sides to all these affairs',
pointing to the ever vicious circle of violence, as in the 'Land
War murders'.[36]

Despite the violence and the curtailment of freedom, Bishop
Hallinan of Limerick, on 8 November, gave expression to the
complexities and paradoxes in Irish life by drawing attention to

the Pope's recent complaint about 'immodest fashion in women's dress' and pointing out contentiously that Irish women 'profess their abhorrence of Anglicisation which is going on in our midst, (and) fall victims to it themselves'! Later in the month, 20 November, the strong moral tone was given further expression by a large demonstration at the Mansion House, organised by the Irish Vigilance Association, in support of 'clean performances in theatres and all places of amusement'.[37]

Governmental terrorism
The year 1920 was a year of terror. On 2 January, the Royal Irish Constabulary (RIC) enrolled the first of several thousand recruits, who were later dubbed 'Black and Tans' and were an ill-disciplined force with the task of stamping out rebellion in Ireland. They terrorised the public in many parts of the country, and were conspicuous in a number of prominent murders. Their violence begot violence in return. Tit-for-tat murder and reprisals continued throughout the year, and on occasion captured American and European attention. The event which captured world attention most of all, however, was the hunger strike of the Lord Mayor of Cork, Terence Mac Swiney, who fasted until his death seventy days later: a symbol of the strength and depth of Irish resistance.

From Bishop Donnelly to Bishop Byrne
In March of this troubled year, Dr Nicholas Donnelly died. On 9 April 1920, Archbishop Walsh significantly informed Edward Byrne, regarding the 'month's mind' service in the Pro-Cathedral on 29 April, that he was writing to Fr Bowden, the administrator, telling him 'that I am asking you to preach the memorial sermon'. He had in mind, perhaps, how the curate, Fr Edward Thomas O'Dwyer, made such an impression by his sermon at the month's mind for the late Bishop of Limerick that he was chosen as his successor.[38] The Dublin curate did not disappoint. His cousin, J. J. Maguire, a member of the congregation, observed: 'It was one of the finest pieces of sacred eloquence that it has been my privilege to hear'.[39]

The archbishop had already applied to Rome for a replacement for Dr Donnelly and was informed to send on three names (the terna). On 11 May, he wrote to the members of the diocesan chapter, asking them to offer Mass for guidance and then in strictest confidence to send him 'the names of three, or any lesser number, of priests of the diocese'. On 3 June, Cardinal De Lai, of the Sacred Congregation, informed Cardinal Logue that three names had been proposed for a new auxiliary bishop of Dublin – Edward Byrne, Gerentium O'Donnell, and Bartholomew Fitzpatrick. The first was Byrne '*ut magis idoneus et acceptabilis ab archiepiscopo indicator*' (whom the archbishop indicated to be the more suitable and acceptable). He asked Logue if in his view Byrne came first in terms of the qualities required for the position.[40] Meantime, on 4 June, Patrick Foley, Bishop of Kildare, expressed the hope that Fr Edward J. Byrne would be appointed. He had been 'greatly struck with the exordium of his panegyric on the late Auxiliary'.[41] Cardinal Logue affirmed Byrne's suitability, and the appointment was announced in August.

The new prelate received numerous letters and telegrams of congratulation. All seem to have been acknowledged, though very few of his responses have survived. One of them was a revealing letter to Fr Hagan, now rector of the Irish College Rome. On 28 August he wrote with style and care.

> My dear Dr Hagan,
> I thank you very sincerely for your kind good wishes.
> Although my correspondence has been of the silent kind, I have always felt that if I wanted a friend I could depend on you. Your letter only gives me another assurance that I was not mistaken. In the difficult years gone by, I have had great sympathy for you in the hard task you had before you, and with my knowledge of Rome no one could realise better than I the influences that were arrayed against Irishmen on the spot.
>
> With real gratitude,
> Believe Me,
> Sincerely Yours,
> Edward J. Byrne.
>
> P.S. Nothing arranged yet. I hope you will be in Ireland for the consecration.[42]

Edward was to receive the title, Bishop of Spigaz. On 2 September, in another of his few extant responses to congratulations, he thanked Fr Michael Curran, now transferred to the Irish College, and then asked him to find out whether the alloca-

tion to him of the see of Spigaz was correct, and if so whether
Spigaz actually existed and where. He observed that Spigaz was
not in the official list of titular sees, and that nobody in Dublin
had been able to identify its geographical whereabouts.[43]

Edward J Byrne was consecrated bishop by Archbishop
Walsh at the Pro-Cathedral on 28 October 1920. It was the archbishop's last major ecclesiastical ceremony. It was the day on
which Terence MacSwiney died. The newspapers on the following day were far more interested in recounting the life and
courage of the dead Lord Mayor of Cork, with photographs of
mourners and of the coffin lying in state in Southwark Cathedral,
than in focusing on the new bishop. The Freeman's Journal, nevertheless, managed to provide appropriate coverage in text and
photographs.

Press Tributes. 'A Dubliner of the Dubliners'
Under the heading 'Our New Bishop', the account in the
Freeman paid particular attention to the 'venerable archbishop'
being present, and to his strength as consecrating prelate during
the long ceremony, at which he was assisted by the bishops,Dr
Codd of Ferns, Dr Patrick Foley, of Kildare and Leighlin, Dr
Foley, Archbishop of Ballarat, and Bishop Miller OMI. On Dr
Byrne, the writer made the observations quoted at the beginning
of this book, that he knew Dublin's life, difficulties and dangers
and was 'a Dubliner of the Dubliners, graced by the culture of
old Rome'. As vice-rector of the historic Irish College in Rome,
the journalist added, he was 'in the heart of the Catholic educational tradition', and busy as his life had been 'he never lost the
interests or habits of the student'. 'To many his appointment
came as a surprise, for Dr Byrne has never sought publicity or
notoriety. But his colleagues in the sacred ministry were not surprised. For a priest of his gifts and eloquence he has been stud-
iously retired. But those gifts are all the richer for his quiet life,
and in their new exercise will find their appropriate field. He
will lighten the burden on the great archbishop, whose unflag-
ging spirit and almost youthful energy, has overcome all the
physical handicaps of age.'

The *Freeman* also carried a rather fulsome appreciation by an
un-named contemporary of the new bishop. He commented on
the manner in which Dr Byrne after his consecration as bishop
went down among the mass of the people 'blessing and being

blessed … in the manner born and every inch a bishop.' Yet no one was more unwilling to be a prelate. 'This man had greatness thrust upon him.' Opportunity after opportunity to come into the public eye presented themselves, 'Invitation after invitation to manifest himself to the world were offered him, but he allowed them to pass by unnoticed or deliberately declined them.' Nevertheless, 'his abounding fitness for high preferment' won out 'despite all his efforts to conceal it …' As a curate in the Pro-Cathedral 'he laboured quietly and unobtrusively' but, almost in spite of himself, won 'golden opinions from all who came in contact with him.'

Drawing to a close, the eulogist drew attention to personal qualities: 'The new bishop is a man of many gifts. Stately in appearance, in manner he is simple and of a charm that is irresistible. By nature reserved, yet he is affable and friendly. Personally endowed with great strength of character, he knows how to be patient with the slow, and gentle with the weak. Of clerical life in all its phases he has had first-hand experience, and his fellow-priests love him very dearly. To a sane and finely-balanced judgement he adds an indomitable courage … Still on the sunny side of fifty, he has already gathered to him much which should accompany old age, "as honour, love, obedience, troops of friends".'

The high-flown eulogy would not have appeared exaggerated to the large number of people who wrote to congratulate the new prelate. In many ways they provide much of what is now known about the person, Edward Byrne. Again and again they talk of his goodness and kindness to them and to the sick and the dying, of his affability, and a number commented that he had long been spoken of as the future archbishop. The letters came not only from the parishes in which he had served, but from all parts of Ireland, and some from England, Rome and Paris. They were written mostly by lay people, but also by religious sisters whom he had helped, by members of men's religious orders and congregations, and by many diocesan clergy not excluding bishops.

A close contemporary, Fr John Waters, wrote from Clonliffe College on the day his appointment was announced in the newspapers: 'All your honours, offices and emoluments are each of them a joy to your countless friends, who are delighted to see the "retiring" friend of so many years come out in a day arrayed in so much glory.'[44] The elderly Jesuit, Edward Masterson, wrote that he was sure that it must be known to him, 'as it is known to everyone else, that the priests have got for their Auxiliary Bishop the man whom they all wished to get. I assure your Lordship that this is, as far as I have been able to judge, true to an extent that I have never seen realised in any other case I can recall.'[45] An old lay friend from schooldays, Dudlegh White, sent a message from Stephen's Green Club, 'I am so glad that what all your friends predicted and hoped for has come to pass.'[46] And in a similar predictive vein, there was a remarkable letter from Dr Denis Hallinan, Bishop of Limerick. Writing to congratulate him and welcome him into the hierarchy, he observed that they had in common that they were both educated in Rome, and he then remarked that he remembered a contemporary of Edward's in the Irish College saying:

> That you were even then looked forward to as the future Archbishop of Dublin. Prophecies of this kind are not always to be heeded. But as time went on I found this belief becoming daily more and more general, so much so that when his Grace the Archbishop asked for an Episcopal helper – the general impression abroad in Ecclesiastical circles was that you would be appointed. I regard this as a happy omen for the future ...[47]

Cardinal Logue rejoiced to have 'a young, active, zealous member' added to the Irish episcopate, 'several of whom, like myself, are getting past their work'.[48] But the message that, perhaps, meant most to the new bishop came on 10 August, before the official announcement. It came from Fr P. J. Walsh, the longtime secretary to Archbishop Walsh. 'Dear Ned', he began, as he sent congratulations and then added: 'With the exception of the time taken, everything has worked out according to programme. Your nomination is a real pleasure and relief to the Archbishop, and I am quite confident that your association with him in the administration of the diocese will be a great comfort and help to him in his declining years and will be a source of blessing to the diocese in these critical times'.[49]

'These critical times' were marked by pogroms against Catholics in the north of Ireland as well as martial law and violence in the rest of the country. Shortly after his consecration, Bishop Byrne sent £5 to Joseph MacRory, Bishop of Down and

Connor, as a contribution towards the relief of evicted Catholics. MacRory thanked him on 4 September on 'behalf of the suffering people and myself'. 'I am the more grateful as I know what great expense you must incur at the present time.'[50] Some weeks later a particular poignancy was added to the troubled days. On 1 November, Kevin Barry, a nineteen-year-old university student just one year out of Belvedere College, was executed in Mountjoy prison for killing a British soldier. His was the first execution since May 1916. The government turned a deaf ear to all appeals for clemency. The ailing archbishop, even though it meant being carried upstairs, visited Sir John Anderson, the Under Secretary, in Dublin Castle, and also called on the Viceroy, Lord French, at the Viceregal Lodge, in vain efforts to save young Barry's life.[51] The young man faced his death with great courage, and took on the status of a national martyr celebrated in verse and ballad.

The government's obduracy with relation to Kevin Barry's execution heralded a New Year of unrelenting government-authorised reprisals and executions. It was also to be a year when Edward Byrne had 'greatness thrust upon him' in a very real way with the death of the patriot archbishop. He was left with the leadership of the diocese in years of strife, uncertainty, and bitterness.

One of his well-wishers at after his appointment as bishop, in August 1920, a Fr P. J. Lynch, from the diocese of Clogher, had enunciated an expectation that was burdensome and bizarre: 'We look to you as our future Edward Thomas O'Dwyer and our Daniel Mannix, Ireland wants you. Be our *Dux* (leader) and lead us on to God and to freedom.'[52] The expectation said more about the writer than about reality. Edward Byrne was not lacking in courage and national feeling, but he had not the temperament that sought confrontation on national or other issues. He was a man who worked for peace by conciliation.

PART ONE

A Hard Beginning in Troubled Years
1921-1925

CHAPTER FOUR

1921

Expectations and the New Archbishop

The death of Archbishop William Walsh, on 9 April 1921, was marked by numerous tributes and newspaper accounts of his life and achievements. He was generally acclaimed as one of the great archbishops of Dublin, a very able ecclesiastic who was very much in the public eye, used the press as his pulpit, and had consider-able influence in political affairs. Bishop Byrne, as vicar-capitular of the archdiocese, was in charge of the funeral arrangements. Bishop Brownrigg writing to him, on 18 April 1921, remarked that he understood from newspapers and those who were present 'that the closing scenes in connection with the obsequies and burial of the Archbishop were quite in keeping with what the occasion called for, and on this I may congratulate your Lordship'.[1]

Edward Byrne's appointment as Archbishop was announced from Rome on 28 August 1921, though he was not formally en-throned until 27 October. As has been seen, he was the choice of Archbishop Walsh and his council as his successor, despite his retiring personality. It was later said of him: 'Tall and stately in appearance, and full of quiet dignity, he was eminently gifted to command respect';[2] but what most likely swayed the archbishop in his regard had to be a long acquaintance with Edward Byrne's zeal and humanity as a pastor, his concern for the poor, deep spirituality, interest in scholarship, and sound judgement. A man of strong faith, he chose as the motto of his episcopate, *In Deo Speravi* (I have trusted in God). His trust was destined to be severely tested in the years ahead.

What might be expected then from this new archbishop? The answer could be largely construed from his temperament and pastoral history, outlined above, and from the ecclesiastical cult-ure dominant among Irish prelates and priests.

Ecclesiastical Culture

The influence of the prevailing ecclesiastical culture would, in-evitably, become more prominent in his role as archbishop. That culture placed a particular emphasis on orthodoxy with respect to church teaching. Intellectual curiosity was not encouraged in the areas of dogmatic and moral theology and sacred scripture, and from the beginning of the twentieth century this had been marked across the Catholic Church, following the condemnation of Modernism, in 1907, by Pope Pius X. Under his pontificate, attempts by some Catholic theologians, philosophers, and historians to build a bridge between the church and developments in their disciplines in the modern world, were viewed with fear and suspicion and seen as Modernism, which the pope in his encyclical *Pascendi dominici gregis* condemned as 'a coherent, organised movement with the intentionally concealed purpose of overthrowing Catholic orthodoxy from the inside'. It was a view that was historically unsustainable, but *Pascendi*, and a following document in 1910, 'prescribed draconian measures for removing modernism from the church. Vigilance committees were to be set up in every diocese; censorship was to be extensive and intensive; delation was encouraged and assured of anonymity; and an oath against modernism was to be taken by office holders in the church.' The sobriquet 'modernist' was to remain for the next fifty years as a convenient label for discrediting theological initiatives.[3]

As a result, during the prelacy of Dr Byrne anything suggesting difference from traditional theological teaching or any leaning towards the new biblical criticism was likely to provide grounds for suspicion. Bishops in different countries were conscious that, with the advances in communication, they could more readily be delated to Rome, and that Rome's intervention was closer than in previous times. In Ireland, moreover, the fear of new ideas extended into secular areas such as social reform, historical interpretation, and even reform of the financial system.

Among the positive contributions of Pius X, however, were his encouragement of the frequent reception of Holy Communion, and of lay Catholic Action.[4] Both of these were to be actively promoted by new Archbishop of Dublin.

Lay involvement in church affairs received a further boost in 1921, when the new pope, Pius XI, devoted his first encyclical, *Ubi Arcano Dei,* to urging strong organised action by the laity. His definition of Catholic Action is instructive to an understanding of Edward Byrne's attitude to Catholic lay organisations in his diocese. He defined Catholic Action as 'the participation of the organised laity in the hierarchical apostolate of the church'. Thus, it was to be under the hierarchy, and to be viewed as part of the overall apostolate of preaching, the sacraments, confraternities, sodalities, involvement in education, Catholic press and publications, and so on.[5]

In addition to the influence of such areas of ecclesiastical culture, there was in Ireland the further dimension of closeness between clergy and the majority population arising from a history of persecution. In the new Irish state, the hierarchy would seek to preserve Catholic/Christian values while otherwise not intervening in political affairs, and the lay leaders would show themselves supportive of Catholic values while preserving political independence. Even the most independent of government ministers, Kevin O'Higgins, in an address, in 1923, to the Catholic Truth Society Conference on 'Catholic Laymen in Public Life', called on the Catholic laity not only to breathe 'powerful life into the nostrils of democracy', and to be up and doing, but to promote 'the Catholic social doctrine, which on examination is seen to be the highest and most distinctive creed ever published'.[6]

What might be expected, therefore, from the new archbishop was that he would be a caring, unostentatious prelate, who would be carefully orthodox in theological, moral and scriptural matters and would take steps to ensure orthodoxy in the archdiocese. He would warmly welcome lay involvement in the works of the archdiocese, especially in the service of the poor, provided it remained subject to episcopal control directly or through a nominee. He had a large area to govern, with a variety of calls and demands on his time and attention, and one of the things he did not want was an active lay organisation operating independently of him.

There were other expectations of a more socio-political nature imposed unfairly upon the successor of Archbishop Walsh by men prominent in public life. Thus, Laurence J. Kettle, a member of a prominent political family, informed him on 1 September 1921: 'You come at a historic time and you will have an historic reign ... There may be a critical interregnum, which will be tided over only by the great power of the church, and that will be where we will lean most upon you and find no weak support.' Even more demanding was the message of the well-known city councillor and former Lord Mayor, Lorcan G. Sherlock, on 30 August 1921:

May I in common with the man in the street express the hope

that your reign will coincide with the settlement of political affairs in Ireland, and give us all freedom to work our futures upon peaceable and Irish lines, and may I further predict that during your reign the most pressing of all our local problems, the housing of the working classes will be tackled and dealt with in a thorough manner.[7]

Such excessive expectations were to induce the new archbishop to act as mediator between the opposing sides in the split over the Treaty: an unenviable task that, apart from the respect due his office, would have required the skill, long experience, and unchallengeable nationalist reputation of a younger Archbishop Walsh, to have any chance of success.

Against the background of political tension and sporadic violence, Edward Byrne, following his appointment, set out to acquaint himself more fully with the various needs and responsibilities of his extensive ecclesiastical region. Five months later, on 5 April 1922, the senior suffragan bishop, Abraham Brownrigg of Ossory, was to urge him to apply for an auxiliary bishop, as 'such sees as Dublin cannot be worked by any one man even having the strength of Hercules'.[8]

The Extent of the archdiocese and its works[9]
In 1921 the archdiocese had 77 parishes, of which 18 were in Dublin city. Some 85,033 Catholics were crowded into the area between the Royal and Grand Canals. During Dr Byrne's time in office there was a dispersal of population. Slum clearance by Dublin Corporation was to lead, from 1926, to a spreading of population to new working class suburbs, while more prosperous Catholics moved towards middle class suburbs on the south side of the city. The ratio of diocesan clergy to laity was estimated at 1: 3,000; but there was also a contingent of priests from religious orders – some 350 regular clergy were working in Dublin and its environs in the 1930s.[10] Many of these were involved in education, and they also had devotional magazines and churches which were very significant as centres of devotion, especially with regard to sodalities and confraternities. In addition, there were convents of enclosed religious sisters whose lives were devoted mainly to prayer, and numerous other convents whose members were involved in educational, social and hospital work. Many of these were directly subject to the archbishop and required visitation and pastoral care and guidance from him.

Distribution of time

The archbishop's day was usually full. Apart from special occasions, including ordinations, confirmations, and attendance at special functions, he was at Archbishop's House each weekday, except Saturday, from 11.00 am to 2.00 pm, and for the convenience of the clergy and others who might wish to see him, his Grace, if communicated with beforehand, was happy to fix a time when he could be seen without delay. On Monday, Wednesday and Friday in each week, from 1.30 to 3 o'clock, the vicars general of the diocese attended at the archiepiscopal vicariate, 47 Westland Row, for the transaction of business.

The Builder

After the first few years, during which, as will be seen, political turmoil added greatly to his concerns, one of the problems was change and development. From 1926 into 1930s new working class suburbs were built in Marino, Cabra and Crumlin, and the archbishop's task was to establish parish structures, schools and churches in those areas. The Marino project, where 1,000 new houses were built by Dublin Corporation, was the model for other developments. A total of 23 new churches were built in the Dublin archdiocese between 1921 and 1940. As buildings they were large and cavernous, with little architectural distinction. It was evident that 'the first consideration was economy'.[11] He also devoted time and planning to the hospital needs of the expanding population. He was frequently consulted by the heads of the Catholic hospitals and sometimes by representatives of other hospitals. He, or his representatives, served on the board of many hospitals, including the National Maternity Hospital and Jervis Street Hospital, and he was the driving force behind the establishment of the Children's Hospital in Crumlin.

A Generous Patron to lay organisations

Despite financial constraints, Archbishop Byrne gave generous support to lay Catholic organisations such as the Society of St Vincent de Paul (V de P), the Catholic Truth Society of Ireland (recently reorganised), and the Catholic Young Men's Society (CYMS), and he also sent regular contributions to needy parishes in the west of Ireland. The Legion of Mary was prominent in the diocese but, as will appear later, was not formally approved by Dr Byrne until the 1930s. The V de P Society, however, was particularly esteemed. It had some 4,000 members in Ireland in 1921, with 285 branches, of which 56 were in Dublin.[12] It took care of the spiritual development of its members, each of whom went to communion once a week for the needs of their conference. The families visited were encouraged to practise their religion.[13]

Living conditions
The annual reports of the V de P Society testified to widespread poverty in Dublin during the 1920s and 1930s. The vast majority of the working class lived in tenement houses. A report of the Housing Committee of Dublin City Council in 1938 was to claim that some 19,874 families lived in dwellings unfit for human habitation.[14] In addition, unemployment remained high, as did the infant mortality rate and the incidence of tuberculosis. The middle classes appear to have had improved living conditions in areas such as Pembroke, Rathmines, Rathgar, Blackrock and Dún Laoghaire. Comfortable rather than wealthy, they were composed principally of professional people, civil servants and a host of clerks. 'As a group', it has been observed, 'they displayed a strong attachment to their church, providing as they did many of the vocations for the archdiocese of Dublin and recruits for lay organisations such as the Society of St Vincent de Paul.'[15]

Religious Observance
The outward practice of their religious faith was strong among the poor. The *Irish Catholic* newspaper might complain, in November 1923,[16] of a decline of respect in the churches, too much rushing and pushing like getting into the cinema, and that many did not wait for the conclusion of the Mass, but, in general, attendance at Mass and the sacraments was very high, and sodalities and confraternities flourished. To visitors to the country the people's religious belief was palpable. One such visitor to Dublin wrote in the *Capuchin Annual*, 1938,[17] of

> Men and women, rich and poor, praying together in crowded churches; of a platform speaker at a recent election meeting stopping at the angelus bell and saying the angelus together with an audience of 15,000 people; and the inspiration it was to see a Dublin man on his way to work saying his prayers unconcernedly in the morning train.

A key factor in the formation of this externally devout laity

was the strict adherence to the diocesan programme of catechet-
ical instruction in Dublin schools. The aim of the programme
was to ensure that all children leaving primary school had a
knowledge of the beliefs, commandments, precepts, sacraments, and prayers of the church. From 1882-1950 the instru-
ment to achieve this goal in Dublin schools was the *Maynooth
Catechism*, an abridgement of the much longer *Roman Catechism*.
The method of learning was by rote. Diocesan examiners sought
to ensure that the questions and answers were remembered by
the pupils, and they visited once a year to test their 'knowledge'
of the catechism and of certain prayers. The examiners' reports
for the 1920s and 1930s indicated that the vast majority of children were being successfully instructed.[18] What was learned in
the schools in those years was reinforced at Sunday Mass, where
the homily often dealt with themes covered in the catechism,
and probably confirmed, and maybe elucidated, for the congregation what they had been taught in school, and its application to
their lives. Those fortunate enough to have a full secondary
schooling had opportunities of deepening their basic catecheti-
cal knowledge by school texts on Christian doctrine and apolo-
getics.[19] By and large, however, the knowledge obtained was
not thought out and thought through, and was likely to produce
a Catholic laity that was conventional and legalistic in its religious and moral outlook, measuring religion by externals such
as Mass attendance and respect for the clergy.

Preaching practices
Among the preaching practices in the first half of the twentieth
century were charity sermons and Lenten lectures. The archbishop was frequently invited to be present for the charity sermons, preached on such issues as proselytism, the work of a
Catholic hospital, the plight of the 'fallen woman', communism
and free masonry. Their main purpose was to raise funds for a
wide variety of institutions in the city. These included the
Magdalene asylums in Lower Gloucester Street, High Park and
Donnybrook, where unmarried mothers and former prostitutes
found shelter and assistance; and many schools and orphanages
founded to protect children of the poor from proselytism – such
as St Vincent's girls' orphanage, North William Street, the
Sacred Heart Home for boys, in Drumcondra, and St Saviour's
orphanage, Dominick Street. The sermons were not infrequently

emotive and fervent, with reminders of the soul's danger of condemnation to hell's fire. It was an era of little state support and of long sermons to packed churches. Some priests were noted for addressing social and political issues affecting religion and morality. Among these were M. H. Gaffney OP, and Edward Cahill SJ. The latter was an influential figure, some of whose activities will be noted in a later chapter. He and fellow-Jesuits such as Tom Finlay and Edward Coyne were actively involved in different social endeavours and did much to popularise the social teaching of Popes Leo XIII and Pius XI.

These somewhat more cerebral activities were set against a variety of popular devotions.

Popular Devotions
Among the more universally popular devotions was that to the Sacred Heart, which the archbishop actively promoted, and Marian devotion. In terms of local devotions, Archbishop Byrne was instrumental in promoting at a very early stage the cause of the saintly working man, Matt Talbot. He attended all the hearings of witnesses testifying to manifestations of sanctity. In addition to the developing devotion to Matt Talbot, there was a popular devotion to the Passionist, Fr Charles of Mount Argus, and to the Jesuits, Frs Willie Doyle and John Sullivan. In terms of practices frequent among Catholics in the archdiocese, it has been suggested that they consisted in the following order: Visits to the Blessed Sacrament, weekday Masses, rosary, spiritual communions, acts of charity, stations of the cross, spiritual reading, and works for the poor.[20]

Publications
Dr Byrne was keenly conscious of the importance of Catholic publications in conveying the church's message to the laity. The *Irish Catholic*, the *Standard*, and even the *Irish Independent* in those days, played their part in this process. The magazine with the highest circulation throughout the country was the *Messenger of the Sacred Heart*, but the key body in religious publications was the Catholic Truth Society, which played an important role by its distribution of cheap religious pamphlets, and by its annual public conferences where papers were read on issues of current significance. A key figure in the CTS in the 1920s and 1930s was Frank O'Reilly, who was to work energetically and

efficiently with the archbishop and to be a mainstay in the country's two great religious celebrations during those years.

The foregoing provides some suggestion of the range of diocesan demands on the new archbishop. In his first months he made a small adjustment, indicative of the new combined religious and nationalist outlook. In relation to the Annual Report of the Royal Hospital for Incurables in which his name appeared as 'Roman Catholic Archbishop of Dublin', a title insisted on under the British administration, he had his secretary, Fr Dunne, suggest to the Registrar of the Hospital that henceforth the title should be 'His Grace the Archbishop of Dublin, (The Most Rev. Edward J. Byrne D.D.), Archbishop's House, Dublin'.[21]

In addition to the many diocesan demands, and running through them as he began his prelacy, was concern lest the political negotiations going on in his diocese fail and the country slip into civil war. He felt constrained to do something to promote agreement.

CHAPTER FIVE

Trying to Avert a Civil War

Offering a Solution
Feeling the responsibility of his position, and conscious, per-
haps, of the respect both sides had for his esteemed predecessor,
Dr Byrne decided to write to the president of the Dáil, Éamon
De Valera, who appeared to be the key figure opposing the
Treaty.

'A Chara', he commenced, 'It will be fresh in your memory
that the Bishops at their meeting, mainly owing to your request,
refrained from making any public pronouncement on the Treaty,
and I myself have followed the same course and hence occupy a
more or less detached position. You will not, then, think that in
putting a suggestion before you I am actuated by any hostile or
even partisan feelings, but on the contrary by the most friendly
and uncontroversial sentiment.

'I venture to put before you the following considerations:
1. The Dail is a representative assembly.
2. Apart from its representative capacity it has no other '*locus
standi*'.
3. The country so far as it has spoken – and it has given no
uncertain voice – seems overwhelmingly in favour of the
Treaty.
4. Your conscience and honour will not allow you to vote for
the Treaty.
5. A formal vote of the Dáil on the Treaty will have one of
two effects. The Treaty will be ratified or not. If the Treaty is
rejected the Dáil will be acting against the will of the country;
if the Treaty is ratified, you and those who act with you will
be placed in the position of acting against the will of the nation. No one doubts your honour and sincerity.
Responsibility for the Treaty does not lie at your door. You
have done everything for the wider settlement. Conscience
and honour demand no more.

And so to his suggestion:

> that to save those who act with you from being placed in the undesirable position of acting against the declared will of the people, and to make it possible for them to act with old friends, to avoid a miserable split in the national forces when all should act in consolidating what has been gained, even if that is not all that has been desired – that you should avoid pushing matters to a division.[1] … Could you not, having made your dignified protest, let things go through without any division, without you or those acting with you taking any part in the ratification. It is division that will create the split.
>
> A significant gesture such as I suggest will enshrine you in the hearts of the people. They will recognise you have done your best. Those who act with you will, if not at present, shortly, be thankful to you that you have not cut them off from public life. Ireland cannot spare a single man of you all.[2] I commend my suggestion to your serious consideration and pray that Almighty God may give you his help to come to a right decision.
>
> In all sincerity,
> Yours very faithfully
> Edward J. Byrne,
> Archbishop of Dublin.[3]

The letter had little effect on the outcome. On 7 January there was a division in the Dáil and the Anglo-Irish Treaty was approved by a small majority of seven, 64 votes to 57. Two days later, De Valera resigned as president of Dáil Éireann and then stood for re-election. It was an attempt to win over a number of those who had voted for the Treaty by making the issue one of confidence in himself. He was opposed by Arthur Griffith. The vote for the presidency on 10 January resulted in victory for Griffith by just two votes, 60 to 58. That narrow margin was to determine the future.

Following the vote in the Dáil, a provisional government was elected by those supporting the Treaty. Michael Collins was chairman. He moved quickly and significantly two days later: formally accepting from the Lord Lieutenant at Dublin Castle the transfer of power to the new administration.

The Dáil vote in favour of the Treaty had to be ratified by the country in a general election. The weeks prior to the election

were filled with tension. The archbishop found himself faced
with something that might add to the general tension as a result
of the death of Pope Benedict XV on 22 January 1922.

Diplomacy and the death of Benedict XV
Some days afterwards, Archbishop Byrne received word that
the Lord Lieutenant, Lord FitzAlan, the first Catholic to hold the
position, together with his wife and two other ladies and gentlemen, intended to be present in the Pro-Cathedral for the requiem Mass for the late pontiff. On 29 January, Dr Byrne wrote to
Mr McMahon, secretary to the Lord Lieutenant, saying that he
quite understood Lord FitzAlan's desire to be at the Mass, but
that in the present delicate situation, with the Treaty in danger, it
was his view that the official appearance of the Viceroy at the
Requiem for the Holy Father could 'do nothing but harm', the
magnitude of which he feared to estimate.

The same day he received a respectful but firm reply. His
Grace's letter came as a 'painful surprise'. Lord FitzAlan felt 'not
only entitled to attend, but bound to do so'. As a Catholic, to be
absent on purely political grounds seemed to him 'not only an
act of cowardice, but an insult to the memory of the late Pontiff
and to the Church'. He assured the archbishop, however, that he
did not plan to attend 'in some state – e.g. in uniform, with escort etc', and in such circumstances felt assured he would be received with that courtesy which his Grace might wish to accord
him.[4] The archbishop, presumably, was happy that at least the
Viceroy was not coming 'in some state'.

The Bishops
Where did the hierarchy stand at this stage as regards the
Treaty? All were prepared to give it a working chance. Already
in December 1921, they had appointed delegates to consult the
Dáil about safeguards for Catholics in the north of Ireland. The
delegates were the Archbishop of Dublin and the bishops of
Derry, Down and Connor, Killaloe, and Galway. On 18 December
1921, Bishop McHugh of Derry reported to Archbishop Byrne
that he and the Bishop of Galway had called on Mr Griffith to
discuss arrangements about his meeting with the delegation.
Their meeting reflected the inchoate state of things, expectations
that seem in retrospect quite unreal. Griffith assured them 'that
he would see that the safeguards required would be inserted in

the Treaty so as to afford the necessary protection in case the Belfast parliament refused to come into the Free State.' He also gave them 'much valuable information about the proposed Boundary Commission' and said 'that as soon as the Dáil ratifies the Treaty he would communicate with your Grace'.[5]

After the split in the Dáil vote in January 1922, Dr Fogarty, Killaloe, found the situation 'heartbreaking'[6] and became bitterly opposed to De Valera. Archbishop T. P. Gilmartin, Tuam, observed that the people wanted peace and sound government and he favoured giving the provisional government a chance. He understood that Childers and Miss Mac Sweeney 'have got hold of De Valera'.[7] Cardinal Logue was so angry at the division in the Dáil that he called a meeting of the bishops for 17 January with a view to denouncing De Valera and his followers. This was something quite inappropriate in the view of Byrne of Dublin and Harty of Cashel. Archbishop Harty composed an alternative statement which was shown to Michael Collins, who approved it and added that 'it would be a fatal mistake to publish any denunciatory statement'.[8] The cardinal's initiative was foiled, but he remained committed to his views. His new co-adjutor archbishop at Armagh, Patrick O'Donnell, informed John Hagan on 23 January that there was anxiety for the future of the state and that 'the Archbishop of Dublin is in a difficult post'. He hoped the republicans would 'give the provisional and Free State (governments) a fair chance in matters of governmental administration ...'[9]

In this interlude before the general election there was much confusion, anger, and a propensity for widespread violence. In such a volatile situation, rumours about a papal intervention evoked a strong reaction from the Archbishop of Dublin.

A Papal delegate for Ireland?

Replying to John Hagan on 2 February 1922, Dr Byrne observed that a delegate or nuncio in Dublin 'would cause us immense embarrassment'. He would have the ear of all kinds of disaffected and disgruntled clergy. The Irish College remained the proper medium between the Irish church and the Vatican. The prospect of an Irish government representative at the Vatican was also not welcome. Indeed, it appeared to him 'that the less the laity have to say to ecclesiastical matters the better'.[10]

Five days later, Hagan informed him that the recently re-

appointed Cardinal Secretary of State, Gasparri, seemed likely
to encourage diplomatic relations with the Free State, and that
Cardinal De Lai was pursuing his 'pet project' of changing Irish
episcopal selection through the terna system. Hagan recommended that, 'along with Cardinal Logue', Byrne 'take the matter up himself in Rome since Logue' was 'not vigorous enough
in combat'. He added that the new pope, Achille Ratti, who was
elected as Pius XI on 6 February, was 'satisfactory enough, but
we have got to wait and see before coming to conclusions', to as-
certain whether the late anti-Irish policies were down to the late
pope or to his secretary of state.[11]

Responding to a 'chaotic' state of affairs
In his Lenten pastoral letter on 26 February 1922, Dr Byrne
struck a positive note. Without reference to political differences,
he publicly welcomed the transfer of power and responsibility
to Irishmen. 'In place of the unsympathetic, wasteful and unin-
telligent rule of men alien to us in blood and traditions, we see in
process of being evolved an Irish government which will have
knowledge of our people's needs and may be expected to take a
real interest in solving the many problems that concern our people's well-being.' He exhorted the faithful to pray that peace
might be established, 'and that their native rulers may govern
them with wisdom, discretion and justice'.[12]

The need to pray for peace indicated the growing state of
disorder and violence in the country. At the end of March the
violence took on a new dimension. A conference of the anti-Treaty
members of the IRA established an executive council headed by
Oscar Traynor, which seemed set on preventing a free election.
On 10 April, Bishop Patrick O'Donnell commented that 'even
those formerly moderate in tone' were now using 'strong language'. He hoped that one section of the army would not come to
draw the blood of the other. 'The difficulty arises', he observed
astutely, 'from the prestige of physical force used as a remedy in
recent years.'[13] The following day, Sean T. Ó Ceallaigh reported
from Dublin to Hagan that 'the state of affairs is much more
chaotic than a month ago'. He judged 'that the extreme stance
taken by the new army executive committee contributed to this.
They did not think even Brugha or Boland good enough fighting men to join them.' They might not survive long without
resources, but they were in a position to prevent a free election

in the 26 counties, especially in Munster. In the same letter, he mentioned that he had delivered Hagan's letter to Archbishop Byrne and found him 'very agreeable', and that 'Byrne and Larry O'Neill are meeting the heads of both parties to find an arrangement to end the shootings and general disorder.'[14] The same day, the archbishop's secretary, Fr Patrick Dunne, sent a similar word to Hagan: 'that the Lord Mayor, Larry O'Neill, and the archbishop were stepping in on Thursday to secure a free election and a truce'.[15]

For some time, Byrne had been quietly trying to engage the participants. Edward Mulhern, Bishop of Dromore, informed Hagan some days earlier that Archbishop Byrne had 'more than once' spoken to De Valera 'but told me that all his efforts were useless'.[16] An irritant to Byrne's quiet diplomacy and his desire to avoid exacerbating the situation was Cardinal Logue's desire to call a meeting of the bishops in order to guide the people – by pointing out 'what is for their good, spiritual and temporal'. He informed Byrne on 5 April that he had 'no confidence in a conference with the Valera party. They would talk and wrangle for days about their shadowy republic and their obligations to it. Judging by the past, I believe, if an agreement were come to, these people would not keep it.' If the archbishop believed it would do good, he would call a general meeting of the bishops.[17]

Three days after that, Archbishop Harty told Byrne that he would approve the calling of a general meeting of the bishops provided they issued a statement 'on the necessity of freedom of election, freedom of speech and freedom of the press'. Any statement taking sides would do more harm than good. He wished to hear from his Grace as he was 'in the centre of political activity in Dublin and can form a better opinion than those of us who are away in the provinces'.[18]

Archbishop Byrne agreed with Dr Harty that any taking of sides would do more harm than good, and it was his experience that something objectively quite small could have unfortunate results. He conveyed his sensitivity to the situation in reply to an invitation from his Church of Ireland counterpart, John A. F. Gregg, Archbishop of Dublin, to join him in a public 'resolution of protest against violence and reprisals'. 'Dear Lord Archbishop', Byrne wrote, 'I thank you for your most Christian letter. The condition of public affairs in Ireland is full of dangers. Casual local incidents might easily lead to widespread disturbance, deplorable bloodshed, and perhaps in the end to civil war. This state of affairs has been to me, as it has been to your Grace, the cause of deep and most anxious concern. Before receiving your letter', Byrne continued,

> the Lord Mayor and myself, feeling that something ought to be done to stay the mischief before it had passed all bounds, had invited the leaders of both parties – Free State and Republic – to meet us and make an effort to explore avenues leading towards the preservation of the public peace. Whether anything useful will come of this conference it is difficult to conjecture. *'Spes mea Dominus'*.
>
> I feel that having this conference in view, it would not be advisable for me to join in any other public measure which might be possibly construed as bringing outside and undue influence to bear on the deliberations of the conference. I think you will understand this position. Again, thanking you for your letter and joining with you in the hope that Easter may see the dawn of peace in our land.[19]

The prospect for an Easter peace receded further two days later. On Good Friday, Rory O'Connor and an anti-Treaty force seized the Four Courts, in Dublin; and De Valera, in his Easter proclamation, compounded the situation by appearing to support the action: 'Young men and women of Ireland, hold steadily on … Yours is the faith that moves mountains … Ireland is yours for the taking. Take it.'[20] By Easter day itself there was, as Archbishop Gregg noted in his diary, 'some public uneasiness as to whether there is going to be a revolution'.[21] Despite this, and numerous other provocations, Collins and his provisional government held back lest intervention might lead to civil war. To observers they seemed 'powerless to intervene'[22] and perpetrators of violence were encouraged to act with impunity.

Cardinal Logue could not hold back any longer. He requested the secretaries of the bishops conference to call a general meeting with a view to issuing a combined formal declaration; and then on Holy Saturday, 15 April, wrote somewhat apologetically to Archbishop Byrne that he had done so before he 'knew of the conference called by your Grace and the Lord Mayor of Dublin'. 'There was a sigh of relief through the country', Logue continued, 'when this conference was announced in the papers; and I hope you will be able to bring the parties to a satisfactory agreement. Even then I fear it will be hard to keep De Valera and his party from wriggling out of any agreement reached …'[23]

In his letter earlier in April, Edward Mulhern, Bishop of Dromore, had observed to Hagan that he now could see little hope of peace as long as De Valera held sway over the Republican ranks. 'The cry in everyone's mouth', he wrote, 'is why isn't there someone to bring the leaders together and the only reason that one can give is that the task is hopeless.' He believed that the Treaty Party would welcome 'an advance of this kind', and he also knew that friends of De Valera had tried to get him to see that the Treaty could be used as a means 'of working towards the ultimate object'.[24] Archbishop Byrne was well aware of the small chance of success. He had experienced the bitter intransigence of many on the Republican side, an intransigence based on a mixture of loyalty to De Valera, loyalty to the Republic, and anger against those who 'betrayed the Republic'. Nevertheless, as he had mentioned to Archbishop Gregg, he and the Lord Mayor felt it necessary to respond to the public cry by doing something 'to stay the mischief before it had passed all bounds'.

The intractable conference

Dr Byrne left no account of the conference. The only reference to it is in passing references in a small diary.[26] On Wednesday, 19 April, his entry read: 'Mansion House 3 o'clock'; the following Wednesday, 26 April, it was: 'Mansion House 11 o'clock'; and on Friday 28 April: 'Mansion House, Labour delegates, 11 o'clock'. The following day, Saturday 29 April, was much the same as the others: '11 o'clock Mansion House'. It was, however, the final and critical day.

It is difficult to establish the exact course of events. It would appear that the archbishop, the Lord Mayor, Laurence O'Neill, and Stephen O'Mara (senior) of Limerick, met in the first days with Collins and Griffith, and with De Valera and Cathal Brugha. Meantime, on 24 April the Labour Party and Trade Union Congress called a successful general strike throughout the Free State against 'militarism'. Subsequently, it would seem, that as the negotiations were not going well, the archbishop and Lord Mayor met with a Labour delegation and invited them to join the conference. They were present at the conference meeting on 29 April.

Archbishop Byrne endeavoured to create a climate of good

will and serious intent by his opening words. A draft of the speech, or part of it, in the Dublin Diocesan Archives gives an indication of what he said. On behalf of the Lord Mayor, Mr O'Mara, and himself, he thanked those present for attending. They had been invited 'not in any way to interfere with the political principles of either side or to dictate political beliefs to anyone'. They had 'not been invited in the interests of any party or any section'. He then proceeded:

> For some time past events have been recurring and incidents taking place that have arroused a grave anxiety and well-grounded fear that the nation is heading straight for civil war. The Lord Mayor and myself, looking on bloodshed amongst brothers as the ultimate calamity, thought we ought to make an effort to stave off such a disaster by calling together the leaders of the people on both sides in the hope that a conference might hammer out some arrangement by which peace could be maintained.
>
> It is a strange thing that we should use the first instalment of anything like freedom to engage in fratricidal strife. Already hearts have been made sore enough by the British bullet and British bayonet without Irishmen bringing more sorrow to Irish homes.[26]

The appeal seems to have made little impression. Some extant but obscure notes of the archbishop suggest little effort to build bridges. On the issue of the occupants of the Four Courts showing open defiance of the government, Cathal Brugha declared that the present government could not be considered to be an Irish government as they had given away their power to another government. Arthur Griffith responded that the Four Courts action had repudiated Dáil Éireann. The Dáil cannot, without abdicating power, sit or talk with mutineers. Michael Collins made three proposals, one of which envisaged having a plebiscite 'for and against the Treaty'. To this, Brugha replied: 'No such issue should be put while threat of war is there' from England. Personal animosities had become part of the problem.[27]

On 29 April, three Labour delegates attended – Thomas Johnson, William O'Brien, and Cathal O'Shannon. From the outset it was evident to them that there was little likelihood of any agreement. The situation, as long-established party member and trade union leader, William O'Brien, remembered it was described in his *Forth the Banners Go*.[28]

'Cathal Brugha made a statement, mainly for our benefit, and from this it appeared that the parties were at daggers drawn.' In the course of the statement 'he referred to Messrs Griffith and Collins as agents of the British government. The archbishop intervened at this, following a protest by Griffith and Collins, and said he was sure that Cathal Brugha would withdraw this statement. Brugha replied that he would withdraw the statement but he regarded any people that did the work of the British government as agents of the British government. This, of course, only added fuel to the flames and the conference appeared to be on the point of breaking up ... Griffith and Collins on one side of the table were standing up, so was De Valera. Brugha remained in his seat and seemed very quiet and composed. Collins showed his irritation more than Griffith and, placing his hands on the table bent over Brugha' and, referring to an earlier speech of his, asked: 'I suppose we are two of the ministers whose blood is to be waded through?' Speaking quietly but distinctly, Brugha replied: 'Yes, you are two.'

There followed a sharp interchange between De Valera and Griffith, at which Archbishop Byrne intervened 'Now, gentlemen, this won't do any good.'[29] Shortly afterwards the meeting concluded. Subsequently, De Valera issued a press statement in which he announced: 'Republicans maintain that there are rights which a minority may justly uphold, even by arms, against a majority.' He proposed a further six-month adjournment before an election so that 'time would be secured for the present passions to subside, for personalities to disappear ...'[30] In fact, events had passed De Valera by. The extreme militants had taken over the Republican movement.

For Archbishop Byrne, the friction and collapse of the conference must have been a chastening experience; but he does not seem to have been particularly downcast. Two days later, in writing to John Hagan about a number of items of business, he mentioned, almost by the way: 'As you may have seen, I have made an effort to secure that Pro and Anti-Treatyites might at least keep their hands off each other. The effort, as I more or less anticipated, resulted in failure.'[31] He remained open, however, to further opportunities to prevent bloodshed. Meantime, he had a backlog of matters requiring his attention.

Catching up on routine

Dr Byrne's involvement with the conference meant that he missed the general meeting of the bishops and, as he informed Hagan in the same letter, 'with the areas of diocesan work to make up, I see no possibility of going to Rome this year. My programme is full well into the summer.'[32] Within days of writing, he commenced a series of confirmations at Rathmines, Clondalkin, Dún Laoghaire, and Sandford.[33]

On top of outstanding correspondence, there were fresh requests demanding attention. On 13 May, Professor Tim Corcoran SJ, professor of education at University College Dublin, reported that following their meeting on 20 March relating to a summer course on Catholic Religious Instruction for teachers in secondary schools, he had contacted members of the bishops standing committee but as yet had not received permission to proceed. As the time for the summer course was now close at hand, he would be very grateful for any indication of his Grace's decision on the matter. Three days later, Professor Corcoran was able to express his thanks for his Grace's 'most kind letter'. The organisation of the course would proceed at once, and he expected very soon to be able to submit it in fair detail for Dr Byrne's approval or further directions.[34]

A week later the archbishop responded to a corporation official on a subject dear to him. He assured Mr Farren that it would give him the greatest pleasure to use all his influence with the trustees of Clonliffe College to secure an amicable arrangement between the college trustees and the Corporation so that the college property known as Donnelly's orchard might be made available for suitable dwellings for the workers of Dublin. He took it for granted, however, that the proposed houses would 'be suitable homes for single families and not undesirable barrack dwellings,' as heretofore, which provided 'neither comfort nor decent privacy to the worker families'.[35]

The previous day, the Minister for Education, Micheál Ó hAodha, wrote about a shortage of trained primary teachers with a sufficient knowledge of Irish to teach the new programme, but his Grace did not reply until 14 June. Then he explained that 'like yourself I have been overrun with work, and have had scarcely time to give the subject of your letter the consideration it deserves'; and then told him that, in any event, the matter concerned the entire body of the bishops and that he should write without delay to the episcopal secretaries at Maynooth. There was a meeting of the standing committee of the bishops next Monday.[36]

The archbishop endeavoured to act with dispatch and in a gracious style, but the range of demands was oppressive. M. J. Curran reflected something of this in a letter from Dublin to Hagan on 14 June, the very day of the belated reply to Mr Ó hAodha: 'The archbishop has aged considerably, but he is popular and is regarded as shrewd by his secretaries.'[37]

This was just two days before the long awaited general election on 16 June. The result showed: Pro-Treaty Sinn Féin 58, anti-Treaty Sinn Féin 36, Labour 17, Farmers 7, Independents 10. Given that Labour and the Farmers supported the treaty, the government was greatly strengthened. The government ministers, generally, had bent to the task of governing with determination. Liam T. Cosgrave provided an earnest of this in a letter to Archbishop Byrne on 22 June. He and Byrne had common views on many social issues. Cosgrave suggested that in view of their recent conference on unmarried mothers, his Grace might take steps to form a central committee, of a federal character, to unify and help the efforts of the existing religious and charitable associations. 'We are in a position to give immediate help (50% grant) in respect of arrangements for attending to the health of expectant or nursing mothers and of children under five years of age.' The government would be glad to co-operate in any way with his Grace if he undertook this proposal. It was felt that the step might suitably be taken by him, as apart from his special interest, the work hitherto had been largely under religious and charitable auspices.[38]

The archbishop was to demonstrate during his episcopate considerable interest in assisting expectant mothers and young children, but his reply on this occasion is not available, and the matter was unlikely to receive attention in the immediate future because of two unwise and provocative events. On that same date, 22 June, Field Marshal Sir Henry Wilson was assassinated in London (for which two members of the London battalion IRA were arrested, and executed); and on 27 June members of the anti-Treaty force in the Four Courts kidnapped the pro-Treaty General J. J. 'Ginger' O'Connell. This, combined with pressure from the British government for strong action, resulted the following day in an attack on the Four Courts by the government forces. It marked the start of the civil war, which the archbishop, the Lord Mayor and so many others, had striven to prevent.

CHAPTER SIX

1922

Trials, Challenges and the Civil War

Efforts towards peace
The shelling of the Four Courts by government artillery led to its destruction and that of the Public Record Office. On 30 June Rory O'Connor surrendered. Meantime, anti-Treaty forces seized the Hammon Hotel and other points throughout the city. On Saturday 1 July, anxious to prevent the struggle spreading and responding presumably to a desire to negotiate on the part of some of the insurgents, the archbishop and the Lord Mayor obtained a pass from Oscar Traynor, brigade commandant of the anti-Treaty forces, allowing them 'to leave and enter the Barracks (*sic*) at all hours'.[1] There is some confusion about the outcome. It is alleged that, as a result of their visit, the archbishop proposed to Michael Collins that the anti-Treaty forces be allowed to march out without giving up their weapons. Collins reportedly replied, 'Let them lay down their weapons and then we will talk to them.'[2] A note, however, from the Minister of Local Government, William Cosgrave, on the same date of 1 July, indicated that the archbishop and the Lord Mayor brought the proposal to him. His brief note reported that he had received a visit from the Lord Mayor and the Archbishop of Dublin accompanied by Mr Cathal O'Shannon (Labour Party) in connection with proposals relative to the Irregular forces. It was decided that these proposals were unacceptable and that the military action in progress against the Irregulars should be vigorously continued'.[3]

Next day, 2 July, Fr M. J. Curran wrote from Jervis Street Hospital, Dublin, to John Hagan, that sniping was going on in Upper O'Connell Street and Gardiner Street, and that De Valera had joined the fighting men, with Robert Barton and Miss Mary MacSwiney, as well as Cumann na mBan. He also commented, 'Fr Albert is much shaken.'[4] Fr Albert, a Capuchin priest well known to Sinn Féin since 1916, had stayed with the Irregulars in the Four Courts, and afterwards joined them in the Hammon

Hotel. He was anxious for an honourable end to hostilities. It is not unlikely that he met the archbishop when he and the Lord Mayor visited Hammon Hotel, and may even have been a spokesman for some of the insurgents. In any event, on the day of the visit he approached a Mr J. F. Homan, of the Dublin Ambulance Brigade, and persuaded him to be an envoy for a cessation of hostilities. A copy of Homan's report of his unusual and ultimately fruitless activities and negotiations was sent to Archbishop Byrne.[5] It captured something of the personalities of key people, and indicated the depth of intransigence of some and their persistent belief in a sacrificial death to rouse the people.

Homan met with Michael Collins, who assured him that nobody wished to hurt or humiliate the men on the Irregular side. 'They are at liberty to march out and go to their homes unmolested if only they deposit their weapons in the national armoury …' Bearing this proposal, Homan then met Robert Barton. The latter did not trust the sincerity of Collins's message. Collins and his men had betrayed the Republic and were killing their countrymen on behalf of the English government. 'We want no terms other than victory or death.' Nothing daunted, Homan contacted De Valera, who seemed to see hope in the proposal but made it clear that the decision lay with the fighting men. That brought Homan to Cathal Brugha, who informed him that they would never lay down their arms. 'We are out to achieve our object or to die. There is no use negotiating with Mr Collins.' Dispirited, Homan reported back to Fr Albert and then sought to meet De Valera once more, but the Hammon Hotel was deserted and De Valera was gone. At this stage the surrender and fall of the insurgents' stronghold in O'Connell Street was a question of an hour or two . Homan met Fr Michael O'Flanagan and gave him an account of his negotiations. Fr O'Flanagan agreed with him that he could do no more.

That same day, 5 July, Cathal Brugha was wounded and captured. He died two days later. As the war in Dublin came to a close, the Free State army in the city moved south to counter the occupation of certain cities and strategic points by the anti-Treaty forces.

Meantime, the behaviour of some clergy brought additional pressure on Edward Byrne. On 8 July 1922, a Fr Costello had called at Lever Brothers, Parliament Street, where Free State troops were stationed and tried to induce them to lay down their arms, calling them murderers and 'Green Black and Tans' working for the British government. William Cosgrave brought Costello's behaviour to the archbishop's attention on 21 July.[6] He also named a number of other priests who had 'used their sacred position as a shelter for treasonable acts': The Capuchins, Fr Dominic and Fr Albert; an Australian priest, a Fr Doyle, with temporary faculties in the Dublin diocese; and Dr P. Browne of Maynooth who visited the Irregulars and heard their confessions thereby encouraging them in the early days of the struggle. Cosgrave went on to supply the names and addresses of priests in the diocese who were known to be sympathetic to the republican side. Of these, 15 were diocesan clergy, three were Passionists, and eight were Capuchins.

The archbishop acknowledged Mr Cosgrave's letter on 23 July and requested him to assure the government that the painful matters he had brought under his notice, would receive his 'most earnest consideration'.[7] One known instance of a diocesan priest who experienced his 'earnest consideration' was a Listowel man, Charles Troy, who was a post-graduate student at Maynooth and a member of the Dublin archdiocese. At home on leave during July, he made an inflammatory speech denouncing the Treaty. Subsequently, he believed that either Cosgrave or a Kerry parish priest had reported him to the archbishop. In the event, he found himself rusticated for several years in a remote parish near Glendalough, Co Wicklow.[8]

Earlier, on 13 July, Bishop Brownrigg of Ossory sent a comforting letter to his archbishop. He offered his 'very heart felt sympathy' in the dreadful tornado of suffering and desolation in which his diocese had been involved. It was a hard trial for his Grace just beginning his career as archbishop, but he who had chosen him to meet the trial would see him safely through it. One good thing sure to come from it was the sympathy of his fellow bishops, and that of the people of the diocese and of the country at large.[9]

During July, Waterford and Limerick fell to the government forces. The elderly Bishop of Limerick, Denis Hallinan, commented that 'since the bombing of the Roman walls in 1870' he had not had 'a comparable experience with the last fortnight's unbroken fusillade of rifle and machine guns. The republican morale was broken down, and they stole out of the city at night.' He believed there was 'no alternative to the present campaign if the country was to be saved.'[10] Most of the bishops seemed to be of a similar mind. M. J. Curran reported from Dublin on 19 July that excommunications were pronounced by the Cardinal and Bishop Morrisroe (Achonry) in cases of destruction of infrastructure and looting; and the following day, displaying his republican sympathies, 'the bishops are as bad as anybody, (and) will follow Killaloe (and) others of our friends into any wild series of denunciation of republicans that forms the staple of their daily conversation. The Cardinal was never so vehement.'[11]

His Grace of Dublin, because of his location, was faced with problems different from most of his fellow prelates. He became the recipient of complaints on behalf of republican prisoners. On 24 July he received the first of three letters from Count Plunkett complaining that republican prisoners in Mountjoy jail were being refused absolution by the prison chaplains unless they undertook not to fight against the Provisional Government, and that they did so on the orders of his Grace. Dr Byrne responded on 25 July that he had 'not interfered in any way with the chaplains of Mountjoy prison in the discharge of their duty in the tribunal of Penance', and he enclosed a pronouncement of the bishops addressed to the people of Ireland which gave the moral teaching of the church on recent affairs. Plunkett next day provided further testimony of republican prisoners being refused absolution, and on 19 August demanded that the archbishop tell him plainly if these men, and the other Republican prisoners in Kilmainham and other Dublin prisons – who numbered now nearly two thousand persons – were still excluded from these sacraments of their faith? The archbishop, clearly under pressure, replied that the chaplains had given a categorical denial to the report and to his having instructed them.[12]

Two days later the issue was raised once more. This time from Art O'Connor in Mountjoy. The chaplains withhold absolution 'unless in defiance of our reason and our conscience we admit that our recent action was wrong and promise not to do the same in future'. 'We are soldiers of the Irish Republic', O'Connor continued, and 'in common with hundreds of thousands of the Irish people and many of the people's elected representatives we deny the authority of the Provisional Government, and we respectfully submit that if a priest holds an opposite view in this matter he is not entitled to force his view as an article of the church's teaching ...'[13]

The archbishop's reply, if any, is not extant. It is not likely that any response, other than full agreement, would have satisfied the writer.

On 24 February 1923, however, the archbishop gave a fuller explanation of his position which, seemingly, he had presumed was evident following the joint pastoral letter of the bishops of Ireland condemning those who took up arms against the lawfully elected government. He was responding to Eithne MacSuibhne (MacSwiney), who had raised the issue on a number of occasions. The bishops of Ireland, acting in discharge of their office as authorised teachers and interpreters of the law of God had declared that certain actions were grave sins and that any person intending to persevere in participating in such actions was not in a fit disposition for the worthy reception of the sacraments, and might not be admitted to them. Consequently, no priest who did his duty could disregard 'this solemn and official teaching of the Pastors of the Church', nor could he with safe conscience admit to the sacraments those who were prepared to act contrary to this official teaching. 'You are quite right', he concluded, 'in thinking that danger of death is not of itself any reason for administering the sacraments to a person indisposed for them.'[14]

Death of Leaders and Signatories

On 11 August Cork fell to the Free State army. The war seemed all but over, but the Irregular leaders decided to continue the struggle by a guerrilla warfare. The conflict, almost immediately, took an unexpected toll of the Free State leaders who had been signatories of the Treaty. On 12 August Arthur Griffith died of a cerebral haemorrhage. Ten days later, on 22 August, the country was shocked to learn of the killing of Michael Collins in an ambush. Edward Byrne participated in the public mourning for both men.

On 20 August 1922, a large number of bishops and priests from almost every parish in the country assembled in Dublin for President Griffith's funeral. A contemporary photograph shows the tall, erect figure of Dr Byrne leading a long procession of clergy to the entrance of the Pro-Cathedral, where he presided at the funeral Mass.[15]

Subsequently, sharing the nation's shock, it was his sad duty to preside at the funeral of Michael Collins. A sombre and poignant painting by Sir John Lavery. which hangs in Áras an Uachtaráin, depicts the moment of the elevation of the Host during the Funeral Mass in the Pro-Cathedral. The coffin of the dead leader is draped in the new national flag, the Tricolour. The first time, it is said, that the flag 'draped the coffin of a slain Irish soldier during a religious service'.[16]

The distress and anger on the government side was palpable during those days. On the day of the announcement of Collins's death, Bishop Foley, writing to Archbishop Byrne on educational issues, observed significantly:

> I don't suppose that the unfortunate Government will be able to deal with such matters for a considerable time, if indeed they will be able to deal with them at all ...[17]

Fortunately, the leadership passed, on 25 July, to the steadying hands of the unobtrusive chairman of the provisional government, William Thomas Cosgrave. The struggle, however, took on an extra bitterness and intensity.

The anti-Treaty forces set about destroying public and private property, especially the houses of unionists and large landlords, and generally preventing the country from settling down and working the Treaty in peace and order. There were atrocities on both sides. Among the government forces there were instances of cruelty and of the murder of prisoners. Laurence Ginnell TD, on 14 September 1922, complained to Archbishop Byrne and to the editors of the Dublin daily newspapers about 'a salaried murder gang having headquarters at Oriel House, paid and maintained with Irish money by William Cosgrave, and operating under the supreme command of Richard Mulcahy'. Recent murders committed in cold blood had their origin in Oriel House. He concluded in his letter to the archbishop: 'The papers are afraid to speak out. The coroner shields the murderers'. A condemnation by the archbishop was called for as 'the highest moral authority'.[18]

The harried and exhausted archbishop was out of the country on holidays when Ginnell's letter arrived. There seems to have been no extant reply. Had his Grace enquired of Mr Cosgrave, as he often did on other matters, it is likely in this case that he would have been met with a denial and a reminder of unscrupulous republican propaganda. Oriel House, a large redbrick building at Westland Row was, in Ernest Blythe's understatement, 'a somewhat doubtful institution'[19] and, according to Colonel Dan Bryan of Irish army intelligence, it was in those years a wild spot, with much drinking, lack of discipline, and ill-treatment of prisoners. The man in charge, P. M. Moynihan, was, in Bryan's view, a particularly insidious, unscrupulous and dangerous individual.[20]

Towards the end of August, Edward Byrne had been happy to get away from Ireland. His journey took him to London, then to Brussels and on to 'Koln' (Cologne). On 4 September, he moved from there to Wurzburg, and thence to Nuremberg and Munich. On 20 September he reached Frankfirt, and commenced the journey home through Cologne and Aachen.[21]

While he was away, the third Dáil assembled and W. T. Cosgrave was elected president of the government. The anti-Treaty deputies did not attend. On 28 September, faced with continuous armed activity by Irregulars, and court delays because of the large number of republican prisoners, the Dáil approved a motion to establish military courts with power to impose a death penalty. It was also a time of renewed efforts for peace.

A letter from Sean T. Ó Ceallaigh to the archbishop and the Lord Mayor, dated 28 August, urged them to make a further effort to bring 'the unhappy civil war to an end'. He believed some of the republican leaders were open to negotiation.[22] The archbishop was out of the country. But John Hagan, home on holidays, followed up Ó Ceallaigh's proposal. A friend of both Ó Ceallaigh and De Valera, he met with General Mulcahy and Rory O'Connor but to little avail. There were a sufficient number entrenched on both sides to prevent an agreed solution.[23] On Dr Byrne's return, he met with P. T. Keohane (Keoghane), a friend of Hagan and sympathiser of the republicans, who sought to promote further negotiations for peace. Keohane was disappointed with the meeting. Byrne, faced with a backlog of work, and with experience of previous attempts, was less than hopeful of the outcome.[24] On 10 October, the date fixed for the bishops' meeting, a further proposal came to his Grace. This time it came from a Thomas Markham, who claimed that he had been a member of Collins's intelligence team. He suggested that his Grace propose at the bishops' meeting 'that a great and determined attempt ... be made to compel a truce'. He believed that the time was opportune, that De Valera and Liam Lynch were 'not averse to a conference'.[25]

It is not evident that the archbishop replied. It seemed yet another unlikely prospect. Besides, the bishops' meeting came at a time when he had so much to do, and he did not welcome, it seems, the episcopal desire to produce a joint pastoral letter condemning the guerilla activities of the anti-Treaty forces. He was uneasy about taking sides in a political struggle, however strongly he felt about supporting the government. Perhaps because he was away for most of September, and felt himself facing a tide of opinion, it is not clear that he strongly challenged the extensive episcopal view at the conference. He put his name to the joint pastoral letter, for which he mainly was to feel the brunt of republican anger.

The pastoral letter was strong and uncompromising and it endeavoured to cover all aspects of the on-going struggle. It was made public after the bishops' meeting, and was read in all the churches and public oratories at the principal Masses on Sunday, 22 October. The sharpness of the republican reaction indicated the importance of the bishops' letter.

The Joint Pastoral Letter

The congregations across the country were reminded that they were 'conscientiously bound' to abide by their lordships' teaching, 'subject, of course, to an appeal to the Holy See'. The letter was both wide-ranging and particular. 'A section of the community refusing to acknowledge the Government set up by the nation, have chosen to attack their own country as if she were a foreign power. Forgetting, apparently that a dead nation cannot be free, they have deliberately set out to make our Motherland, as far as they could, a heap of ruins ... They carry on what they call a war, but which, in the absence of any legitimate authority to justify it, is morally only a system of murder and assassination of the nationalist forces – for it must not be forgotten that killing in an unjust war is as much murder before God as if there were no war'... Side by side with this destruction of life and property there was a running campaign of plunder, raiding banks, seizing land and the property of others, burning mansions and country houses, and slaying cattle.

Religion itself was not spared. A certain section had engaged in a campaign against the bishops, 'whose pastoral office they would silence by calumny and intimidation'; and in spite of all their sin and crime, they claimed to be good Catholics, 'and demanded at the hands of the church her most sacred privileges, like the sacraments, reserved for worthy members alone.' The bishops' document pointed out that the long struggle of centuries against foreign rule and misrule had weakened respect for civil authority in the national conscience, and that if Ireland were ever to overcome its miserable record of anarchy, all classes of her citizens must cultivate respect for and obedience to the government set up by the nation. Hence, they decreed that all who carried on war against the government in contravention of the bishops' teaching were 'guilty of the gravest sin' and might not be absolved in Confession, nor admitted to Holy Communion, if they purpose to persevere in such evil courses'.[26]

Turning to the issue of priests supporting the Irregulars' insurrection, the pastoral letter declared that if there were any such, they were 'false to their sacred office', and guilty of the gravest scandal. They would not be allowed to retain the faculties they held. Furthermore, each bishop for his own diocese, hereby 'forbade under pain of suspension, *ipso facto*, reserved to the Ordinary, any priest to advocate or encourage this revolt, publicly or privately'. Finally, with respect to young men who were deterred from seeking peace by the oath they had taken, their Lordships insisted that 'no oath can bind any man to carry on a warfare against his own country in circumstances forbidden by the law of God. It would be an offence to God and to the very nature of an oath to say so.'[27] The bishops denied any political bias. They issued the document out of a responsibility to preach the doctrine of the Divine Master and to safeguard the rule of faith and morals.

Republican reaction

Archbishop Byrne received an immediate response. On 11 October, a Cathleen O'Moore, Drumcondra, wrote several pages presenting 'the Republican side of the picture'. 'Your Grace has all the nice points of the "Treaty", that shameful thing that no Irishman worthy of the name should consider for a moment. Surely if you had known our motives, our ideals, our sacrifices in the cause of justice and truth, you would never consent to put your name to the Pastoral, which I assure you has shocked and hurt many of your people.'[28] There were voices of criticism also among the clergy. One priest was quoted as declaring that 'the Irish bishops gave their solemn benediction to a murderous and traitorous usurpation'.[29]

A printed republican reaction appeared on 14 October, which was quite blunt and unrelenting:

The latest Pastoral of the Irish Bishops demands immediate and decisive action on the part of Republicans. It is literally 'Now or Never'. Three things should be done at once:
1. A Republican Government and ministry must be set up and proclaimed
2. A supreme effort should be made to wipe out the Provisional Government; or at least to paralyse it at its centre – Dublin
3. In the present divided state of Catholic opinion – lay and clerical – in Ireland, Rome should be asked immediately to appoint an Apostolic Delegate for Ireland from Italy or some neutral nation.[30]

On 26 October, the concern about the effect of the pastoral letter, resulted in the Republican Dáil Éireann passing a resolution asking the president, De Valera, to make representation immediately to the Vatican 'against the unwarrantable action of the Irish Hierarchy in presuming and pretending to pronounce in authoritative judgement upon the question of constitutional and political fact now at issue in Ireland – viz: Whether the so called Provisional (Partition) Parliament, set up under threat of unjust war and by a *coup d'état*, was the rightful legislature and government of the country or not – and in using the sanctions of religion to enforce their own political views …'[31] They were availing of the opening mentioned in the pastoral letter that people were bound by the bishops' teaching 'subject, of course, to an appeal to the Holy See'. This now became a means of negating the episcopal teaching pending the result of an appeal to Rome. The resolution came a day after the Dáil supporting the Treaty approved the Constitution of the Irish Free State.

Defiant clergy
What Edward Byrne found particularly trying was the defiant attitude of some clergy, especially among religious orders, towards the episcopal pastoral letter. The depth of his feeling was reflected in a letter to the provincial of the Passionists on 31 October 1922. The provincial had requested permission to open a further house in the Dublin archdiocese.

The archbishop apologised for his delay in replying to the

provincial's letter of 31 August: 'I was away from home for some time and since my return I have been rushed to overtake arrears of work.' He refused the request as he had done with similar requests from other orders. It would cause dissatisfaction to make an exception. He continued: 'Besides, I may add quite frankly, the attitude of some members of your community towards the Pastoral Teaching of the Irish Bishops has not inspired me with any particular desire to have another such community in this diocese. The attitude I allude to, must be well known to the superiors of the congregation as it is certainly well known to the people of Dublin, and I can only draw the inference that the superiors of the congregation do not wish to detach themselves from methods which have given anything but edification to our people.'

On 3 November, the provincial, Malachy Gavin CP, replied from London in a conciliatory and astute manner. Of course he accepted his Grace's decision regarding the new foundation and could not reasonably expect preferential treatment. As regards the other matter to which his Grace had 'alluded in confidence', he wished to explain that there were two priests in Mount Argus who were active in political matters, Frs Joseph and Kieran. They were 'estimable and convinced priests' but believe 'they have a mission to save Ireland from herself'. Their dislike of England was so intense that they cannot be moved to England or the North of Ireland. He cannot very well denounce them in public for this would only accentuate the evil. A number of extremists in Dublin would immediately raise a clamour. There remained, Fr Gavin confessed, 'only the endeavour to persuade them that it is altogether against the spirit of our Rules to intervene in political matters; and this I have striven to do, with at least some success'. After some further remarks, he was sorry if they had unintentionally added 'to his Grace's worries', and assured him of his 'profound esteem'.[32]

Mary Mac Swiney's case

Someone who sought to 'add to his Grace's worries' was Mary MacSwiney, who was on hunger strike and wrote to him from prison on 5 November 1922. With fervent republican fundamentalism, she informed him that with God's help she would carry her hunger strike through 'as bravely as my sainted brother did, for the same cause and with equal justification'. She accused

Byrne and his episcopal colleagues of supporting, by their October Pastoral, 'perjurers, job hunters, materialists; and driving away those who stand for Truth and Honour and who refuse to take, or sanction others to take, false oaths'.[33] She challenged his Grace by asking if he was going to have it on his conscience that he deprived her of the sacraments in the days of her suffering and in the event of her death.

Dr Byrne replied on 8 November that 'in all humility' he, too, loved his country and his people 'as much as many who make more open profession of patriotism', and that in their pastoral letter the bishops were acting as 'divinely authorised interpreters of the Divine Law'. He refused to yield to her principal demand for the sacraments, telling her firmly that if anyone in Mountjoy prison 'openly manifested to the chaplain an intention of contravening this authorised teaching, it is clear that he, the chaplain, is not free to do otherwise than to follow the directions set forth in the Pastoral'. Those who contravened the teaching of the Pastoral manifested that they were not in fit disposition to receive the sacraments.[34]

Eight days later, nevertheless, Byrne wrote to Cosgrave expressing his concern at the consequences her death might provoke. After all, she was the sister of Terence MacSwiney. 'Personally I have little sympathy for this Lady and politically none', but to allow her to die 'would be a thoroughly unwise policy'. Her death would have a more harmful effect than her release.[35] Cosgrave replied, on 18 November, that if she persisted in her indefensible position and died, it would be 'of her own volition'.[36] After further consideration, however, she was released on 28 November without explanation.

The fate of Erskine Childers

One of the men most wanted by the Free State leaders was Erskine Childers, who was depicted as one of those primarily responsible for the civil war. He was captured on 11 November, and was tried in camera before a military tribunal on the charge of 'being in unlawful possession of a colt automatic pistol', which, in fact, had been a present from Michael Collins. On 17 November, four republican prisoners were executed for the possession of revolvers without proper authority. Archbishop Byrne protested to the government against the executions. Cosgrave, in his letter of 18 November, stated with reference to the executions that the government was obliged, with the security of the nation in jeopardy, to take many stern but just actions. And referring to the Bishops' Pastoral, he announced that in taking these stern actions they were acting 'in the spirit of the solemn teaching of our highest moral authority', and that there was no question of mere politics involved but rather 'what is morally right or wrong according to Divine Law'. The archbishop, one suspects, was disturbed at having the October Pastoral used in this manner.

Following the executions, great concern was felt for Erskine Childers. Archbishop Byrne personally intervened with the authorities on his behalf. He was shot at dawn on Friday, 24 November, without an opportunity to appeal his conviction. There was widespread sadness and pain among all who knew Childers. Hagan wrote to Byrne on 2 December to congratulate and thank him: 'Your action to have him spared does honour to you and him; and I am glad to know that even one voice was raised on the side of mercy'.[37] Another prelate who interceded and probably knew Childers better than Edward Byrne was Patrick O'Donnell, Auxiliary Bishop of Armagh. Writing on the day after the execution, he commented: 'All executions are deplorable, especially that of poor Childers.' He had been saying Mass for him frequently of late, and had 'fruitlessly intervened to prevent' his death. They had worked together during the Irish Convention in 1917 and he had come to respect and admire him. His execution saddened him unlike any other event in recent years. He hoped it would not lead to reprisals. Up to then the Irish government seemed to him to have done well on the whole. 'In them (the executions), if I can judge, wisdom left them. I trust it may soon return ... Our cardinal and the Archbishop of Dublin are against the executions.'[38]

Frank Gallagher's view and republican pressure
Meantime, Archbishop Byrne had received on 12 November a further letter from a prisoner concerning the pastoral letter. The writer was Proinnsias Ó Gallchobhair (Frank Gallagher, destined to be the first editor of the *Irish Press* newspaper), who commented: 'It is said that your Grace signed this letter with reluctance and misgiving. This attitude is not surprising to any who analyse the Pastoral in the cold light of today, when it is clear to all that it has failed in its political purpose and has suc-

ceeded only in dishonouring the Beloved Spouse of Christ, in whose name it was issued.' He went on to analyse in much detail the 'wording and temper' of the document and concluded:

I submit to your Grace that on these most relevant and serious grounds the Pastoral and its awful penalties cannot be allowed to stand, especially by those who teach that the Church of Christ is the Church of Truth, Justice, and an all-embracing Charity.[39]

This was followed on 17 November by a telegraphic message from the London District Committee of the Irish Self-Determination League (Great Britain), conveying a strong unanimous protest 'at the scandalous un-Christian action of clergy in your diocese in depriving Mary MacSwiney of consolation of the sacraments during her heroic struggle … All here are shocked to think that such acts of cruelty which was avoided by the English Government in case of Terence MacSwiney should only two years later be used by Irish Catholic clergy against his equally noble sister.'[40]

Such comments, however, were of far less concern to Edward Byrne than the possibility of a papal delegate being sent from Rome.

An unwelcome Papal Delegate
He was concerned that anti-Treaty propagandists were seeking to discredit the Bishops' Pastoral in Rome, and endeavouring to have a delegate sent from the Vatican to scrutinise the situation. He suggested to Cardinal Logue that he discuss the matter with his friend Cardinal Gasparri. The Cardinal replied firmly on 22 November that the question of a papal delegate coming to Ireland had no foundation. He personally would welcome some one coming 'in a temporary way to report on the condition of Ireland', because in Rome they had a very hazy notion of the state of Ireland. At present they were flooded with De Valera's propaganda from Ireland and America, most of it quite intemperate, especially resolutions from America. He had sent the Bishops' Pastoral to Rome and some choice specimens of the abuse of the bishops. He did not agree with Byrne's opposition to asking the Pope for a pronouncement. The authority of the bishops was impeached, vilified and condemned; and it was 'the part of the Holy See to support and maintain the authority of the Bishops.'[41]

Archbishop Byrne, however, determined to express his concerns to Mgr Hagan. He had seen references in newspapers that some people were agitating in Rome against the Bishops' Pastoral and suggesting that a Papal Delegate be sent to Ireland. He was sure the Holy See was too wise to follow the lead of people seeking to minimise the influence of the bishops in Ireland. Such a course as sending a Delegate would be most inexpedient, not to say dangerous, both to the best interests of religion and to the prestige of the Holy See in this country. Such an appointment would 'raise a "No Popery" cry all over the North – and would be a permanent bar to the ultimate union of North and South. This would leave the Holy See open to the charge of placing the unfortunate Catholics in the North permanently under the heel of the Orange oppressor. Moreover, there would always be the suspicion that the Delegate was acting under English influence.

The only reason a Delegate was 'mentioned by certain people', Byrne continued, was not out of respect for Apostolic Authority, but to spread the idea 'that the Irish bishops have not the confidence of the Holy See as teachers of the people'. The encouragement of such an idea would be ruinous to religion in Ireland. He underlined his final sentence: 'Those who disregard the Bishops would have scant respect for either the Holy See or its representative'. In the background was a fear of a permanent Papal representative, especially an Italian, in Dublin, the archbishop's own diocese, and that, given the strength of British influence in Rome, such a development would strengthen British control over the Irish church.[42]

Matters of episcopal routine

In November, following the capture and trial of Erskine Childers, the archbishop's range of duties and engagements continued much as usual. In addition, on 19 November, he blessed the foundation stone of a new parish church at Lusk, where he had served as a curate. After the ceremony, accompanied by the clergy and a large gathering of parishioners and visitors, he went to the temporary church, where he presided at a public meeting, at which he delivered what was described as 'an interesting address'.[43] Three week later, on 10 December, he was at Finglas, Co Dublin, to bless a new church, and was given a very cordial greeting by a large number of parishioners.[44]

At the beginning of this final month of the year, a letter came from W. T. Cosgrave reminding him that a governor-general, T. M. Healy, would be appointed during the next few days, in accordance with the terms of the Treaty, and that the question of a chaplain would arise. The name of Rev George Byrne SJ, Gardiner Street Church, had been suggested to him, and it would afford him the greatest pleasure if his Grace 'would take steps to have his services made available when required'.[45] Three days later, on 4 December, the governor-general-to-be made a similar request in his own inimitable, more relaxed way. He requested a chaplain for Sundays and Church holidays, especially for his wife, who had been unable to attend Mass since January. He left the choice of clergyman entirely to his Grace, but added that his wife had 'a great grá for Fr George Byrne SJ'.[46] Fr Byrne was appointed and remained as chaplain and friend until 1926, when he was sent to head the Irish Jesuit mission to Hong Kong and China.

On the same day that he received the letter from T. M. Healy, the archbishop wrote to the commander in chief, General Mulcahy, enclosing a letter from Miss Ffrench-Mullen on behalf of two prisoners, Waters and Archibald, who, 'if the facts are as she states them, would seem at first sight to be cases in which clemency might be exercised'. The following day, Mulcahy agreed to have enquiries made. On 30 December, Dr Byrne thanked him for the release of Archibald, which had taken place ten days earlier.[47]

Various State Affairs

Meantime, on 5 December, the Irish Free State Constitution Act ratified the Constitution; and the following day the Dáil approved nominations to the executive council of the Irish Free State: W. T. Cosgrave, President and Minister for Finance, Kevin O'Higgins, Vice-President and Minister for Home Affairs, Richard Mulcahy, Minister for Defence, Eoin Mac Neill, Minister for Education, Ernst Blythe, Minister for Local Government, Joseph McGrath, Minister for Industry and Commerce, and Desmond Fitzgerald, Minister for External Affairs. On that day, too, T. M. Healy was sworn in as the first Governor-general of the Irish Free State, and on the 12 and 13 December received messages of good wishes and prayers from, respectively, Pope Pius XI and from George V, King of England.[48]

One of the most disturbing occurrences in these days was the murder of a Dáil representative, pro-Treaty deputy, Sean Hales. The killing of elected representatives threatened the political life of the country. The government decided to send out a harsh message to the anti-Treaty forces. As a reprisal for the assassination of Sean Hales, the republican leaders, Rory O'Connor and Liam Mellows, and two other republicans, were executed without trial on 8 December.

On the eve of the executions, Archbishop Byrne paid a lengthy visit to President Cosgrave to plead with him not to put into effect the decision of the executive council taken earlier that day. Cosgrave stood firm, despite his sympathy for the archbishop's point of view.

Byrne was deeply outraged when he read in the newspapers that the executions had been undertaken as a 'reprisal'. He sent a stern protest to the President on 10 December 1922. He reminded him that he, Cosgrave, had previously said that he did not consider his letters on a public matter 'as anything like undue interference'. Encouraged by this, he again took the liberty of addressing him 'on a matter on which I feel very keenly'.

It was with something like dismay that I saw by the Army Communications to the newspapers on Friday that the four men were executed as 'reprisals' for the death of General Hales. Now, the policy of reprisals seems to me to be not only unwise but entirely unjustifiable from the moral point of view. That one man should be punished for another's crime seems to me to be absolutely unjust.

Such a policy, Dr Byrne continued, was bound to alienate many friends of the government, and it needed all the sympathy it could get. If anyone were to suffer (and he hoped that the road of clemency was not closed) – let it be after fair trial and without the appearance of heat or haste.

'I do not write this to embarrass the Government', he concluded, 'but I think it only fair to the position I hold to put you in possession of my honest views.'[49]

His was not the only ecclesiastical criticism of the government. This occasioned concern to key members of the cabinet. Archbishop Byrne was invited to a meeting with government ministers to discuss the matter. He attended with his secretary, Dr Dunne. The meeting lasted about a half-hour and, according to Dunne, was effective in moderating government policy. Executions continued, but no other prisoner was shot 'as a reprisal'.[50]

Following the government's executions, there was a real fear on the republican side that the lives of other prisoners were at risk. Sean T. Ó Ceallaigh's wife, Cáit, informed Hagan, that a delegation was about to set out for Rome to make an appeal for clemency for the prisoners. The appeal was not signed by De Valera, and when the petitioners approached Archbishop Byrne on the matter he received the people courteously but said he was powerless to help. He had already failed to obtain mercy for prisoners. On 12 December, writing again, she added that she had heard 'rather indirectly, that those people who went to see the archbishop learned that he was broken-hearted'.[51]

A difficult priest, and further distressing news about Childers

As the grueling, troublesome year drew to a close, Edward Byrne received two unwelcome letters. The first was sent on 20 December by the Vice-President, Kevin O'Higgins. He reported that at the eight o'clock Mass, at Mount Argus, the Passionist priest, Rev Joseph Smith, asked the congregation to 'pray for Sean Hales TD, whom the CID murdered to give the government an excuse to murder the men who are fighting for the Republic.' A woman who was present subsequently spoke to the rector about the matter and received the reply: 'I cannot stop him. I am utterly powerless. He won't be stopped by me.'

'I think it better to refrain from comment', O'Higgins observed. 'I make no request for intervention. My colleagues and I are absolutely content to leave the matter entirely in your discretion.'[52]

This letter, coming after his earlier communication with the provincial of the order, was very disheartening; but the second letter must have come as a bomb-shell. It was written by Mrs Childers on 31 December 1922.[53] Her late husband's cousin, Robert C. Barton TD, was very ill in Mountjoy Military Prison Hospital, and her fear was that the same circumstances might arise in his case that arose in the case of her husband, Captain Erskine Childers, 'who repeatedly asked to see the Rev Father Albert or the Rev Dr Browne for spiritual help in preparation for death and was denied.' She asked his Grace that in the event of Mr Barton being near death, if he expressed the desire to see some particular priest, this might be accorded him. If his Grace consented to do this, she further asked him in his kindness to communicate the decision to the chaplain of Mountjoy Military Prison.

CHAPTER SEVEN

1923

The Civil War and the immediate aftermath

Various grievances and Complaints
In the early months of the New Year, the archbishop was besieged by complaints on behalf of republican prisoners. One of these in the early weeks came from Conn Murphy MA, PhD, a Corkman who lived in Rathgar, Dublin. He complained that his daughter had been arrested. She was not involved in violence but in constitutional action such as the bishops had advocated. He asked whether his Grace considered the treatment accorded his daughter, a faithful member of the church, to be just? If it was unjust and tyrannical and an interference with the constitutional action, which the bishops advised, then his Grace had a responsibility in the matter. Not content with the archbishop's reply, he claimed to be entitled to a little more sympathy from the shepherd of the flock, who was the representative of the Good Shepherd ready to lay down his life for even the least member.[1]

Replying to a request from General Mulcahy, Minister for Defence, with respect to a weekend retreat for newly-commissioned officers, Dr Byrne mentioned the strong polemic from Conn Murphy and also seems to have urged a renewed movement towards peace. Mulcahy replied on 14 February that he too wanted 'to reach peace', but that if it was not clear now it would probably be clear in time that 'we are really dealing with people with whom one cannot negotiate'.[2]

Shortly afterwards, Murphy himself was arrested for republican activities and went on hunger-strike. He desisted, however, and was released after signing the required undertaking – 'I promise that I will not use arms against the parliament elected by the Irish people, or the Government for the time being responsible to that parliament, and that I will not support in any way such an action. Nor will I interfere with the property or person of others.'[3]

Pressure from republican prisoners continued during February.

Eithne Mac Suibhne (Mac Swiney) wrote from Kilmainham jail, on 21 February, asking was it by his orders that she was deprived of the sacraments as her sister had been. This evoked the assurance from the archbishop that he had given no directions regarding her personally in respect of the reception of the sacrament, and he went on to outline the episcopal policy given earlier.[4]

Complaints about priests
On 13 February, Dr Byrne drew the attention of the Passionist provincial to the complaint of the Vice-President, Kevin O'Higgins, about Fr Joseph Smith. 'I would suggest', he wrote, ' that he be transferred to some other house of the congregation, where he will not have the same opportunities of doing harm that he has had in Mount Argus.' He, as archbishop, could deprive him of the power of preaching, but this would not meet the situation since he took occasion for political remarks from the reading of simple notices and even from the announcement of prayers for the deceased. It was his impression, Dr Byrne went on, that if a member of a religious congregation was put under strict obedience to a certain course he could be dealt with severely in the case of disobedience. The provincial's response was less than helpful. He was evidently fearful of Fr Smith. Previously when the President made a complaint about him, Smith was in such a temper that he consulted a solicitor with a view to instigating a libel action against the President. To remove Fr Joseph without confronting him with his accusers would lead to some very disagreeable consequences. He had a certain amount of backing in Dublin and would be urged to hold out as a martyr to the cause. 'All things considered', the provincial, Fr Malachy, concluded, 'I think it best for your Grace to demand an explanation from him personally, and if it be not forthcoming to dispense with his services.'[5]

It is not clear what happened following this washing of hands, but the archbishop's relations with the Passionists were strained for some time.

Pastoral Letters, Lent 1923
On 11 February the Lenten Pastoral Letters were read in all the churches. Despite the criticism of their earlier pastoral, the bishops re-emphasised the people's duty to support the duly constituted government, and issued solemn warnings to those

who, directly or indirectly, participated in the campaign of law-lessness. On the social/moral state of the country, their lord-ships condemned illicit distillation, intemperance, immoral lit-erature, and foreign dances. With reference to their previous pastoral, his Grace of Dublin observed that the counsel the bishops of Ireland gave their people some months ago had fallen on many unheeding ears. Acts which were declared to be grave sins were still being committed with appalling frequency. He prayed, and asked for prayers, that the Holy Spirit might turn the hearts of 'those misguided ones' to thoughts of peace, and breathe into their hearts the spirit of brotherly love and unity. His pastoral letter also reminded hearers and readers of the sen-tences of excommunication pronounced by successive Sovereign Pontiffs against secret societies as detrimental to both public order and the interests of religion. Hence, Catholics were warned against becoming Freemasons, Fenians, or members of any sim-ilar secret society.[6]

The archbishop's criticism of 'those misguided ones' was very circumspect and mild compared to the blunt northern elo-quence of Cardinal Logue. 'The plague of bloodshed, destruc-tion, pillage ... even sordid theft ...' had been conducted 'with a virulence which left in the shade even the most outrageous ex-cesses of the Black and Tans'. The agreement reached under the Treaty brought a sense of relief, and the vision of a brighter future, but a destructive hurricane had been unleashed based on a thin, unsubstantial vapour: 'The difference between some equivocal words in an oath, the difference between external and internal connection with the British Commonwealth – men versed in the subtleties of the schools may understand them, but men of sound, practical sense would hardly succeed.'[7]

Intimations towards peace

Early in February, Mary Mac Swiney became aware of De Valera inching towards the cessation of hostilities, and on 10 February she warned that a personal statement from him on his own would be disastrous. She reiterated the republican position: 'Majority rule ... does not apply when the majority under duress wants to give away the independence of their country. That is a case where it is not only the right but the duty of the minority to take up arms.'[8]

Around the same time, Archbishop Harty of Cashel, with

some laity and clergy, was in communication with Tom Barry, a leading republican activist, with a view to an immediate cessation. Nothing resulted from the initiative for some time.

In March a new dimension was added with news of the arrival of a delegate from Rome.

Mgr Luzio's mission of peace

On 13 March it was announced that Mgr Salvatore Luzio, formerly professor of Canon Law at Maynooth, had been sent to Ireland with a mission from the Holy See to learn at first hand from the bishops and other leading people the real position of affairs, and to endeavour, in conjunction with the bishops, to develop an atmosphere of peace.[9]

Fr Michael J. Curran, writing from the Irish College, to Dr Patrick O'Donnell, Coadjutor Archbishop of Armagh, was sceptical about Mgr Luzio's mission and the prospects for peace. In his view, the real object of the mission was 'to pave the way for an Apostolic Delegate', who would be, in effect, 'an unaccredited nuncio to the Court of St James, or rather to Downing Street politicians and Westminster ecclesiastics'. English influence was dominant in Rome. In his experience, the Secretariat of State was hostile, in practice, to Ireland. The timing of the mission was clever. The Free State wanted some recognition, or something they could call recognition from the Vatican, the cardinal wanted the republicans condemned by the Holy See, the republicans wanted the bishops condemned for their censures, the British wanted some ecclesiastical weapon in Ireland to replace the Irish bishops since the conscription issue, and lastly the Holy See would not be happy till it got it. In Curran's view, as long as the connection with England remained, a permanent delegation could not but be a grave evil, dangerous to the Holy See itself on account of the suspicions it would generate in Ireland.'

Then, feeling perhaps that he had overstated his case, he explained that he had been schooled by Archbishop Walsh, who was very much alive to the danger, but now that he had gone the business was being reopened and there was no one but Dr O'Donnell to take his place. 'The new Archbishop (Byrne) is thoroughly sound but he's new, dislikes a fight, and may not push things too strongly from the delicacy of his own position.'[10]

Monsignor Luzio arrived in Dublin from Holyhead on 19 March. He got off to a disastrous start by omitting to visit the local ordinary, Archbishop Byrne, in whose diocese he took up residence. He travelled north to visit Cardinal Logue, who favoured the Roman visit as a mark of papal support for the bishops, and alienated his Eminence by requesting him to join in a peace mission to the rebels. Logue did not believe it was possible to talk profitably to the anti-Treaty representatives and, according to T. M. Healy, 'sent Luzio away with a flea in his ear'.[11] In 1924, when Archbishop Byrne visited Rome, with his secretary Fr Dunne, the Pope informed him that when he heard that Luzio had not called on the archbishop he knew that his mission was a failure.[12]

Luzio's arrival, however, coincided with renewed attempts at a ceasefire. The archbishop was brought into the lengthy process of negotiation. On 15 March he received an appeal from a Fr Duggan in Co Cork to use his influence with the government to get them to stay their policy on executions, as Tom Barry was engaged in efforts towards peace.[13] On 18 March, Byrne exchanged letters with Cosgrave on the matter. He enclosed the letter from Fr Duggan, and urged the government to be patient on the matter.[14] Cosgrave replied that extreme measures would be stopped if there were a real prospect of peace, but he was not convinced. There was increased republican activity in Cork. It was the government's view that a real peace could only come from good military results, and the defeat of the enemy in the field. He assured his Grace that in that event they would not exercise severity, though some show of it might be necessary in view of the large number of prisoners – now over 10,000, who were so ridiculous in their notions that they might want some thousand different peace arrangements.[15]

At 5.30 pm on 19 March, Byrne wrote again. Father Duggan had just been with him and had assured him that the movement towards peace was genuine. The Irregulars in the Southern Command, despite some unfortunate incidents, had adopted a 'non offensive' policy.[16]

Meanwhile, Luzio, whose coming had not been formally heralded to the Irish government and who was kept at a distance by government ministers, had met with such republican figures as Count Plunkett, Dr Cleary, and Mary MacSwiney. The latter, in a letter to De Valera on 21 March, advised, in relation to Mgr Luzio, that republicans should represent themselves as Irishmen determined to achieve the independence of our country and in no way anxious to disregard but always uphold the lawful authority of the church. She warned him against those who said 'We don't need Rome, we can do without the priests'; the Vatican did matter.

Luzio showed himself sympathetic to the views of republicans. He urged them towards a peace settlement. He left the country during April, following the intervention of the Irish government, without seeming to have achieved much; but he brought back to Rome a favourable impression of the republicans he had encountered. He had met secretly with De Valera. The latter commented with accustomed circumspection some weeks later that the visitor's attitude was so sympathetic that people thronged to visit him. He had an interview with him, in which he discussed matters generally. What his ecclesiastical mission was, he did not know, but he seemed to have received scant courtesy from the bishops. Some of our people, he added, seemed inclined to petition for a permanent delegation. He had to persuade them that that might be very far from a blessing. It was much easier for a powerful Empire to secure friends than it was for a struggling small nation.[17] It was no coincidence that an identical view was maintained by Mgr John Hagan and Michael J. Curran. It was shared, as has been seen, by his Grace of Dublin.

On 10 April, perhaps a major obstacle to peace was removed with the fatal wounding of Liam Lynch, chief of the Irregular IRA, in an engagement with government forces in the Comeragh Mountains, Co Waterford. Less than three weeks later, on 27 April, De Valera, in conjunction with Frank Aiken on behalf of the Irregular IRA Council, announced the suspension of offensive operations. Making the most of the ceasefire announcement, he attributed it to Mgr Luzio in a politic letter to him on 30 April. He regretted the public discourtesy shown to the representative of the Holy Father. His coming had raised possibilities for peace for which 'our people have been sighing and longing', and at local assemblies had given voice to their wishes. He hoped that the suspension of operations would be of some consolation to him and the Holy Father. His public offer, he assured Luzio, was the proximate result of his meeting with him. If peace were the outcome, the Pope's representative would certainly have more than a share in bringing it about. He concluded expediently:

Please give to the Holy Father my dutiful homage. Though nominally cut away from the body of Holy Church, we are still spiritually and mystically of it, and we refuse to regard ourselves except as his children.[18]

Despite De Valera's public announcement, some of his followers continued the struggle. He felt it necessary, on 19 May, to emphasise that the armed struggle was over.[19]

Dealing with Roman interventions

Prior to that, the republican appeals to Rome had impinged directly on Archbishop Byrne. Cardinal Pietro Gasparri, on behalf of the Pope, requested him to approach the Irish government with a view to securing the release of Dr Conn Murphy. The cardinal was under the impression that Murphy had been arrested because he had presented a petition to Rome on behalf of republicans. Byrne was taken aback by the intervention, and Cosgrave even more so. The government negotiated for the recall of Mgr Luzio to Rome, and pointed out that Murphy's arrest was not because of his petition to the Holy See but because he was a conduit for documents between republicans. Desmond Fitzgerald was sent to Rome. He had a lengthy audience with the Pope, during which he emphasised the attachment of the Irish government and the Irish people to the Holy See. The Irish party left Rome on 8 May well pleased with their visit. That same day, Cosgrave wrote to Gasparri requesting him to convey to the Holy Father the government's sentiments 'of grateful appreciation of the gracious consideration of His Holiness ... whereby the embarrassment caused by the manner of Right Rev Monsignor Luzio's intervention in our affairs has been brought to an end and Monsignor Luzio has been able to take his departure without further difficulties ensuing'.[20]

A postscript to the Luzio visit was added some months later by John Hagan, in a letter to Archbishop Daniel Mannix of Melbourne. He commented that since Mgr Luzio's return to Rome he had expressed bitterness against most Free State ministers. Hagan added that having himself seen the Pope a few times since Luzio's return, his impression was that His Holiness was 'sick and tired of Ireland'. Cardinal Gasparri had been severe on the bishops' behaviour towards Luzio. Nothing would be done, however, against the political situation in Ireland because the Vatican was always going to appease Britain if it is seeking diplomatic triumphs. A deal seemed to be on the cards to recognise officially a Free State representative at the Holy See.[21]

More Representations for Prisoners

The on-going requests for Dr Byrne's intercession from prisoners, or those connected to them, was a testimony to his reputation for compassion and readiness to help. In the weeks as the Civil War drew to a close the requests seemed to increase. He wrote again and again to Cosgrave on behalf of prisoners who claimed to be innocent,[22] or to have been threatened by Free State personnel, or who were on hunger strike. On this last, he was approached by a Mrs O'Kelly, presumably the wife of Seán T. O'Kelly, with respect to three women on hunger strike in Kilmainham Jail. He assured her that he would do what he could, but that his power in these matters was very small.[23] He wrote to President Cosgrave about the three women.[24] 'Don't you think', he asked, that 'the government has the rebellion sufficiently in hand without allowing them to die even through their own fault?' He was aware of the government's view about the machinations of women in the movement but, at the risk of being tiresome and perhaps illogical, he would put in a strong word for clemency for these women. Their deaths would cause a wave of sympathy through the country. The government was strong enough, and peace was sufficiently in sight, not to expose itself to the criticism of making war on women.[25]

Cosgrave replied on 19 April. The government had given long consideration to the question of those on hunger strike and were not satisfied that it would be safe to release them. They had decided, however, that if they signed the same sort of undertaking as Dr Conn Murphy they would be released. The demands, the propaganda, and the general demands of prisoners indicated that only stern methods could bring them to their senses. 'We all wish sincerely', Cosgrave continued, 'that it might be otherwise and feel keenly that your Grace should be disappointed.' The government was prepared to contribute towards peace and the restoration of order in every way consistent with public safety. But their experience was that those in arms against them were opposed to any limitation imposed by any government and *the more serious opposition came from the women, who apparently were a law to themselves.* He concluded by assuring the archbishop that the other members of government joined him in sending their very good wishes.[26]

Subsequently, Cosgrave replied concerning a letter by a Mr P. Soden, who had written to Dr Byrne claiming to be wrongfully imprisoned and which the archbishop had forwarded to the president. After an examination of Mr Soden's case, it was clear that he was far from being an innocent victim and that his account of conditions in Tallaght were greatly exaggerated. There was never more than seven in the room in which he was detained, not twenty as he had claimed![27]

The tendency of the republican prisoners to exaggerate about their conditions was highlighted in the 'Report of the International Committee of the Red Cross Mission in Ireland, April-May 1923', extracts from which were sent to Archbishop Byrne in June by the Irish Government Publicity Department. These noted that there were grounds for complaints of overcrowding in Mountjoy prison, that while the government refused the status of 'prisoners-of-war' to the prisoners, in reality it treated them as such. That there was a carefully organised medical service and that the serious accusations made on this subject appeared unfounded, and that the complaints regarding the prohibition of correspondence with prisoners' families, sanitary conditions, and food in the camp were unfounded. In the circumstances, the Publicity Department was delighted to send typed extracts to bishops and to all who might have received complaints.[28]

Praise for the Government
The cessation of hostilities gave rise to much praise for the government from members of the Catholic hierarchy. On President Cosgrave's visit to Limerick on 17 June 1923, Bishop Hallinan, unable to be present owing to a mortal illness, sent a letter to be read which declared that the government with clear vision, undaunted courage, unfailing patience and perseverance, had accomplished their task in the face of unparalleled difficulties, and hence deserved well of the Irish people.[29] The Bishop of Kerry, Dr O'Sullivan, voiced similar sentiments;[30] and on 20 June he had joined with Cardinal Logue and fellow prelates, Browne, Fogarty, McKenna, and Mulhern in a courtesy call on the Governor-General, T. M. Healy, to wish him every success in his high office and to express the gratification of the hierarchy that the Free State Government, notwithstanding its want of experience, was working so efficiently in the face of many difficulties and obstacles.[31]

Archbishop Byrne was noticeably absent from the visit to the Governor-General, and he was also absent from the funeral for Bishop Hallinan, which the cardinal and very many bishops attended. There is no extant evidence to explain the absence, but a remark of Fr Michael Cronin on 19 June – 'the archbishop was very attentive, but looked worn'[32] – might indicate a condition of exhaustion or illness.

In the summer, during the shadowy interlude following the calling off of offensive action by the Irregular IRA, the Dáil passed a variety of Acts, including Land Law, Public Safety (Emergency Powers), and the establishment of a police force. Also, on 15 August, De Valera, who had remained elusive, was arrested while addressing a public meeting in Ennis, Co Clare. Previously, he must have felt in danger of execution for his role in initiating and promoting the civil war, but at this stage he was just arrested and kept in imprisonment without trial for most of a year until July 1924. In captivity he was treated well.[33] On 27 August 1923, twelve days after De Valera's arrest, a general election was held. The government party, Cumann na nGaedheal, won 63 seats, the Republicans a surprising 44 seats, Labour 14, Farmers 15, and Others 17.

To Bobbio: International Recognition

On 2 September 1923 a special occasion drew together representatives of church and state. Some 300 Irish pilgrims travelled to Bobbio, in Italy, for the thirteenth centenary celebrations of St Columbanus. Among the participants were Cardinal Ehrle, the Papal Legate, and twelve archbishops and bishops, including the archbishops of Dublin and Tuam and the bishops of Cork and Down and Connor. In the Irish party were President Cosgrave, Professor Eoin MacNeill, Marquis MacSwiney (who was to represent the Free State in the Vatican), and the Lord Mayor of Dublin. At the Basilica of St Columbanus, Cardinal Ehrle celebrated a solemn pontifical Mass and delivered a homily, in which he extolled Ireland's renown as the Island of Saints and praised the virtue and zeal of St Columbanus and other Irish saints. The cardinal and distinguished guests then visited the crypt and prayed at the remains of Columbanus.

A banquet followed at the episcopal palace. The Bishop of Bobbio delivered a speech in Latin in which he eulogised Cardinal Ehrle and greeted the Irish delegates in warm terms.

Then, Dr Byrne, as Archbishop of Dublin, spoke highly and fluently of Italy and emphasised Ireland's spirit of attachment to
the Holy See. At the end, Cardinal Ehrle gave a short speech of
thanks for his reception, and the sub-prefect, representing the
Italian government, paid a tribute to the Irish government and
authorities, and thanked the Archbishop of Dublin for his courteous references to Italy. Finally, Marquis MacSwiney, who
spoke fluent Italian, conveyed, on behalf of President Cosgrave,
the thanks of the Irish party for the enthusiastic welcome they
had received.

The celebrations were brought to a close by a procession
through the streets carrying relics of the saint. The procession of
15,000 people was headed by the Cardinal Legate and 14 Italian
and Irish bishops, and included President Cosgrave.[34]

The international dimension continued eight days later,
when the Irish Free State was admitted to the League of Nations.
'Members rose to their feet and cheered enthusiastically.'
Cosgrave addressed the League in Irish and in English, celebrat-
ing Ireland's entry into a bond of union with other nations.[35] In
further corroboration of his government's standing, President
William T. Cosgrave, addressed the opening meeting of the
Imperial Conference in London on 1 October 1923.

Signs of stability
The archbishop initiated a major mark of stability in September.
He sent invitations to the president and to the members of the
Oireachtas to come together for the celebration of a votive Mass
to the Holy Spirit to ask God's blessing on their deliberations.
Mr Cosgrave, on 26 September, expressed thanks on the part of
the government 'for the great thought which prompted the
Votive Mass, and for the many kindnesses and generous assist-
ance we have at all times received from your Grace'.[36] On 3
October, Archbishop Byrne presided at a solemn votive Mass of
the Holy Spirit to implore Diving guidance in the deliberations
of the Oireachtas, and to obtain the blessing of the Almighty for
the well being of our country. His Excellency, the Governor-
General, the President, and members of the Oireachtas attended.
Subsequently, the Governor-General expressed his thanks 'for
today's splendid ceremonies in the Pro-Cathedral. Everything
was due to the archbishop, including the original idea.'[37]

Three weeks later, 21 October, his Grace presided at another distinctive gathering: the religious ceremonies marking the opening of the academic year in University College Dublin. The ceremonies took place in the church associated with Cardinal John Henry Newman, University Church, St Stephen's Green.

Appealing for multiple hunger strikers
Even as this last event was taking place, Edward Byrne was seriously concerned about a massive hunger strike, involving several thousand prisoners. On 28 October, he considered it his duty to the position he held to let the President know his views on the matter. A draft of his letter has him stating boldly that he would consider it a downright calamity for the country if any of the hunger-strikers were allowed to die. He made his argument first of all on humanitarian grounds, and further pointed out that the leaders of the hunger-strike had declared that the reign of violence was over and that they were committed to presenting their views in a constitutional manner. This made their claim to conciliation seem strong before the world. The archbishop continued with a variation on the argument used previously in relation to smaller numbers of hunger-strikers, namely, that no government, however strong, could allow thousands of men to die. It would arouse a revulsion of feeling that would shake the foundations of the Free State. Mr Cosgrave had to weigh in the balance whether the release of these people would be a greater danger to the state than allowing them to die of hunger-strike. He distinctly inclined to the view that the latter course would be fraught with far more danger to the state.

The President's response, the same day, was on the firm, predictable line that the government would not yield on the issue of hunger-strike. There were some grounds for releasing people prior to the Public Safety Act, but these no longer existed. They were now held by law. The government's policy was showing results. There were 7,400 on strike (from memory) a month ago – today, there were 6,400 more or less. 425 came off that day. His information was quite the opposite to that of his Grace, namely, that the government would fail in their duty if they were to permit these people to demand and secure their release in this manner. He was satisfied that generosity or mercy was thrown away on those people, and that the change which they claimed had taken place was a change of necessity – not conviction or any sense of wrong doing; and he thought it only fair to draw the

attention of his Grace to the fact 'that government in this country' would 'have an impossible task if the weapon of hunger-
strike' was 'to be regarded as proof against the law of the state'.
In conclusion, the President assured the archbishop that he
would be in his office at 10.30 the following morning should he
wish to communicate further with him on the matter.

Mr Cosgrave felt it necessary to add a long postscript. There
were some 13,000 prisoners. A week ago it was down to 9,000. It
was planned to get the number down to about 4,000 by
Christmas, and to have all released by St Patrick's Day or Easter.
The government decided, however, to suspend the releases of
those on hunger strike. That day's report from the officers commanding the internment camps indicated that, in their view, the
end of hunger-strikes was in prospect. 'I myself, however,'
Cosgrave concluded, 'think there will be some casualties, which
I think would have the contrary effect to that expressed by your
Grace'.[38]

The archbishop continued to respond to individual requests
for help from prisoners or on their behalf. During that month of
October he was happy to write to Mrs Margaret Mac Sherry that
he had heard from the President that James Mac Sherry's release
had been sanctioned by the Minister for Defence, to whom the
archbishop's letter had been communicated.[39]

Meantime, the hunger-strike continued into November. The
archbishop's role as a mediator was publicly acknowledged by
republicans towards the end of the month. The Sinn Féin standing committee made out an offer to the government on 20
November. They arranged with Mr Eoin O'Keefe to bring it to
the archbishop and to request him to mediate with the government. The committee's statement guaranteed an end to the
hunger-strike if the government announced the release of all
prisoners by Christmas. The archbishop met with President
Cosgrave on 21 November. The response, as might be expected,
was unyielding. The government would make no promise, give
no undertaking. There would be no negotiations with hunger-
strikers. The archbishop conveyed the government's response to
Eoin O'Keefe that day.[40]

Pastoral links with government leaders
The following day, T. M. Healy, the Governor-General, expressed his thanks to his Grace for his kindness in his 'promised

remembrance of my dear brother (Maurice). He was rare in type and I am very lonely.'[41] Earlier, President Cosgrave's brother had died. The archbishop assured him of his sympathy and prayers, and received from Mr Cosgrave, on 3 November, a grateful note for his kind letter of condolence. The blow was a heavy one to him and to his family. They were comforted by the sympathy extended to them and the kind promises of His Grace and members of the clergy of remembrance in their prayers. A month later, following a bout of illness, the President, through his secretary, informed Fr T. O'Donnell, the archbishop's secretary, that he wished to thank his Grace for the photographs taken at the celebrations in Bobbio, at which it was his 'high privilege to assist', and he was much obliged for his Grace's enquiry after his health, and says he feels much improved.[42]

As is evident from the correspondence between Edward Byrne and William Cosgrave during the civil war period, their relationship was characterised by mutual respect and openness. Neither stood on dignity, both valued humility, and tried to understand the other's position and situation. The relationship was important to church-state relationships throughout the 1920s.

Ecclesiastical considerations: educational, military, and representational

Amidst the various concerns arising from the civil war, there continued not just the daily diocesan demands but also those as a member of the hierarchy. Thus, on 8 July 1923, he had received from Bishop Foley, secretary to the bishops' conference, a copy of the response made to the Senate of the National University regarding their scheme for training National School teachers. The response, as agreed by the bishops at Maynooth, was quite definite. They were 'altogether opposed to the proposal of making a professional degree a necessary qualification for the first recognition of a National teacher'. In Germany and France, which, in educational matters, were supposed to be the most progressive of all countries, there was, as far as they knew, no requirement of this kind. Moreover, they were convinced that a mere pass degree would add little to the efficiency of a National teacher, and would place a greatly increased burden on the tax payer. They were of the view that the best way forward was improved methods of training in the training colleges, together

with 'the better material' which, it was hoped, would be attracted
to them by the new scale of salaries.

The bishops went on to make what was an essential point –
namely, that they had no wish to scrap denominational residen-
tial colleges, which had given so much satisfaction in the past
(and were, of course, under their control), in order to make way
for experiments which probably would prove expensive fail-
ures.[43]

The position of archbishop touched on a range of interests
that brought him into contact with different government departments: education, home affairs, defence, among others. The appeal for prisoners brought contact with the Department of
Defence, but there was also contact, as noted earlier, relating to
retreats for officers and especially to the question of chaplains.
Quite early in 1923, Dr Byrne corresponded with the Adjutant
General, Gearóid O'Sullivan, in relation to providing suitable
priests for chaplaincy work.[44] Subsequently, such issues as uniformity of services in the different barracks, uniforms, and
domicile of the chaplains arose, and the need for the appointment of a head chaplain. On this last, the archbishop, during
July, sent eleven names to General Mulcahy asking him to chose
three names and return them to him.[45]

Towards the end of the year, Cardinal Logue raised questions about the continuance of Mgr Hagan as the bishops' representative in Rome. Hagan's strong republican sympathies raised
doubts about his primary loyalty to the wishes of the Irish bishops. On 11 December, Byrne responded to the cardinal's letter of
criticism. It was difficult to know what to say, he conceded.
There was no doubt that Dr Hagan was not in political sympathy with the bishops and, as a result, the bishops had been bereft
of a great deal of help in Rome that the rector of the Irish College
was in a favourable position to give. Nevertheless, Byrne firmly
believed that, notwithstanding Dr Hagan's own political way of
thinking, since the issue of the Bishops' Pastoral he had not done
anything against the interests of the bishops, and furthermore
he would be prepared, if definitely instructed, to further the interests of the bishops.'[46]

Within a week, the cardinal wrote back, furious with inform-
ation which seemed to point directly to Hagan. He informed
Byrne, on 17 December, that he had heard from Cardinal
Gasparri that Messrs Donald O'Callaghan and Conn Murphy

arrived in Rome, presented a memorandum to the Vatican, and asked to be received by the Holy Father. How could two private gentlemen, Logue asked, manage not only to see the Cardinal Secretary of State, but even get an audience with the Holy Father to make charges against the bishops without warning and without the knowledge of the bishops?[47] Archbishop Byrne sought to spare his friend, Hagan, by deflecting some of his Eminence's outrage. He responded on 19 December that he, too, had heard from Cardinal Gasparri about these two republican gentlemen, but what encouraged him was the refusal of the Holy Father to see these men and the message he sent them.[48] 'I have always had an uneasy feeling', Byrne explained, 'ever since Mgr Luzio's ill-starred mission,' that the Holy See, misled by intense propaganda against the bishops, might issue some pronouncement that would be misinterpreted and twisted into a criticism of the bishops' action. It now seemed, thank God, that the danger was over. But if his Eminence thought so, it might be well to point out to Cardinal Gasparri that the Holy See would be much safer in taking its information from the bishops themselves rather than from interested Republican sources.[49]

Winter and Christmas

The winter months brought their own scale of needs. On 6 November, his Grace of Dublin sent a cheque for £250 to the Dublin Council of the St Vincent de Paul Society;[50] and on 22 December, Sir John Irwin JP, thanked him, on behalf of the Mansion House Coal Fund, for his 'generous subscription of one hundred pounds. The assistance you have rendered since you assumed your present exalted position is highly appreciated by the committee and doubtless by the citizens themselves.'[51]

Dr Byrne's pastoral role continued to be extended to republican prisoners. On 11 December, General Mulcahy's secretary informed Fr Dunne that the General was having investigated the cases referred to him by the archbishop – Daniel Stonahan, William Stonahan, and James O'Hanlon.[52] On 1 January 1924, the archbishop would learn that O'Hanlon had been released.

The cardinal, meanwhile, had called on the government to release by Christmas all internees except those convicted of or liable to be tried for crime.[53] No such conciliatory gesture was manifested, however, by Bishop Cohalan of Cork, who refused to accept into any church the body of hunger-striker, Denis

Barry, and pronounced unrelentingly: 'Anyone who deliberately takes his own life is deprived of Christian burial, and I shall interpret the laws of the church and refuse a Christian burial. I feel bound to do it.'[54]

As Christmas drew near, a cheerful and helpful note was struck by Fr John Fahy, clearly an admirer and friend of the archbishop. He was forty-seven years of age, a few years younger than Edward Byrne, and he had just completed the first year of a benign and successful term as Jesuit provincial. In a spirit of personal gratitude and appreciation, he wrote, on 23 December, from St Francis Xavier's community, Gardiner Street:

> I venture to send to your Grace a little personal note to express my deep gratitude for your many kindnesses to myself. When I think of the year, I realise that I have never left the doorsteps of the Archbishop's House without feeling enlightened and comforted by your Grace's kind words and advice.
>
> We are passing through grim days, and even Christmas does not seem to soften men's hearts. Still we may take some comfort. Already we have the dawn – cloudy and grey; but it is the dawn.[55]

A consoling thought at the ebb-tide of public morale and confidence.

CHAPTER EIGHT

Pastoral Activity as Disorder changes to Order and Comparative Stability

In the mid-1920s, Edward Byrne and his fellow bishops faced a world very different from that in which they had spent most of their lives. In Europe, after the deprivation and carnage of the First World War, there was a reaction in terms of expansive living, self-indulgence, a new freedom in the behaviour of women, and a pursuit of pleasure stimulated by a popular press. These features were reflected in Ireland after a civil war following on years of revolutionary struggle. In addition, there was political disunity, a crippling trades union war between the country's largest union, the Irish Transport and General Workers' Union, and the recently formed Workers Union of Ireland under James Larkin, widespread unemployment, heavy emigration, costly reconstruction, and general political apathy. It was a most unpromising situation in which to create the first independent Irish state. The government, however, brought to the task a single-minded determination to lay firm foundations and bring about general stability irrespective of popularity or unpopularity.

Despite any disagreements he had with the government during the civil war, Archbishop Byrne remained generally supportive of its policy in subsequent years. From his personal acquaintance with many of its key members, he had no doubt about their determination to do what they thought best for the country. He was acutely aware, in 'the cloudy grew dawn' as civil strife ended, of the mammoth task facing them.

An immediate challenge was to secure the rule of law throughout the country. The Free State army, following its defeat of the anti-Treaty forces, had become ill-disciplined. In different parts of the country armed bands looted, terrorised people, and indulged in drunken orgies and sexual abuse. The report to the archbishop from the army's head chaplain, Fr Dominic Ryan, on 7 January 1924, announced that in his visits to various posts throughout the Free State he found 'post-war listlessness, drink, immorality and venereal disease'.[1] He observed, perhaps sweepingly, 'any vice at present in the army is due directly or indirectly to over-indulgence in drink'. The civil war had undermined the already strained social fabric and contributed to an extensive moral collapse.

In the subsequent months and years, Dr Byrne's contact with government ministers and personnel was more occasional than during the civil strife. It tended to be in relation to educational and moral issues. These last focused on the rights and safety of the family and included issues like divorce, drunkenness, immoral literature, certain dances and films. From time to time there was communication with the Department of Defence regarding military chaplains and special church celebrations, and with the President of the Executive Council in connection with combined church and state functions. On a personal level, he remained in friendly communication with T. M. Healy, the Governor General.

The state and religion and morals

In matters of religion and morality, Archbishop Byrne was unlikely to find himself on a collision course with the government. Its members were Christians, the vast majority Catholics. They viewed themselves as governing a Christian state, and they endeavoured to apply Christian values in their administration. Where differences arose between the Christian churches on religious/moral issues, such as the legislation of divorce, the leaders of government, during Dr Byrne's lifetime, followed the position that reflected the official teaching accepted by the majority population. Not that the government was under church control, as is sometimes suggested. From what has been seen of Byrne's and Cardinal Logue's relations with the Cosgrave administration during the civil war, it is evident that while their views were treated with courtesy they only had effect when it suited the government. Besides, in most areas of government the hierarchy had nothing to say. In the two areas in which they demonstrated strong views, namely, education and morality, the government tended to come up with policies acceptable to them; but, then, the members of government, in any event, were likely to hold views similar to the hierarchy.

A moral aftermath

After nine years of war and the frequent proximity of death, from 1914-1923, the country, as noted above, indulged in outlets for pleasure and amusement and, almost inevitably, to an excessive extent. This was a prominent theme in the *Irish Catholic* on 26 January 1924, and aspects of that theme were to figure prominently in episcopal pastoral letters for a number of years.

It was an observable fact, the paper commented, that the love of unwholesome pleasure was on the increase, that 'tons of pornographic literature' from across the Channel was being dumped into Ireland every week and finding a ready sale, that many exhibitors of pictures were finding that it was 'the unwholesome variety of films' paid them best. Moreover, the current craze for all-night dancing had no parallel in the time of anyone living, while immodest fashions in women's dress had such a vogue as had compelled the Holy Father himself and ecclesiastics of all degree to utter protests and stern warnings. The writer added that one of the most potent sources of evil in the great cities was the exhibition of obscene or immoral pictures. It had engaged the legislators in the United States of America and other countries. He was now delighted to find that the Free State government, despite its many other pre-occupations, had not overlooked the necessity of dealing with this very grave matter, and last autumn the Oireachtas passed the Censorship of Films Act, which had just been brought into operation.[2]

Not surprisingly, Archbishop Edward Byrne, in his desire to preserve his people from occasions of sin, echoed some of the above concerns in his Lenten Pastoral Letter of February / March 1924. He avoided sweeping condemnations, however, and concentrated on excesses. He praised innocent recreation and reasonable relaxation from work but contrasted this with 'the feverish rush for pleasure which seems to absorb the minds and energies of so many'. Again, dancing, of course, was not intrinsically bad in itself but it could become a prolific source of evil, if not conducted under the strictest supervision. He had particularly in mind 'suggestive dances imported from countries whose outlook is largely pagan'. Many of the abuses, he suggested, would soon be abolished if there were a sound, strong Catholic opinion operating amongst the people. Such an opinion would refuse its sanction to theatrical and cinema representations, or to the public display of posters which pandered only to debased tastes and degraded instincts. Moving from moral dangers, the archbishop emphasised the need for reverence in the use of 'the Holy Name of our Saviour', and respect for the just rights of one's neighbour. The all-devouring desire for worldly riches, he concluded, had driven many to commit outrages on the property of others, and even to the heinous crime of sacrificing human life itself.[3]

Widespread diocesan changes. Diocesan engagements

M. J. Curran, writing from Dublin to Mgr Hagan, in Rome, on 14 January 1924, observed that ecclesiastical Dublin was in a ferment of excitement because of 'the forty-one changes that have been applied to the clergy … I need not say how disgusted all the bigwigs of the old days feel.'[4] It was scarcely the wisest way for a new archbishop to avoid enemies. A fortnight later, Byrne himself, in a letter to Hagan, remarked in passing how the senior clergy and the parish priests placed the blame 'on the appointment of a curate bishop'.

In the same letter, he welcomed the appointment of his secretary, Fr Paddy Walsh, as vicar-general, and he reported that the canonisation process on the Irish martyrs was proceeding to the fifth period. This last served as a reminder of the on-going work involved in this process, and also of the daily round of engagements facing an archbishop.

Apart from contact with priests of the diocese, fellow prelates, numerous Catholic organisations, and occasional unexpected eventualities, there was the interchange with the various religious congregations, especially those convents that came directly under his care. These involved him in visitation and consultation, supplying priests to say Mass and hear confessions, and at times dealing with sisters seeking to leave congregations or having complaints against their superiors. In the extensive field of hospital work, much time and attention was devoted to the Catholic hospitals, especially those run by the Sisters of Charity and the Sisters of Mercy. In addition, there were the requests of congregations seeking permission to set up novitiates or to open houses, or to attract candidates to their overseas work. Among the foreign groups seeking candidates in Ireland were: the Sisters of Mercy from California, the Congregation of Our Lady of the Assumption in Manila, a convent from Sydney, and a nursing body, the Sisters of St John of God. Many were fortified with letters from their bishops. In several instances, his Grace, in granting permission, sought protection for those joining the organisation. Thus, on 13 February 1924, his secretary, in a letter to a Sister Patrick, conveyed Dr Byrne's permission 'on condition that he gets from you a written guarantee that in the event of any subjects acquired by you in Ireland not proving suitable for any reason whatsoever, they will be returned to their homes in Ireland at the expense of the institute'.

In the case of religious organisations coming to Ireland to quest for money, the archbishop often refused permission because of the burden on the generous public. Among the male congregations, the Irish Christian Brothers expanded considerably in numbers and buildings during Dr Byrne's episcopate. They were generally kindly received and supported by him.[5]

Care of those who are poor and in difficulties
As noticed previously, he was supportive generally of lay Catholic organisations, but especially of those directly concerned with the poor and the unemployed; and in this respect, the St Vincent de Paul Society held pride of place. On 22 March 1924, he wrote to Mr Lalor, the president of the Dublin Council of the Society, that because of the accounts reaching him about the shortage of employment in the city, he was enclosing a cheque 'for £100 for immediate distribution by the Society to relieve the distress of families of those temporarily unemployed'.[6] On 21 December, in connection with another V. de P initiative, the Back Lane Night Shelter for men, he contributed £250.[7]

His pastoral care for the poor, as noted earlier, led to each priest being supplied with a *Liber Familiorum* (a book of families), which contained the addresses and names of the members of the parish, to enable the clergy to make contact with their people, and also to provide continuity at a time of change of clerical personnel. He urged priests to visit houses/homes. At ordinations and confirmations, the archbishop found time to meet with parish priests and curates and to enquire about their practice of visitation and their use of the *Liber*. Where he found these being neglected he could be very firm. It is believed that three men were assured of not being appointed parish priests during Dr Byrne's lifetime because of such pastoral neglect.[8]

Correspondence with members of the administration
Correspondence with members of the government, as mentioned, was much less than during the civil war years. There are

extant, however, a number of widely different communications. Early in 1924, Ernst Blythe TD, Minister for Finance, wrote announcing the establishment of a Savings Certificate Committee to encourage thrift in the Free State. It would be non-political and widely representative, and he requested his Grace to become a member. After some consideration and enquiries, Dr Byrne provided a representative on the Committee into the late 1930s.[9]

A quite different relationship was reflected in his communications with the Governor-General, T. M. Healy. On 21 March the latter thanked the archbishop for consenting to ordain 'our dear son'. His son, Paul, a Jesuit, was to be ordained in his first year theology by a special exception because of tuberculosis. It was a high additional joy, Healy added, 'that such a friend should perform the ceremony'. On 3 July, Dr Byrne received an invitation by card to dinner at the Vice-Regal Lodge 'on Thursday at 8 o'clock'. He, like Fr Tom Finlay, some other clergy, and a variety of people, enjoyed such occasions. Healy was the most gracious of hosts, noted for his wit and his capacity to stimulate lively conversation. On 4 November, the Governor-General, supported by the archbishop, sent a request in Latin to His Holiness seeking the privilege of having the Blessed Sacrament reserved in his house. On 12 December, Dr Byrne was able to inform Mr Healy that he had had a letter from Cardinal Gasparri granting him the privilege of the Blessed Sacrament for five years.[10]

An exchange of letters with General O'Duffy demonstrated flexibility on church matters on the part of the archbishop. On 7 March 1924, O'Duffy wrote about a date for a concert by the Garda Band. The only date available clashed with a church feast day. If Dr Byrne considered it embarrassing or objectionable to have the concert on that date, he, O'Duffy, would readily call it off. On 12 March, the archbishop thanked him for his courteous letter. 'It was unfortunate', he added, 'that the day selected … was Passion Sunday – a solemn religious anniversary, and in addition just at the heart of the Lenten season … However, as the arrangement was made unwittingly it would seem too hard to defer the performance until winter. Perhaps if the band master would introduce a few items of sacred music into his programme the performance would not bear a purely secular aspect.' He appreciated that the Gardaí wished to give good example in comporting themselves with propriety in external religious matters, and he concluded: 'May I take this opportunity of congratulating you on your taking up the highest honour in the Free State army.' A pleased O'Duffy replied on 15 March, assuring the archbishop that the band programme had been revised to include some items of sacred music.[11]

It was a comment on President Cosgrave's approach to the teaching of the Catholic Church that, before dealing with the issue of divorce, he sought an interview with Archbishop Byrne to familiarise himself with the church's position. They met on 7 February 1924, and subsequently Cosgrave requested, through his secretary, Mr Duggan, that his Grace summarise the teaching on marriage in a series of clear propositions. Dr Byrne did so under different headings and with an explanation covering 5 foolscap-size typed pages. The headings were: A. Marriage in Natural Law. B. The Catholic Church and Marriage. C The Church and marriages of people not baptised.[12] Cosgrave acknowledged receipt of the document on 4 March. He did not anticipate any difficulty whatever in the matter of a correct interpretation or action by Catholic members of the Oireachtas.[13] Later he confided to Bishop Downey, the Coadjutor Bishop of Ossory, 'I was a child so far as my information and knowledge of the subject was concerned.'[14] When he spoke in the Dáil in February 1925 on his own motion to prevent the introduction of a Divorce Bill, his comments reflected the archbishop's document:

> The majority of the people of this country regard the bond of marriage as a sacramental bond which is incapable of being dissolved. I personally hold this view. I consider that the whole fabric of our social organisation is based upon the sanctity of the marriage bond and that anything that tends to weaken the binding efficacy of that bond to that extent strikes at the root of our social life.[15]

A further insight into religious sentiments among major figures in the administration was provided in a letter from General McKeon, which was written on behalf of a foreign ecclesiastic who hoped to seek funds in Ireland for his mission.

Dr Byrne replied carefully on 12 May 1924 that he had received similar petitions from foreign ecclesiastics in similar need. 'From the very beginning of my episcopate,' he explained, 'I had been obliged to adopt the policy of giving an equal refusal to all.' The people of Dublin had many calls on their charity and they responded nobly. He felt strongly that it would not be fair to them if he by his approval gave a free hand to foreigners to collect money in Dublin for charities in which the people had a very remote interest. Softening his refusal, he added: 'If it were not a question of principle with me, I should have been only too pleased to grant the request of one like yourself, of whom I have heard such golden opinions on every side.'[16]

Irish College Rome insight and development

On 22 March 1924, Archbishop Byrne sent a telegram to Hagan granting permission to sell the site of the Irish College in Via Mazzarino and acquire the former Capuchin novitiate on the Coelian Hill.[17] The following day, M. J. Curran wrote from Dublin that Hagan would also receive a letter from the archbishop. Both he and Coadjutor-Archbishop O'Donnell were very keen on the project. Dr Byrne thought that there was 'no better college in Rome' than the Capuchin premises. Curran had succeeded in extracting a promise from him that he would ask the bishops for subscriptions.[18]

Byrne and O'Donnell got on well. In a letter to Hagan on 12 May, O'Donnell observed that Archbishop Byrne had shown him Hagan's letter;[19] and on 26 June they sent a joint telegram to Hagan informing him that telegrams were being sent from the bishops' standing committee to Cardinals Lucici and Sharetti in thanks for their efforts to secure the Capuchin site on proper terms.[20] Finally, on 9 July, Curran assured Hagan that having met the archbishop, he could say with certainty that his Grace would support the college, with its current plans for moving, all the way.[21]

Special occasions in the diocese

Always, in addition to the archbishop's routine, there were occasions of special celebration held not only in the Pro-Cathedral but in other locations. On 3 February, to mark the beatification of the celebrated scholar-Cardinal, Robert Bellarmine SJ, in the presence of an overflowing congregation, Dr Byrne presided at Mass in the Church of St Francis Xavier, Gardiner Street.[22] Two months later, on 9 April, he presided in the Pro-Cathedral at the anniversary requiem high Mass for the late Archbishop Walsh, at which there was a large congregation and upwards of 200 priests in the choir.[23] In June he was the consecrating prelate in

Blackrock College, when Dr. H. Gogarty CSSp, vicar-apostolic of Kiliman-jaro (sic), East Africa, was consecrated Bishop of Themiscyra; and on 29 June, the archbishop presided at the high Mass to mark the jubilee celebrations of the foundation of the Arch-Confraternity of the Sacred Heart of Jesus in St Peter's Church, Phibsboro.[24]

His on-going purpose to provide churches to meet the movement of population was further manifested during July 1924. On 6 July he dedicated the temporary Church of Corpus Christi at Home Farm Road, Drumcondra, in the presence of a large congregation; and a week subsequently, 13 July, he blessed and laid the foundation stone of a new chapel of ease at Donore Avenue, South Circular Road. On this last occasion there was an immense gathering of parishioners, and an ample banner pronouncing 'Welcome to our Beloved Archbishop'.[25]

Another aspect of building construction required his attendance on 12 November. As archbishop he had a particular interest in and responsibility towards Catholic-owned hospitals. Consequently, on that date, he was present at St Vincent's Hospital, which was run by the Irish Sisters of Charity, to formally open a new extern department.[26]

Meantime, on the political front, a particular occasion was greeted with a widespread enthusiasm that took the government by surprise.

De Valera released and welcomed

There was understandable rejoicing among republicans at the release of De Valera from prison in July 1924, but what surprised and overjoyed them was the warm reception he received from so many others. On 22 July, Sean T. Ó Ceallaigh commented, in a letter to his friend Mgr Hagan, about the release of Austin Stack and Éamon De Valera: 'You would have been charmed beyond measure witnessing the thousands greeting De Valera and lining the streets; even the most optimistic did not expect such.' Likewise thousands appeared when a reception was held that evening. De Valera spoke well and effectively, and he seemed 'to have gained ground rather than lost it'.[27]

Mrs Childer's unexpected letter

Late in October, Archbishop Byrne received a most surprising and embarrassing letter from Mary A Childers, wife of the executed

Erskine Childers. It cast an unexpected light on the inner life of
her much maligned husband.

My Lord Archbishop,
I am to receive tomorrow, Tuesday, the remains of my husband, Erskine Childers, and I write to request your Grace's
consent that they be admitted, along with the remains of the
other executed men, to Whitefriar's Street Church on
Wednesday night.
    I do so because I know that my husband did not wish to
have a Protestant burial, and, though not actually a Catholic,
did wish to have a Catholic one. This he expressed to me
often during his last years. His religious life was a progress
from a rigid Protestant upbringing, through doubts which
gave him intense suffering, to absolute faith in God and the
Divinity of Christ, and at the same time, as the years passed,
often he told me that if he learned his way to a Christian
communion none other would be the one that he would
choose than the Catholic Church.

Mrs Childers continued: 'Towards the end of his life, he acquired and practised an intense devotion to Our Lady, and his
devotions were such as Catholics practise. During his last sum-
mers he said the rosary daily and in his farewell letter to me he
wrote of how he had come to understand the "meaning of the
Blessed Mother".'
    'He never gave formal adhesion to the Catholic Church, but
in the hour of death he asked for first one and then another
Catholic priest. To me who for twenty years was his close com-
rade and wife, and to whom his profoundly earnest and spiritual
nature was known, that choice can bear only one interpretation.
I believe that he desired to profess and to give himself to the
church in the hour of his death, and that he was still not certain
and wished instruction, longed for admission. In those hours as
I watched here I know how it would be for him then.'
    'I have not spoken of these things or of the denial that was
made to him, for I felt these things too sacred. But now that the
choice is placed before me, that I am asked to decide, it is an
agony of mind to me to think of ... still being refused to him
what I know he desired – to arrange Protestant rites when in the
hour of his death he wanted those of the Catholic Church.'
    She wished she could see his Grace and tell more of her hus-

band and of what it meant to her to carry out for him what he would have chosen. 'I do hope Your Grace', she concluded, 'will see your way to granting my earnest prayer and will send the reply to reach me in the course of tomorrow – Tuesday.'[28]

The archbishop's reply is not available. He was placed in an impossible situation within a very short time-span. Erskine Childers had not been received into the Catholic Church. The two men who guarded him in prison, and protected him from attack, may not have passed on his request for a priest, but they readily allowed Dr Craig, the Church of Ireland Archbishop of Dublin, to visit him before his death. Writing to Hagan, 26-27 October, Cáit, wife of Sean T. Ó Ceallaigh, observed that 'Fr P. Browne (Pádraig de Brún) will find it difficult to deal with Mrs Erskine Childers' wish to have her husband buried with Catholics; he cannot be taken to the church in Whitefriar Street. The Bartons, on the other hand, see it would be just as good to have one Protestant patriot and saint in a Protestant church-yard.'[29] Erskine Childers was buried according to the rites of the Church of Ireland.

Death of Cardinal Logue

Archbishop Edward Byrne joined thousands of mourners at the funeral in Armagh, on 25 November, of Michael Cardinal Logue. Following the High Mass, he gave absolution at the catafalque together with Most Revd Drs O'Donnell, Harty, Gilmartin and MacRory, and then walked in procession with his fellow archbishops. The vast attendance included twenty-three bishops, and such lay dignitaries as the Governor-General, Mr T. M. Healy, Mr Kevin O'Higgins, Vice-President of the Executive Council, a number of other government ministers and representatives, and a representative of the Governor of Northern Ireland.

Dr Patrick O'Donnell succeeded to Armagh. With his elevation to the primacy, the tension between Dublin and Armagh, which remained from Archbishop Walsh's time, came to an end. Archbishops O'Donnell and Byrne continued to work together as friends, and were determined to keep the clergy out of partisan politics.

Supporting worthy causes and closing the year

Also during November, Dr Byrne sent a letter of encouragement and £250 to the Dublin branch of the St Vincent de Paul Society.[30] A further letter of support was sent to the annual general meeting of the Dublin and District Centres of the Pioneer Total Abstinence Association, encouraging its members to continued their endeavours 'with spirit and strength until the vice of intemperance was completely banished from the land'.[31]

Closing a momentous year
On 19 December 1924, the *Freeman's Journal* was published for the last time. It had recorded aspects of Irish life and history for 161 years. Four days later, Archbishop Byrne returned to Armagh for the Month's Mind of the late cardinal. The year came to a close for him with a solemn service of thanksgiving at the Pro-Cathedral. Although the service was timed for 4.00 pm the large church was thronged. After an end-of-year sermon, there was exposition of the Blessed Sacrament while the Pro-Cathedral choir sang under the direction of Vincent O'Brien. The ceremonies concluded with Benediction of the Blessed Sacrament given by his Grace. Two days later, on 2 January 1925, he heralded not just a New Year, but issued a pastoral letter marking a Holy Year Jubilee.

Signs of stability, 1925
On 25 December 1924, the Archbishop of Tuam, Thomas P. Gilmartin reminded his congregation that 'now that we are enjoying comparative peace' it was the duty of all to pray for peace and to co-operate with the officers of peace in stamping out all elements of disorder such as robbing mails and holding up people with revolvers.[32] Despite still suffering from what he termed 'the paralysing effect of national strife', the country had taken on a sense of identity and stability. Green pillar-boxes and green post-vans had replaced the red which had been prominent for so long; the people in Dublin and in garrison towns were becoming accustomed to a green-clad national army, and to the navy-blue of the Civic Guards (or Garda Síochána) in place of the black jackets of their predecessors. Motors and buses were becoming a frequent sight, and there was the occasional excitement of a plane overhead.

There remained, of course, intense poverty and widespread unemployment, and the proselytisers continued to function with their hymns and songs. They were, however, widely un-

popular and Dublin ballad-singers retaliated with their own dit-
ties, such as the relentless ballad to the air of *Nóra Críodhna*:

> O, Come with me to Merrion Square
> An' sure as my name is Reilly,
> Each 'murdherin' thief will get mutton an' beef
> If he prays with Mrs Smyly.

After years of strife, and latterly of internecine bitterness and
even hatred, 'there was a feeling of spring making its way
through a heavy soil'.[33]

A helping hand

Archbishop Byrne, early in the New Year, was happy to perform
the blessing and opening of another new church, this time at
Lusk, Co Dublin, which held many happy memories for him.[34]
Then, once again fulfilling his role as dispenser of aid to those in
need, he sent £100 to the Dublin council of St Vincent de Paul.[35]
Four days later, on 4 February, Bishop William MacNulty wrote
from Letterkenny to express appreciation of his Grace's
thoughtful financial aid to the people of Donegal: 'two bad sea-
sons in succession, especially turfless ones, test the endurance of
even the hardiest mountaineers'.[36] A further expression of appreciation came from President Cosgrave, whose wife had been
ill. On 12 February, he wrote from his home at Beechpark,
Templeogue, Co Dublin: 'It is with deep joy and gratitude that I
received your Grace's kind letter enclosing the Apostolic Brief
according me the cherished privilege of maintaining a private
oratory in my house at Beechpark.'[37]

The President felt under pressure following the split in the
government's party over the handling of the army revolt, and
the establishment of the rival National Party, and also because
of the persistent complaints that the civil service was being run
by Free Masons, and concerning taxation. Bishop Fogarty received a reply from him on 29 January, which almost certainly
he communicated to Edward Byrne and some other friendly
prelates. Cosgrave explained that he had tried hard over the
summer to unite the National group with his party, but did not
succeed. He was greatly concerned about this split with old personal friends and colleagues. As regards the charges being made
against the government, they were 'untrue in substance and in
fact' but were difficult to answer satisfactorily. It was quite un-

true that the government was dominated by Masons. Out of ten ministries there was not one head of department a Mason. Moreover, the clerk and assistant-clerk to the Dáil were old Dáil officials, and the clerk to the Senate was Major-General Dalton. He did not think 'a more grossly unfair allegation' could be made. As to the taxation being 'too heavy', he regretted that most of the Acts passed by the government made enemies. He agreed with Fogarty, however, that the small farmer had a hard time and that it would be a great thing to do something for him.[38]

Appointments, opportunities, problems

On 8 March, the archbishop wrote at some length to Hagan at the Irish College. He requested him, first of all, to obtain approval for certain capitular appointments,[39] and then with reference to some other clergy, he mentioned Fr Patrick Dempsey, with whom he had much difficulty and who, for his part, had appealed to Rome and kept expressing his grievances against the archbishop. 'Our Friend Fr Pat Dempsey', he explained, had applied for a transfer from the diocese and got it immediately. The application arose because he had been transferred to a chaplaincy 'after his appearance on that roll of fame *Stubs Gazette* for a debt of £80. Another instance of my episcopal tyranny. I am only afraid that the Bishop of Auckland ... will not accept him.' He did not think that Dempsey would come knocking in Rome on this occasion, but he was 'so queer and self-righteous' one never could tell.

Byrne added that he and Fr Dunne proposed to be in Rome some day during Easter Week, and they hoped that Hagan would be able to give them a corner under his hospitable roof. He would let him know the day of their arrival nearer the date. He looked forward with a great deal of pleasurable anticipation to his visit to Rome and 'particularly to passing some time in the Old College before it ceases to be our Roman Home'.[40]

In September it was confirmed to the archbishop that Fr Dempsey had been adopted by the diocese of Brisbane. Dempsey requested and received a final financial gift from Dublin, and stated that he would have no future claim on the archdiocese.[41]

Educational matters

The archbishop's diplomatic skills were tested in negotiations with the Irish Christian Brothers. Based, no doubt, on experience as well as principle, the Brothers did not wish to have a parish priest as manager of their primary schools. The Superior-General had been quite blunt on this matter in a previous meeting. On 6 April, however, Dr Byrne explained to Bishop Patrick Foley, of Kildare and Leighlin, secretary to the bishops' standing committee, that he had 'a long and very friendly chat' with the Superior-General and his assistant, who wished to settle the matter in Ireland, without having recourse to Rome. They made three suggestions: '1. The bishops should be patron of the school and should appoint as manager the brother nominated by the superiors of the Christian Brothers; or 2. The bishop should be patron and manager; or 3. The bishop should be patron and should appoint as manager either the nominee of the brothers or the parish priest in exceptional cases. It being distinctly understood that no. 3 only holds for exceptional cases and is not to be the normal state of things.' If any of these suggestions were adopted, the brothers would depend on the bishops to secure such legislation in Rome as would accord with the agreement.

He gathered, Dr Byrne explained, that the Brothers would never accept parochial management as a normal thing, but would be immensely relieved if the bishops saw their way to accept any of these proposals. His own personal view, Dr Byrne concluded rather characteristically, was that compromise was indicated on the part of the bishops. He would be content with proposal no. 2, which safeguarded the managerial system and left independence to the brothers. The alternative to compromise was 'a disedifying squabble in Rome and who knows how it would end.'[42]

Subsequently, Bishop Foley suggested that the appointment of the parish priest and the brother in charge as a possible 'stand off of our present difficulties', or no. 3 above. Archbishop Byrne was prepared to accept this. He would not bring up the matter with the Congregation in Rome until he had carefully seen how the wind was blowing.[43] On 26 May 1925, Foley informed him that the Standing Committee were impressed with how well he had negotiated with the brothers.[44]

Education, in its different forms, was to take up much of Archbishop's Byrne's time and attention during his episcopate. This was because he was in a developing situation. The government was endeavouring to stamp its own educational ideals on the Free State. In 1924 the Department of Education had been set up. Forthwith, the system of state grants was changed to a capitation per pupil basis, and agreement was reached with the Christian Brothers which enabled them to bring their schools into the national system, and the general trend of government policy was made clear: 'In the administration of Irish education, it is the intention of the new government to work with all its might for the strengthening of the national fibre by giving the language, history, music and traditions of Ireland their natural place in the life of Irish schools.' The ideal was attractive, but the implementation had many problems, not least the training of teachers to implement the new ethos. Bishops with training colleges had a deep interest in this area, especially with respect to the teaching of religion. Archbishop Byrne, with two training colleges, felt a particular responsibility that was to continue for some years.

Matt Talbot: Death and Devotion

June proved a particularly significant month for him. On 7 June, Matt Talbot died on his way to Mass. He was well-known to Edward Byrne from his years in Marlborough Street. Matt spent hours in prayer in the Pro-Cathedral, as he did in Gardiner Street and some other churches. A labouring man, he had overcome alcohol addiction by prayer and penance. He ate little, gave alms from his small income, and after death was found to wear chains about his body. Within a short time of his dying a popular devotion developed to him.

To the archbishop and many others he was seen as a providential figure at a time when the country was struggling with excessive alcohol consumption and a preoccupation with self-indulgence and the pursuit of pleasure. He encouraged Sir Joseph Glynn, noted for his work for the St Vincent de Paul Society, to write an account of Matt's life. His biographical pamphlet was published by the Catholic Truth Society in March 1926, less than a year after Matt died. Ten thousand copies were sold in four days. Within a few months 120,000 copies had been sold. Glynn's pamphlet was translated into more than thirteen languages.

Official enquiries into the life of Matt Talbot were conducted by the archdiocese of Dublin. They led to the publication of a pastoral letter by Archbishop E. J. Byrne DD, dated 1 November 1931, which noted that popular devotion had 'grown up and spread beyond the limits of our diocese and country' ... and 'it seemed that the hand of Providence must surely be here, and that God had chosen one of our own beloved poor to show forth to the world the working of the ever abiding principle of holiness which is in the Catholic Church ...'[45] The archbishop's special interest in Matt Talbot helped the latter's cause, but it was not until some years after Dr Byrne's death that the Holy See established the apostolic process for his canonisation. In 1952 his body was exhumed and he was declared 'the Servant of God', a title short of beatification. That was to remain the situation into the twenty-first century.

The problem of Archbishop Mannix

At the end of June, the arrival of the formidable Archbishop Mannix of Melbourne in Ireland was an occasion of embarrassment for the Free State government and the Irish hierarchy, because he came on the invitation of anti-Treaty supporters and was noted for his republican sympathies. His presence offered republicans a welcome manifestation of support and understanding from a senior churchman.

When his ship, the *Cambria*, docked at Dún Laoghaire, he was met by De Valera and members of the Sinn Féin Party – Countess Markievich, Mrs Tom Clarke, Madam Maud McBride, J. J. Kelly, Dan Breen, and Austin Stack. Dr Mannix travelled with them on a special train to Westland Row Station, Dublin. There a crowd of several thousand was assembled to greet the archbishop. The party then made its way, pointedly, to the Pro-Cathedral for prayers, and from there to the Shelbourne Hotel, where, not having been invited by Archbishop Byrne to stay with him, Mannix was lodged. Wisely, however, he declined to make a statement to the press.[46]

The embarrassment to Archbishop Byrne was augmented by republican planning. Despite his moderate stance in the civil war and his many appeals for republican prisoners, he was viewed as an enemy to the republic.

The appointment of a Cardinal

Since the death of Cardinal Logue there had been speculation about the appointment of a cardinal to Ireland. From New York, on 2 June 1925, Sean T. Ó Ceallaigh expressed to Hagan his view that Archbishop Mannix was likely to be promoted, and also either

Armagh or Dublin. He favoured Archbishop Patrick O'Donnell of
Armagh because he was 'the bigger man and more reliable from
Hagan's own standpoint'. At the same time, Dublin was raised in
his estimation through his unstinting support for Hagan.[47]
Nothing happened, however, until November. Meantime, both
Byrne and O'Donnell received strong support. O'Donnell, of
Armagh and Primate of all Ireland, was favoured by people
with strong republican sympathies, and by many others for his
ability, presence and charm. In a partitioned country, there
would be a strong assertion of national as well as ecclesiastical
unity in offering the 'red hat' to the Primate of All Ireland.[48] In
that context, O'Donnell was favourite for the promotion. As
against that, the strong English lobby in Rome might be expected
to support the Irish government in its promotion of Byrne's can-
didacy. The Governor-General, T. M. Healy, was said to have
expressed his backing for Dublin; and President William
Cosgrave and Oliver St John Gogarty (senator, surgeon, poet,
former friend of James Joyce, and *bon vivant*), an unlikely
combination, went to Rome to plead his cause.[49] In the event,
Archbishop O'Donnell was named as cardinal.

O'Donnell's appointment was received with much enthusiasm by Catholics north and south of Ireland. Byrne must have
been disappointed, given the publicity the issue of cardinal had
stirred up and the high expectation in Dublin, but he was also
aware that his reaction was likely to be sharply scrutinised. He
determined to join in the rejoicing, and to invite the new cardinal to stay at Archbishop's House on his return to Ireland. He
did so all the more readily in that, as noted earlier, he liked and
got on well with O'Donnell. His letter of invitation was written
with particular care, combining friendship with respect for the
new 'Prince of the Church'. He wrote on 2 December 1925, while
O'Donnell was still 'Cardinal-Designate'. Addressing him as
'My dear Lord Cardinal-Designate', he proceeded:

> I don't know if you are yet able to decide how soon you will
> be able to leave Rome after the Consistory. Of course the cer-
> emony of taking possession of your titular church and other
> functions will naturally cause your stay to be further pro-
> longed. But when you are returning I should take it as a great
> favour, and indeed it will give me the greatest pleasure if, on
> your way back to Armagh you would stay with us as long as
> you find convenient.

It seems scarcely fitting that on such an occasion as the return of our Irish Cardinal from Rome, with the sacred Purple newly-conferred upon him, that any other house in Dublin should have the honour of being the first to offer hospitality to the new Prince of the Church, when this house is heartily open to him and where he will have a hundred thousand welcomes.

He would request all the bishops to meet him at Archbishop's House and to give him his first welcome home. Of course it would be difficult to assemble them all but he would like to have as many as could come. His car would meet the Cardinal at Westland Row Station and bring him to Drumcondra.[50]

The cardinal arrived back in Ireland on 23 December. He was officially welcomed by President Cosgrave at Dún Laoghaire on his arrival, and had an enthusiastic reception from people who thronged the pier. 'His Eminence also had enthusiastic receptions *en route* to the residence of his Grace the Archbishop of Dublin, and outside the residence, and subsequently at Amiens Street Railway Station, when he entrained for Armagh.' There were demonstrations of rejoicing at different places on his journey northward until at Armagh he found the city illuminated and witnessed memorable scenes of joy and enthusiasm.[51]

A sense of relief and heavy challenges

The year drew to a close with the debacle of the Boundary Commission. The three governments – Britain, the Free State, and Northern Ireland – agreed to leave the existing boundaries unchanged. Despite a feeling of concern and anxiety for the Catholic population in the North, and that population's sense of betrayal by the Free State, the result was greeted with relief by many. The people had been through too much. They were apathetic and in shock, and there was so much poverty, unemployment and emigration. Something of the weight of it all and the need to focus on essentials was conveyed on 4 December, the day after the result of the Boundary Commission was announced, by the archbishop's friend and admirer, John Fahy, the Jesuit provincial:

This morning brings news about another pact. It is to be hoped that the country will accept it and ratify the actions of our ministers. We have had too much fighting and anarchy and need time now to heal our wounds. There is great distress among the poor, we need time to bring them relief in their suffering and poverty. We should avoid at this time a general election which would only engender fresh bitterness and waste the little money we have. May the ministry insist on some amicable compromise with Labour – sit on Mr McGilligan if necessary! – and get on with its schemes for the relief of unemployment.[52]

That he was echoing part of the concern felt by the archbishop was indicated by the latter's increased donation of £500 to the Vincent de Paul Society on 17 November, and his reminder that the 'dead weight of unemployment' was the most difficult problem to solve, and that its necessary consequences were the poverty and misery that were evident to all. The human need and struggle for existence close to home was focusing attention to the exclusion of other considerations in the cold final weeks of 1925.

PART TWO

Times of Sadness and Exhaltation
1926-1933

CHAPTER NINE

1926-1928

Censorship. Catholic Action. Tragic Deaths.
Signs of the Archbishop's Illness.

Regulating behaviour

The 1920s were deeply marked not only by political change but by a welter of other changes: increased communication by means of radio and, as noted earlier, a greatly increased influx of foreign press and publications, a new freedom in women's dress and behaviour, the discovery of jazz, a variety of new dances and the multiplication of dance halls (some quite unhygienic), the spread of smoking and excessive alcoholic indulgences by both sexes, and the widespread appeal of the 'picture house' as films attracted people of all ages. In February 1926, Archbishop Byrne, though more circumspect than many of his colleagues, observed that 'the moral fibre of our people' had become relaxed 'in these later years'.[1] A similar concern was felt by many members of the government with respect to behaviour and external conduct, and was reflected in legislation.

Legislation and films

As early as 1923, the Free State government introduced a Film Act which envisaged a film censor with power to cut films or refuse a licence to those which, in his opinion, were 'subversive of public morality'. This development reflected what was happening in the United States of America and some other countries. On 5 November 1925, the Minister for Justice, Kevin O'Higgins, informed Archbishop Byrne that a Film Censorship Board was being established and requested him to nominate a clergyman to serve on a Cinema Appeals Board. He had to write a second time, on 4 January 1926, before receiving the nomination of Canon Michael Cronin PP, the fellow-student and friend of Byrne's, who was called on to fulfill many roles.[2]

The Foreign Press and publications

An issue that occasioned widespread interest and protest was the proliferation of British publications, many of which were deemed objectionable. The fact that they were 'British' provided an additional impetus and edge to the criticism. The reaction was not unusual. In the history of emergent nations control of communications has been a major concern, especially when the media of the former foreign administration continues to exercise considerable influence. In Ireland in the 1920s there was a growing feeling that the foreign press, which had maligned the efforts of the Irish people to achieve independence, was now seeking to win over the minds and moral outlook of Irish people to a hedonistic naturalism. The first person to give strongly coherent expression to such views appears to have been a Jesuit, Rev Richard S. Devane (formerly a priest of the Limerick diocese), who was well known for his concern at the treatment of juvenile offenders, and for his picketing of the Dáil to assert the rights of unmarried mothers – a circumstance which earned him the waggish sobriquet 'the Father of unmarried mothers'. His arguments, in a landmark article entitled 'Indecent Literature', which appeared in the *Irish Ecclesiastical Record* in 1925, helped to develop a strong public demand for legislation prohibiting literature that contained 'obscene' material, including under that heading all birth-control literature. He won the support of the bishops, but also that of more extreme bodies such as vigilance committees and publications like the *Catholic Bulletin*. Devane was careful to point out with regard to birth-control literature that federal legislation had been drawn up in the United States of America limiting the sale of all contraceptive articles; and in Britain a Joint Select Committee of the House of Commons had recommended that it be illegal to advertise drugs or articles for the prevention of conception, while the Church of England at its Lambeth Conference, in 1925, had condemned such practices. Other English-speaking countries, like Canada and Australia, had also adopted similar attitudes to the same issue.[3]

The weight of opinion encouraged the Minister for Justice to establish a Committee of Enquiry into 'Evil Literature' in 1926. This led to the Censorship of Publications Act. Subsequently, on 16 October 1929, Monsignor Boylan, St Patrick's College, Maynooth, informed Archbishop Byrne that the Minister for Justice had invited him to be a member of the Censorship of Publications Board. He was loath to accept the invitation, but if he thought the archbishop would like him to accept it he would accept it without further hesitation.[4] He was to chair a five member board for two terms of three years. The other distinguished members were: Denis J. Coffey, Esq, President of University College Dublin; R. Fearon, Esq, MA, FTCD, professor at Trinity College Dublin; William Magennis, Esq, MA, professor at UCD; and W. G. Williams, Esq, MA, lecturer in Education at UCD. Professor Fearon was a Protestant, the others were Catholics.

Explaining the working of the Act to the archbishop, Mgr Cronin pointed out that any person might complain to the Minister for Justice that a book, or a particular edition of a book, was indecent or obscene, or advocated the unnatural prevention of conception, or the procurement of abortion, or miscarriage, or the use of any method, treatment, or appliance for the purpose of such prevention or procurement. On receiving the complaint, the minister might refer it to the board which, in turn, was required to report back to the minister. The board might also examine and report to the minister on their own initiative on any book or particular edition of a book. Indeed, in practice, very few complaints were made by the public. The majority of reports on books were made by the board on their own initiative. Practically all the effective work of censorship had hitherto been done by the board itself and its staff. Neither the clergy nor the laity had shown any real interest in the working of the Censorship of Publications Act.

Diocesan Censorship
A point of special interest to the archbishop was Mgr Cronin's reminder that the board could not recommend the prohibition of a book because its teachings were anti-Christian or anti-Catholic, or because it advocated dangerous views in theology, philosophy, or the social sciences.[5] His Grace considered such literature, with respect to the Dublin archdiocese, to be matter for the diocesan censors, Mgr Cronin and Fr J. J. Dunne, of the Church of the Sacred Heart, Donnybrook. Both men, and especially Cronin, acquired a very conservative reputation among theologians, and among clergy and laity involved in social studies. The grounds for that reputation merit consideration. They turn a sharp light on the prevailing episcopal ethos of control and caution in matters relating to theology, social philosophy, and morals.

Generally, there was no great problem with devotional books, though exaggerated devotion was likely to be criticised and sometimes quite devastatingly. Thus, of a book by the well-known Fr Fahy CSSp, on *The Mystical Body of Christ in the Modern World*, it was pointed out that the 'Mystical Body' was made to prove and disprove everything and that the book was not needed; while Frank Duff was reminded, with respect to his work on devotion to Our Lady and the teaching of Simon de Montfort, that while the work as a whole was 'most edifying' it was advisable to correct certain extravagances, which were certain 'to be seized by Protestants as good ground for their Protestantisms'.

When it came to works by theologians or men immersed in social thought and teaching, the Dublin censors' protectionist conservatism became evident. In this they largely reflected the thinking of their archbishop and of the Irish episcopacy. The official church, ever since the condemnation of Modernism, as noted earlier, had become cabined and confined within a very traditional theology, and prized 'orthodoxy' above all. On 19 January 1926, J. J. Dunne informed Cronin, with reference to a pamphlet by Fr Peter Finlay SJ, one of the leading Irish theologians, that he agreed with his (Cronin's) letter and reasons and had written to Fr Finlay to say that he looked upon the reasons and suggestions as sound and was in agreement with the censor that the pamphlet should not be published until the suggested changes were made. Dunne added that he was sure the Archbishop would be of the same mind. 'Somebody said to him that you were very conservative. He replied: "If you mean by conservative, orthodox, Dr Cronin is very conservative." So say we all.'[6]

But was such conservatism part of the role of a diocesan censor? The previous archbishop, a former distinguished professor of theology, did not think it was. When it came to deciding what deserved the *imprimatur* of the archbishop, Dr Walsh gave clear instructions, which Dr Cronin preserved among his papers:

> An Imprimatur is not a recommendation of the book to which it is attached. It conveys no sort of approval of the work. A Bishop for whose imprimatur a work is submitted may perhaps disapprove of the views expressed in it by the author. He may even regret that the author should have thought of publishing the work at all. But this will not justify him in withholding his imprimatur, or official licence, for the

publication of the work, if it is found to be free from error in the matter of faith or morals.

Concluding his instructions, Archbishop Walsh observed that as a rule, the book to which the imprimatur was attached was not seen by the bishop. His responsibility in the matter began and ended with the selection of one or more ecclesiastics, sufficiently learned, prudent, and painstaking, to be entrusted with the important duty of the censorship of certain classes of works, published in his diocese.[7]

The key determinant was the book's freedom from error in matters of faith or morals, not whether or not the censor disapproved of the views of the author. Fr Patrick Gannon SJ, emphasised these points in his response to Dr Cronin as censor of his work. He returned his paper with the required emendations but remarked that he could not change the view put forward without destroying the whole contrast he had drawn between authority in church and state. He added:

> I acknowledge that the view I hold is not quite in line with that supposed in the Leonine encyclical … But equally I hold that the encyclical was not an ex-cathedra definitive document and left the question still open. The alternative opinion was taught in Rome even during Leo's pontificate and has been taught since. Hence it is free, and appeals to me much more than Taparelli's thesis.[8]

The striking case of Dr Coffey

The man most aggrieved by the diocesan censors was Dr Peter Coffey, professor of philosophy at Maynooth, who had long been a leading exponent of Catholic Social Teaching and who had sought a viable alternative to the capitalist system. He, Fr Lambert McKenna SJ, and a few other priests, were among a small minority of clergy who gave a sympathetic hearing to James Connolly's brand of socialism, and struggled to enable leaders of the Labour movement to find a *via media* between much of Connolly's teachings and those of the Catholic Church.

On 7 March 1923, Coffey had complained to Dr Mac Caffrey, a fellow professor at Maynooth, of the treatment of his pamphlet *A Sinn Féin Money Policy* and of his *Catechism of the Labour Question*. Both, he explained, had received 'the nihil obstat (approval) of Fr Peter Finlay, who is at all events one of our best theologians', but the bishops appointed as Visitors or Examiners at

Maynooth had prohibited their publication even anonymously. The bishops were so afraid that the public would learn anything about economics or finance from an Irish priest who was a Maynooth professor. The cardinal had stated that there must be no hint of 'socialism' in Maynooth.[9]

Seven years later, in 1929, as the capitalist system came under intense strain in the western world, Dr Coffey's projected publication, *The Flaw in the Money System – an Elementary Analysis of Currency and Credit, Costs and Prices*, was rejected. He was informed that in the present state of Ireland a professor of Maynooth should be very cautious. It was not a time to launch a revolutionary economic policy.

On 11 December 1929, a concerned and exasperated Coffey sent a forthright, confidential memorandum to the archbishops and bishops of Ireland. He sent it under a covering letter to the episcopal secretary, Dr P. Morrisroe, Bishop of Achonry, requesting that Archbishop Byrne bring it to the attention of the episcopal conference. The memorandum commenced:

> Certain happenings within the past decade have caused me some concern and perplexity regarding the official attitude of the Church in Ireland – mainly as evidenced by the attitudes of some theological censors – towards the efforts of Catholics, especially the priests, to foster a genuine and earnest study of the social and economic question.

He drew to a close with the blunt comment that in Ireland there were numerous priests, and some laymen, who would willingly devote themselves to the study of the Social Question in the light of Catholic teaching but who were deterred from doing so by the belief that such study would lead to conflict with an excessively strict and reactionary theological censorship, and by the feeling that their motives and competence for such study would be distrusted by the bishops.

His appeal to the body of the episcopate failed, as did his subsequent appeal to Rome. A concluding comment on his campaign, was written in ink at the foot of his covering letter to Bishop Morrisroe: 'The Committee of Bishops reported that, having examined the writings of Dr Coffey, it was inadvisable to appoint Dr Coffey to the Chair of Ethics.'[10]

Pastoral activity in 1926
During the years 1926-1928, Archbishop Byrne took part in a range of public functions. The year 1926 was particularly busy in that respect: especially with the blessing of the foundation stones of new churches, and the opening of new schools or extensions to existing buildings. He also responded positively to an invitation to be a joint manager of a Department of Education initiative to establish in Dublin 'schools for juvenile street traders' – one for boys and one for girls.[11]

Two church celebrations had a special significance that year: St Patrick's Day, and the new feast of the Kingship of Christ. The former, as the *Irish Catholic Directory* noted, was a day of sobriety beyond all precedent, thanks to the new licensing legislation, which ordained the total closing of the public houses on St Patrick's Day. The archbishop presided at High Mass in the Pro-Cathedral at noon. There had been Masses every half-hour from 5 o'clock. Seven months later, on 25 October, his Grace led a crowded congregation at High Mass in the Pro-Cathedral to mark the inauguration of the new feast of the Kingship of Christ. The feast was celebrated throughout the country and gave a distinctive fillip to public devotions.[12] Not the least of its effects was the foundation of a very important lay organisation, *An Ríoghacht*, the League of the Kingship of Christ, in Dublin on 31 October 1926. It grew in influence during the years of the Dr Byrne's episcopate.

An Ríoghacht. Training for Catholic Social Action
The founder, Fr Edward Cahill SJ, informed the archbishop on 20 October that the body had been at a tentative stage for some months, and named its provisional committee.[13] He was conscious of the intellectual weakness of Irish Catholicism. He sought out able men and women, as Associates of the League, with a view to involving them in a serious study of Catholic social principles. Shortly after founding An Ríoghacht, he published a pamphlet which defined its object as 'a society for social study and Catholic action'. Such a body was essential, he believed, to counteract organised anti-Christian forces and movements. Already for many years, Catholic lay organisations were an immense force in many continental countries. Ireland had a special need for such an organisation because, although the people were predominantly Catholic, the framework of the society

in which they lived was still largely un-Christian. The civic institutions and social organisation still reflected anti-Catholic foreign influences and this had resulted in Ireland losing touch with the traditional Catholic culture of Europe.

The constitution of An Ríóghacht sent to Archbishop Byrne noted in its first article that it assumed as its basis the fundamental laws of Christian society and the principles of Catholic Action as laid down by the great encyclicals of Leo XIII, and several later pronouncements of the Holy See, and explained that An Ríóghacht was not associated with any political party, and took no part in political controversy or activities except where, and in so far as, its objects (viz. Catholic social interests) were involved.[14]

One of the effects of the organisation was that it attracted men and women of different political persuasions to reorganise the public life of the nation in accordance with Catholic standards and Catholic social principles and, in the process, it served as a force for healing the bitter divisions of the civil war. Within a few years it had six branches in Dublin, two in Cork, two in Kilkenny, and one each in Waterford, Mullingar, Nenagh, and Bray. Cahill viewed the organisation as a training area, and once the members had a good grasp of the social principles and ideals he urged them to move on and to spread the good news. By means of public lectures, pamphlets, summer schools, a major public conference, a magazine, the numerous articles of Fr Cahill, and by word of mouth, An Ríóghact made its name known. The cumulative effect of Fr Cahill's lectures and articles resulted in the publication in 1932 of his major work the *Framework of the Christian State*, which became a textbook for Ríóghacht meetings. The members of the body were to have considerable influence in the 1930s. The organisation came to be represented in areas of importance such as the Banking Commission, 1934-1938. On the silver jubilee of the League of the Kingship of Christ, a founder member, John Waldron, commented in the *Irish Monthly*, of January 1951, p 179, that not least among the achievements of An Ríóghacht had been the training of members, who carried into their various spheres in public life a sound knowledge of Catholic social principles, in the judiciary, the professions, the civil service, trades unions and in commerce.[15]

The Maynooth Synod and Catholic Action

Fr Cahill's pamphlet on An Ríoghacht appeared in 1927, the year in which a national synod was held by the bishops at Maynooth. It was one of the most important occasions in which Archbishop Byrne participated. It was largely concerned with bringing conformity in church law and practice across the country in keeping with the requirements of the new code of canon law issued in 1917. It reflected the official church's policy of promoting greater unanimity in law and practice throughout the world.

The Irish synod also expressed the bishops' on-going concern at the pursuit of pleasure, and their wish to promote Catholic Action in the service of the church and under the control of the clergy. The synod called on the laity 'to unite in suitable societies to form an organised army ... to mould the public conscience in accordance with Catholic principles, to foster religion, to defend it in public and private and to restore the Christian mode of life.'[16] Much of this was in accordance with Byrne's appeal from the start of his episcopate for a strong spirit of social responsibility among the Catholic people. The synod drew attention to the work of particular societies which it recommended to the laity. These were: the Catholic Protection and Rescue Society (against proselytism), the Society of St Vincent de Paul, and the Catholic Truth Society of Ireland. The synod's message in this regard was reinforced the following year by the publication of *The Handbook of Catholic Action*, which made special reference to the CTSI, whose function it was to develop Catholic Action. Catholic organisations were encouraged to counteract the forces and enemies arrayed against the church, and to create in Ireland a thoroughly Catholic environment, a thoroughly Catholic atmosphere, a thoroughly Catholic public opinion.[17]

Catholic Action and the Freemasons

But how was such an environment and atmosphere to be accomplished given that, in Cahill's view, the framework of the society was still largely un-Catholic and much of business and the important positions in the civil service were held by Freemasons? This view was widely held, and was to feature in Fianna Fáil's criticism of the government in the 1927 election. Freemason sources acknowledged that there were some 70,000 Freemasons in Ireland. Fr Cahill's name became associated with a vigorous campaign against freemasonry. He wrote five lengthy articles against international freemasonry in the *Irish Ecclesiastical Record*, 1927-28. Other writers took up the same theme in the *Catholic Bulletin* and the *Irish Rosary*. It was not, however, just an Irish reaction. As in some other issues, Ireland was reflecting a wider trend. In England, the United States of America, France and Belgium, there was, during the 1920s, an upsurge in publications examining the anti-Christian movement of 'Masonry and its Jewish allies'.

Archbishop Byrne, like most of his fellow prelates, was likely to have had some knowledge of the more extreme manifestations of freemasonry. In his 'memorabilia' he had noted, from the *Observer* newspaper of 7 June 1931, the comment of General Sir Ian Hamilton that the members of the masonic body known as the Grand Orient were 'an ultra malignant crowd. Compared to them Bolshevists are lambs'.[18] He was also very conscious of Pope Leo XIII's critical views on Freemasonry in his encyclical, *Humanum Genus* (1884). views frequently adverted to by Irish Catholic publications dealing with the topic.[19]

In 1929, Edward Cahill was to publish *Freemasonry and the Anti-Christian Movement*. It became an immediate success. Within a few months a second edition was published. The contents were accepted as factual. *The Leader*, still edited by D. P. Moran, was greatly impressed and raised the question 'Should Freemasonry be suppressed? Mussolini put an end to it in Italy.' It declared that in the Catholic Saorstat the people had been dragooned, bludgeoned, and legislated into a Protestant country, and it urged that the book be widely read so that people could wake up to the reality of masonic influence in the banks, railways, Dublin University, the Royal Dublin Society, and some of the medical institutions.[20]

It has long been acknowledged that Cahill's case was overdrawn, and that the Freemasons in Britain and Ireland were much less anti-Christian than their counterparts on the continent. Nevertheless, there is no doubt that in Ireland of the 1920s and 1930s there was a widespread belief in the reality of Freemason influence, especially in business and commercial life where most of the largest enterprises were owned by Protestants. Various Catholic agencies, such as the Knights of St Columbanus, the Ancient Order of Hibernians, and the Catholic Young

Men's Society which, by 1928, saw itself in the vanguard of an organised campaign of Catholic Action to promote and strengthen
the influence of the Catholic Church,[21] received an injection of energy in the face of this international enemy. The AOH brought the
iniquities of the Masons to the bishops' attention on a number of
occasions. It perceived direct links between Bolshevism, Jewry,
and Freemasonry, which it described as 'this unholy combination'. The secretary of the Mountjoy branch of the AOH in
Dublin, John D. Nugent, not only published several pamphlets
against Freemasonry but at a public conference urged Catholic
organisations to counter the forces that were 'always the deadly
enemies of Irish nationalism and Irish Catholicism'.[22]

Political empathy through the 1920s
Politically, Dr Byrne continued to empathise with the government. The year 1925 had ended with the failure of the negotiations in the Boundary Commission, and the New Year brought
continued grounds for public frustration with high unemployment, financial entrenchment, and little to raise morale. In such
circumstances, there is a tendency to look for scapegoats and for
a saviour. The desire for scapegoats focused on the government
but did not stop there. Authority figures generally, including
the bishops, found themselves objects of criticism. De Valera, on
the other hand, became a saviour figure for many, including
clergymen. During 1926, reading the times, he broke from Sinn
Féin and launched the Fianna Fáil party with the intention of en-
tering the Dáil. In the Dáil, the party became a formidable critic
of the government and, by 1928, was increasingly viewed as the
means towards an alternative government.

Even though friends like Hagan and Curran of the Irish
College, and some episcopal colleagues, were avid supporters
of De Valera, Edward Byrne remained unmoved. Despite the
rigidity of Cosgrave and his ministers on matters of policy, and
the continuance of unemployment and extreme poverty, he still
had confidence in the high values of most members of government and of many government officials, and continued to believe that they were doing their best for the country and had
manifested by their legislation a concern for the moral wellbeing
of the people. Indeed, had he known AE's (George Russell)
striking endorsement in the *American Quarterly Review*, January
1929, he would most likely have strongly approved.

The leaders of government, AE observed, found a country distracted after years of conflict and made it as crimeless as any country in the world. They took some forty government boards and welded them into a few departments that had reason for their existence. They had lowered taxation. The income tax was lower than in Great Britain and Northern Ireland, and duties were abolished on tea, cocoa, coffee, and reduced on sugar. They created an unarmed police force, and managed, what seemed impossible, to put an end to jobbery. 'Never did a government coming to power after a revolution, throw over so completely the doctrine of "the spoils for the victor". Not in England, not in Europe, and not in America, has there been such a determination to have honest administration ... This kind of honesty makes enemies. But our ministers have not sacrificed honesty for popularity.'[23]

With some such view of the government's aims and achievements, the archbishop co-operated with it as far as he could without open partiality. Two notable instances of his support occurred in these years.

Prior to the 1927 general election, he made a contribution to the government's election fund which evoked from W. T. Cosgrave, on 16 September 1927, an expression of gratitude for the big subscription to the fund for the General Election. Personally, he had not expected a subscription at all, but the size of the subscription had surprised him. He felt very grateful for this mark of confidence and could only hope that they would prove worthy of it.[24]

The second notable instance was in connection with the Tailteann Games in 1928. The archbishop received an invitation from J. J. Walsh, the former Minister for Posts and Telegraphs, who had broken away from the government, to perform the opening ceremony of the Tailteann Games and, in the event of his being unavailable, it was hoped it would be in order to invite Dr MacRory, Archbishop of Armagh. Dr Byrne's secretary, Fr Tom O'Donnell, replied on 16 July expressing his Grace's regret that it would not be possible for him to perform the ceremony and that he could not see his way to invite another bishop to replace him.[25] The Tailteann Games Committee forthwith invited Dr MacRory, who consulted Archbishop Byrne as the ceremony was to be in the latter's archdiocese.[26] The archbishop replied that he had no objection to his performing the ceremony – 'My regard for yourself and our mutual friendship will assure you of that' – but it would give a good deal of offence to the clergy and many people in Dublin if the Archbishop of Armagh performed such a public ceremony in Dublin. That apart, the advisability of any bishop performing the ceremony was in question. J. J. Walsh had invited them, not out of any regard for the church or for themselves but simply to give a snub to the government by not inviting President Cosgrave to open the games. Having severed his connection with the ministry himself, he wished to ignore them publicly on this occasion, and desired to make the church a cat's paw to help him carry out his idea. It was questionable whether it was wise to help him in this design. After receiving the letter, MacRory wrote on it that he had turned down the invitation 'in the interests of peace and charity – not because I regarded as reasonable the Dublin feeling here spoken of'.[27]

Also of some interest in the political sphere was a letter from Seán Lemass to the archbishop, on 8 July 1927, requesting his advice about taking the oath to be faithful to his Majesty King George V his heirs and successors, which was required before entry to the Dáil. Was he morally justified in taking the oath seeing that he was publicly pledged to his constituents, and privately determined also to nullify, by every honourable means available to him, the authority of the British Crown and cabinet in Irish affairs? Sensing a political purpose behind the question, Dr Byrne had his secretary reply on 13 July that he had been very busy and was gone away for a fortnight and would look into the matter on his return. Meanwhile, the archbishop would be glad if Mr Lemass would inform him if he wished for confidential advice between pastor and his spiritual son, or if it was his intention to communicate his answer to his political colleagues.[28] Lemass replied with characteristic brevity to Rev Patrick Dunne on 19 July that he did not consult his political colleagues on his intention to ask his Grace's advice with reference to the Oath of Allegiance. He would, however, prefer to be free to communicate his answer to them.[29]

Mr De Valera, for his part, did not need the archbishop's advice. He had his own 'theologians' to advise him; and on 11 August, three weeks after Lemass's reply, he and other Fianna Fáil deputies took their seats in the Dáil , having signed the parliamentary oath as merely an empty political formula. The action was precipitated by government legislation following the assassination of Kevin O'Higgins.

Tragic events

The year 1927 was a fateful year in Irish political and church history. It witnessed the unexpected deaths of two of the outstanding Irishmen of the period, Vice-President and Minister for Home Affairs, Kevin O'Higgins TD, and Cardinal Patrick O'Donnell.

Response to the murder of Kevin O'Higgins

The assassination of Vice-President O'Higgins, on 10 July 1927, sent shock waves through the country and raised fears that the bloodshed of the civil war might be revisited. The response of the hierarchy, especially that of Dr Byrne, was considered inadequate by some supporters of the government. Thus, J. P. Walsh, the eloquent and able secretary of the Department of Foreign Affairs, in a long typed document for the Minister, Patrick McGilligan, dated 16 July, denounced the bishops as acting as if they were outside the state and not viewing 'the Saorstat ... as a living reality' to be given mental allegiance and loyal service. Although Archbishop Byrne devoted a pastoral letter to the assassination, to Walsh it was a profoundly disappointing document. Instead of denouncing Kevin O'Higgins's murder as a moral offence against God of the very gravest kind because it was a crime against the state, against the natural law, and against the highest order imposed by God on human society, he merely denounced the act as if Kevin O'Higgins were an ordinary citizen struck down in private vengeance. He almost narrowed down his denunciation to describing it as a crime against Catholic piety. He had wasted a magnificent opportunity to use all the weight and majesty of the church to uphold the supreme power of the state. In the Irish church, Walsh insisted, there was disaffection towards the state, and there was an urgent need to appoint a minister to the Vatican and to have a papal nuncio sent to Dublin. 'We have too many enemies at Rome – Irish and others – to allow our interests to look after themselves any longer ...'[30]

Walsh was less than fair to Edward Byrne and to the hierarchy as a body. Some of its members may have become dissatisfied with the government and even supportive of De Valera, but they did distinguish between the Saorstat and its transient government; and however unpopular O'Higgins may have been in some circles, there was horror at his assassination and great sympathy for his wife and family. Many bishops, including Cardinal O'Donnell, sent messages of condolence.

Archbishop Byrne presided at the Office and Requiem Mass for the late Kevin O'Higgins on 13 July, and four days later, Sunday 17 July, his pastoral letter was read at all Masses throughout the archdiocese. He was concerned above all lest the crime precipitate a return to national violence. The reader may judge whether J. P. Walsh's strictures were justified.

He felt, he said, that he would be altogether lacking in his pastoral duty if he did not appeal most earnestly to all men of good will 'to set their faces steadily and fearlessly against such murderous deeds of blood as that which shocked our people last Sunday'. This cowardly assassination of an unarmed man, who was on his way to perform the usual Sunday duty of a Catholic had displayed a most callous disregard of religion, and had aroused a deepened horror amongst our Catholic people. This crime, deplorable in itself, was all the more lamentable because it occurred at a time when the vast bulk of our people had turned to constitutional ways of peace in seeking their political ideals. Sad and deplorable things took place in years not long gone – tragic events happened in the heat and turmoil of our fraternal strife; but lovers of Ireland had thought that we had put these terrible things away like evil dreams of the past. It was to be hoped that our people would not be led astray by specious phraseology toning down and palliating the crime of Sunday. 'Here at a time of peace is murder stark and hideous. Let us not fear to call it by its name'.[31] That the sympathy of our people was not with such evil work was demonstrated by the public declarations of many leaders of different schools of political thought. Its perpetrators could not expect the blessing of God to follow such lawless deeds.

The archbishop concluded with a warning he had issued over and over again to young men 'to avoid secret societies, which are forbidden by the church'.

It seems evident that, despite his concern for the wider implications of the assassination, he was deeply moved by the horror of the event itself. Indeed, it is not unlikely that his large contribution to the government's electoral fund was influenced by the murder of its ablest member.

The Loss of Cardinal O'Donnell
The unexpected death of Cardinal Patrick O'Donnell, on 22 October 1927, also brought a sense of national loss. For Edward Byrne the loss was felt at a deep personal level.

Patrick O'Donnell had established himself as a much respected national figure. To exceptional ability, charm and bearing, he added a capacity to express views that crossed the years in their relevance. During the course of a highly successful North American visit, he assured the Irish-American Historical Society in New York, with reference to Irish political unity, that the surest path to a united Ireland was the path of goodwill, the path of sympathy, the path of friendship between North and South, the path of good feeling between Catholics and Protestants, the path of friendship as far as principle would allow, between even conflicting parties'.[32] And he concluded that when good men on both sides, North and South, had put forth their best endeavours, division would cease, but it would not come, as it ought, by consent until people on all sides were convinced that unity was good for them.[33]

Cardinal O'Donnell's influence on his fellow bishops was considerable. To Edward Byrne's deep regret, however, he was not in Ireland at the time of the death and funeral. He was in Rome for the celebration of the third centenary of the Irish College, together with a large number of prelates from Ireland and other countries. The college had recently moved to its more spacious location, and the archbishop's admiration for the new colleges was said to be 'only diminished by his tiredness'.[34] He presided at a Solemn Pontifical Mass in the college, in the presence of a range of archbishops and bishops, and later, on 24 October, headed the Irish archbishops and bishops at their reception by the pope, who joined in their grief on the death of his Eminence Cardinal O'Donnell.[35]

All creeds and classes, and numerous representatives of church and state, including Governor General, T. M. Healy, President William T. Cosgrave, and government ministers, attended the funeral Mass for the cardinal, and joined the vast cortege that took half-an-hour to pass a given point. The Archbishop of Dublin was represented by Rt Rev Mgr Wall, PP, VG.[36]

Dr Byrne was back in Ireland for the 'month's mind', and he presided at the Office and Solemn Requiem Mass in St Patrick's Cathedral, Armagh.[37] A week later, on 30 November 1927, John O'Donnell, secretary to the cardinal, wrote to him:

Probably no one knows better than I do the affection that existed between you and the poor Cardinal. Certain it is that none greater, if as great, ever existed between him and any of his colleagues.

O'Donnell went on to explain the circumstances of his Eminence's death. 'He was bathing in the mudpit of a place in Carlingford. Thinking that there was more depth, in jumping in he hit his leg against some rocks.' He damaged his knee and his leg swelled. Some time later he developed pleurisy and pneumonia. After a long struggle he appeared to have overcome these when he 'got a clot in a vessel of his heart' and died within minutes.[38]

Concern for the archbishop's health and the cardinalate

Two months later there were rumours in Ireland that, following Dr O'Donnell's death, the cardinalate would go to Dublin,[39] but already there was concern being expressed about the state of his health. On 15 February 1927, Sean T. Ó Ceallaigh informed Mgr Hagan that Dr Byrne at a recent chance meeting looked better than expected.[40] At the end of 1927, P. Dunne, the archbishop's secretary, referred to 'the chatter about the archbishop's health';[41] and in February 1928, Fr Michael Browne SJ, wrote from Gardiner Street Church that all were greatly disturbed 'at the rather uncertain condition of your Grace's health.'[42]

By the end of 1928 the serious state of Dr Byrne's health was the subject of much clerical discussion. Fr E. R. Morrissey, who often wrote under the pseudonym of the 'Brewer' or other inventions, spoke of Dr Byrne's health and his performance as archbishop. He informed his friend, Hagan, on 29 November 1928:

Clerical news is very little here. We seem to have sat down to a general mode of criticism of N. B. (Ned Byrne), and to talk the more freely because he is supposed to be only ... a short time for this world.

In his view he had been 'a perfect failure'. P. T. Keohane (of M. H. Gill and Son Dublin) agreed with him. He was the first to remark to Morrissey that Ned Byrne was not *big* enough for the position, and was too narrow.[43] He was proving that every other week. He was most unpopular, but that was caused by some undesirable friends he has, more so than by his own actions.[44] It was generally believed here that Armagh would be an easy winner of the colours.[45]

The 'winner of the colours' referred to Joseph MacRory, who

At Belvedere, 1887. *Top row, l to r:* Michael Cronin, Edward Byrne.

Edward Byrne, following BA graduation.

Front l to r: Rev Michael Cronin, Edward J. Byrne, James P. Nolan

Standing: John G. O'Reilly, Augustine Farrell

Jim Larkin rallies his followers, 1913. (National Museum)

O'Connell's statue still standing amidst the ruins of 1916.
(National Museum)

British soldiers on patrol in Kildare Stree, 1920.
(National Museum)

Archbishop Byrne blesses the people on his way to enthronement in
the Pro-Cathedral following his appointment as archbishop.

Edward Byrne, shortly after his appointment as archbishop.

Archbishop's Staff

Rev Richard Glennan STL

Rev P. Dunne DPh

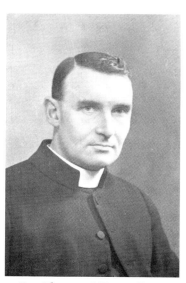

Rev Thomas O'Donnell BD

'Peace for Ireland's sake.' A Shemus cartoon in *Freeman's Journal*,
12 April 1922.
(Courtesy Felix M. Larkin, *Terror and Discord: The Shemus Cartoons in*
Freeman's Journal, *1920-1924*, Dublin, 2009; courtesy of the National
Library of Ireland)

The Four Courts in flames, 1922. (National Photographic Archive)

Michael Collins and supporters about to enter the Pro-Cathedral
for the funeral service for Arthur Griffith, 17 August 1922.
(National Photographic Archive)

28 August 1922, funeral Mass for Michael Collins in the Pro-Cathedral.
(Painting by Sir John Lavery, August 1922.)

'Ireland's Via Dolorosa'. Shemus cartoon in *Freeman's Journal*,
24 August 1922, two days after Collins was shot.
(Thanks to Felix M. Larkin; courtesy of the National Library of Ireland)

Crowds greeting de Valera on his release, 1923.
(National Photographic Archive)

President Cosgrave with the Governor-General T. M. Healy

The Irish Pilgrimage to Bobbio, Italy, September 1923, for the 13th centenary of St Columbanus. Cardinal Ehrle, Papal Legate, in the centre, Archbishop Byrne on his right.

President Cosgrave and Archbishop Byrne exchange views,
in the early 1920s.

A portrait of Archbishop Byrne by Professor G. Bravi, c 1927,
in the Irish College in Rome.
(Courtesy The Rector, Irish College, Rome)

Aeroplanes in the formation of a cross escort the Papal Legate's ship
into Dún Laoghaire harbour.

Cardinal Legate Lauri descends the gangway,
with Archbishop Byrne in the doorway, Dún Laoghaire harbour

The Cardinal Legate, accompanied by President de Valera and Archbishop Byrne, blesses the military guard of honour at Dún Laoghaire.

Lord Mayor, Alfred Byrne, welcomes the Papal Legate, Cardinal Lauri, to Dublin at Merrion Gates as Archbishop Byrne alights from the car.

The Papal Legate, Cardinal Lauri, with Archbishop Byrne, and the Papal Legate's suite at Archbishop's House.

Decorations in Marlborough Street during the Congress

Men's Meeting during Eucharistic Congress week,
with the Lord Mayor of Dublin, Alfred Byrne, and members of the Oireachtas.

TREMENDOUS CONGREGATION HEARS MASS.

ALL NATIONALITIES AND ALL ORDERS REPRESENTED.

PARK BECOMES WORLD'S GREATEST CATHEDRAL.

POPE LISTENS TO ENTIRE CEREMONY AND GIVES ADDRESS.

By NICHEVO.

TRUMPETS broke an unearthly silence with the " General Salute "; the gleaming swords of a score of officers flashed against the dull white of the High Altar, and away up in the sky a flock of snowy gulls wheeled easily out to sea.

Mitred figures moved to and fro on the altar as the imposing ritual of Pontifical Mass drew majestically to its close. · Nearly a million worshippers knelt and rose in rhythmic unison as the sonorous Latin of the Celebrant was carried to the uttermost ends of that tremendous congregation by means of a marvel of science, which seemed but a trifling thing in the presence of a mystery older than time and deeper than space itself.

The exquisite beauty of the ceremony seemed to be enhanced by the occasion and the memorable mise en scène. · It was a blaze of lovely colour.

For some time before the Mass was due to start thousands of priests had begun to assemble in the reserved enclosure before the altar. They were of all nationalities, and representative of all Orders. Irish and American, Dutch and German, Italian and Indian, French and Syrian—even a full-blooded Red Indian—they had come from the ends of the earth to bear witness to the might of Rome. On either side of the altar they gathered in their multitudes—young and old, grave and gay, priests of every sort and condition, until one marvelled that there should be so many of their cloth in the world.

Under the beautifully-built colonnades that flanked the altar some hundreds of bishops and Monsignori had taken their places. The brilliant purple of the Latin prelates blended with the luxurious green of hanging ferns, while here and there the spotless cream of an abbot's habit threw into sharp relief an Eastern bishop's sombre robes. In that riot of grandeur one noticed the ascetic features of Jerusalem's olive-skinned prelate, and the dusky dignity of the Archbishop of Bethany, holding aloft his golden cross, while the Papal Nuncio, in his Franciscan grey and his scarlet biretta, was a prominent figure among his archiepiscopal peers.

Front: The Archbishop of Dublin with, on his right, the Bishop of Thasus, Dr Wall, and members of the Congress committees. Frank O'Reilly is on the extreme right of the picture.

Most Rev Paschal Robinson, OFM,
Apostolic Nuncio to the Irish Free State

Archbishop Byrne and President de Valera chat
at the Blackrock College Garden Party for the
British Medical Association, June 1933.

Fr J. C. McQuaid, Archbishop Byrne and President de Valera at the Blackrock College Garden Party for the British Medical Association, June 1933. (Blackrock College Annual)

Members of the Oireachtas and clergy at the Blackrock College Garden Party, June 1933.

Front row, l to r: Conor Maguire, Sean McEntee, French Minister, Seán T. Ó Ceallaigh, President de Valera, Archbishop Byrne, Nuncio Paschal Robinson, Lord Mayor Alfred Byrne, and Fr J. C. McQuaid CSSp

The remains of Archbishop Byrne are borne through O'Connell Street
on their way to the Pro-Cathedral.

had succeeded to Armagh. Morrissey's report that his Grace was 'only a short time for this world' proved greatly exaggerated. Archbishop Byrne was seriously unwell, but he was to struggle on for a further twelve years.

A more immediate report on his Grace's health came from his secretary, Patrick Dunne, on 29 December 1928. He commented to Mgr Hagan: 'Our friend has not been in the best of form for the past week or two. He had first a cold, and then last Saturday got a bit weak at an ordination. But he is pulling round again. The weakness gave him a shock, as he began to fear that he would not be able to finish the ceremony – of course it will start more talk.'[46]

Before long, it became clear that the archbishop was suffering from progressive muscular atrophy or 'wasting paralysis', which often commences in the hand and spreads gradually. Indeed, there may be a long delay – in some cases a matter of years – before the initial wasting of the hand muscles begins to spread to other parts of the body.[47] Inevitably, there were days when Dr Byrne felt much better than others, but public social occasions were to become progressively difficult for him. For the most part, however, he was to remain mentally alert to the end.[48] Meantime, he faced years of special challenge: years of great public ceremony and celebration as the country honoured the centenary of Catholic Emancipation, 1829-1929, and hosted an International Eucharistic Congress in 1932.

Towards a positive portrayal
Before leaving the years 1926-1928, it seems right to balance the negative estimation of the archbishop attributed to the clergy of the diocese with information of a more positive nature from religious congregations. John Fitzgerald CSsR spoke for the Redemptorists in thanking Dr Byrne for his 'great kindness' during the visit to them of his Eminence Cardinal van Rossum, head of Propaganda Fide.[49] The Franciscans praised his support and kindness at the feast of their great founder; and the Passionists under a new superior, Fr Sebastian, expressed their appreciation of his kindness and his readiness to heal the breach of earlier days.[50] The link with the Jesuits was perhaps closest, because of his years in Belvedere. Fr Fahy, the provincial, readily expressed his appreciation of his Grace's 'kindness' (a word so often used in regard to Dr Byrne) and his support, and thanked

him for his graciousness to the Society. Fr Michael Browne, who wrote a number of letters to the archbishop, reflected revealingly and movingly, on 1 August 1927, as he was about to leave Gardiner Street Church for another post:

> Ever since I first met your Grace in Rome in 1904, I felt so drawn to you that I always wished to call you my friend; and though it may seem presumption for me to do so now, I must admit that these last years have deepened in me that wish.
>
> I came here inexperienced and frightened of the task imposed upon me, and when I knelt to get your Grace's blessing in 1922, I looked fearfully at the years to come. In retrospect they are brightened by the recollection of many things, but beyond all others by the recollection of your Grace's help and encouragement.[51]

Edward Byrne undoubtedly had a gift for friendship. He was close to Cardinal Patrick O'Donnell, but also claimed his assertive successor, Joseph MacRory, as his friend.[52] Extant correspondence also indicates closeness to Bishop Fogarty of Killaloe, and to his own suffragan bishops. He also surrounded himself with his friends of many years and, perhaps, out of loyalty to them, allowed some of them to continue on in positions of responsibility for which they were unsuited. Outside the episcopal and clerical ranks, his good relations with Cosgrave survived various differences, but the most marked of such friendships appears to have been his relationship with the elderly Governor General. From the Vice-Regal Lodge on 9 January 1928, T. M. Healy, who was due to leave office, wrote how touched he was that his Grace wished to pay him a farewell visit here. 'Any day your Grace fixes to come here will be a day of joy and happiness. I thank Y. G. for your attendance at the dinner on Saturday night, which with the presence of the Protestant archbishop and the Presbyterian moderator, made it so notable an occasion that words fail me to suitably acknowledge it.'[53] Courtesy, ease of manner and a desire to help, seem to have been frequent, perhaps constant, features in Edward Byrne's relations with people.

An unusual feature of these years helpful to biographers was the introduction of Pathé newsreels and their portrayal of certain public events. Archbishop Byrne was shown blessing five new churches: the church of St MacCullin in Lusk in 1922; the church of St Brigid in Killester in 1925; the church of St Vincent de Paul in Marino in 1926; the Garrison Church in Arbor Hill in 1927, during which he is seen inspecting the guard of honour accompanied by an officer; and Crooksling Sanitorium (later St Brigid's Hospital) in 1928. In these it is noticeable that up to 1925 he is tall and vigorous, but at Marino in 1926 there is a suggestion of a shake in his left hand, which he tended to hold against his body when not holding a crosier, and a newsreel of him that year at the Irish Catholic Truth Conference shows the open signs of his illness, he is slightly stooped, no longer the tall, erect figure of his first years in office. Despite that, he is seen to walk and act with vigour in blessing the churches and their foundations.

In 1928 there was an event which figured prominently in newsreels, namely, the first transatlantic air flight from East to West, which took off from Dublin and had an Irishman among the crew of three – Captain James Fitzmaurice, Captain Hermann Köhl and Baron Ehrenfried von Hünefeld. They made their flight in April, and in July they received a State Reception in Dublin. The newsreel depicts the pilots emerging from a car surrounded by a crowd of people and then being photographed with the President, William Cosgrave and the Governor-General, James McNeill. Afterwards they visited Archbishop's House, where they are shown exiting the imposing building with his Grace, coming down the steps chatting together, and then posing for a photograph. The archbishop stood erect for the camera but noticeably held his hands behind his back. As they were leaving, the men either kissed the archbishop's ring or bowed to him, and as they departed in their car, Dr Byrne is seen doffing his biretta and waving it with a wide smile.[54]

As 1928 drew to a close, the Archbishop of Dublin seemed to have become smaller physically, and was more prone to colds and unexpected set backs. The future medically was bleak, yet, from the indications available, he faced the coming years of intense preparation and organisation with dignity, and a fortitude based on deep faith in God's providence.

CHAPTER TEN

1929-1930

The great Centenary Celebrations. The Cardinalate. An Exchange of Envoys. A Cathedral for Dublin, Preparing for 1932

The political scene towards the end of the 1920s showed support for Fianna Fáil growing to the point that even its more moderate supporters were resorting to impatient and intolerant language in their desire for power. Sean T. Ó Ceallaigh, a regular correspondent of Mgr Hagan, commented on 17 November 1928 that the Cosgrave government showed all the signs of weariness but would have to be 'literally kicked out'.[1] Wrongly, in the event, he saw no prospect of they freely relinquishing office.

The archbishop's health
If the fall of the Cosgrave government seemed, one way or another, just a matter of time, it seemed so too with the archbishop. On 5 February 1929, Fr Richard Fleming, the presbytery, Rathmines, Co Dublin, informed Hagan that the archbishop looked quite weak when he saw him last. He had been given no more than two years by one source.[2] Two days later, another maximising report came from Fr E. R. Morrissey, Donabate, Co Dublin. 'The archbishop is not well and is in London; he went with Cronin, who is not popular.' Such reports and rumours reaching Rome were to tell against Byrne's prospects of becoming a cardinal. Morrissey also mentioned that P. T. Keohane, whom he earlier quoted as saying that Byrne was not big enough for the job and was a failure as archbishop, was now looking very well and his attitude had changed for the better through his illness![3]

Preparing for the Centenary
In fact, despite his fragile health, the archbishop carried on his ordinary work and was also actively involved in planning for the centenary celebrations of Catholic Emancipation (1829). The plans, indeed, were well under way by the end of 1928. They envisaged a week of celebrations focused on certain venues

throughout the country, but the celebrations were to begin and conclude in Dublin. In acknowledgement of the national nature of the celebrations, each archbishop had a part to play, but his Grace of Dublin was to remain the central figure.

In his Lenten pastoral letter, Dr Byrne reminded his people that it was not to revive old feelings of bitterness that we recall the trials our fathers were obliged to suffer to keep the lamp of faith burning. Their faithfulness in days of trial was the pride of the Irish church. Nowadays a great deal was said about Irish tradition. The greatest glory of Irish tradition was not to be found in the pagan story of the wars of ancient Irish kings and the fights of misty Irish heroes, but in the patient endurance and high courage with which, God helping them, our fathers faced the loss of all things, lands, freedom, and life itself to keep the pearl beyond price – the Faith of Christ.[4]

When it came to organising for a massive event attracting people from all over the country and from abroad, the archbishop and his clerical colleagues turned to lay Catholic organisations, the younger clergy, and the government, especially the departments of defence and justice. The army and police force had a key role to play in terms of crowd control. It was recognised that the centenary celebration was a preparation for the Eucharistic Congress. If it could be run successfully, without incidents reflecting the national reputation for violence and drunkenness, the approval of Rome for a Eucharistic Congress was likely to be granted; otherwise the Congress might go to South America.[5]

Previously, at a meeting of the hierarchy on 21 June 1927, Archbishop Byrne had written on the back of the Agenda sheet that he had 'promised to give answer', and that he 'was bound to accede to the desire of the bishops'. If they agreed to support the venture financially, he was prepared to host the Congress. He required, however, and this was sanctioned at the meeting, that the hierarchy would be the supreme governing body of the Congress, and that the executive work would be done by the priests of Dublin, to avoid jealousy. After this agreement, the minutes noted that Dr Byrne, after due consideration, thought it possible to carry out the plan.[6]

The archbishop looked to two particular bodies, the Catholic Truth Society and the St Vincent de Paul Society, for the effective running of the centenary celebrations. Speaking to the quarterly meeting of the Vinvent de Paul Society, at the Mansion

House Dublin, on 9 December 1928, he praised their work, expressed his pride in the young men coming in strong numbers to join the Society, and assured them of his complete sympathy and that he had complete confidence in their loyalty as a body and relied on them to carry out with zeal now and always such works, however difficult and unpleasant, as he might entrust to their care.[7]

Chief among the organisers of the centenary celebrations was Francis (Frank) O'Reilly, executive secretary of the Catholic Truth Society of Ireland (CTSI), and also a member of the Knights of St Columbanus. He had been appointed secretary of the CTSI in 1918, and in 1926 received the papal decoration of *Bene Merenti*. Two years later he received the further distinction of Knight of the Order of St Gregory. Despite the honours, he preserved a low profile, and was unlikely to arouse suspicion of being ambitious for power or position.[8] Also present as a significant figure, trusted by the archbishop and his close associates, was Sir Joseph Glynn, chairman of the CTSI and prominent in the Vincent de Paul Society.

In addition, there was the strong personality of Eoin O'Duffy, commissioner of the Garda Síochána and a devoted Catholic. A gifted orator and organiser, his relations with the archbishop began shortly after his appointment as commissioner, when he requested a resident chaplain for the Garda depot where large numbers of recruits were being trained.[9] Some 98.7 percent of the police force were Catholic, and a Catholic ethos was promoted. O'Duffy also encouraged the spread of the Pioneer Total Abstinence Association of the Sacred Heart (PTAA) among the Garda. In a country ravaged by drink, he wished the members of the force to lead by example.[10] In 1928, he led a 250 strong Garda pilgrimage to Rome, where they were received in special audience by Pope Pius XI. At this stage in his life, therefore, O'Duffy was a much respected figure, and an ideal choice as grand marshal of the vast crowds that gathered for the Emancipation Centenary and subsequently for the Eucharistic Congress.

The CTSI established a special sub-committee in 1928 to begin the preparations for the centenary celebrations. On 28 December 1928, it met with the Minister for Defence and, on 1 January 1929, with the Archbishop of Dublin.[11] It had a heavy task. Finance was sparse and poverty widespread. The young state had little experience of public celebration, and there were deep political divisions. The sub-committee, however, was given virtually a free hand by both government and hierarchy. The bishops opposed a national collection fearing it would adversely affect a later collection to defray the expenses of the projected Eucharistic Congress in 1932,[12] but otherwise stood back, even refusing to have a representative on the organising committee.[13]

The success of the centenary celebration was to be the outcome of a co-operative yet independent approach. The Catholic Truth Society of Ireland, which was well established in many parishes, had a national network and an efficient administrative apparatus. Public lectures were arranged that would provide a view of Irish history that intimately linked Irishness and being Catholic, in order that all political divisions could be united in pride in a common religious history. Daniel O'Connell, as the central figure of the centenary, was acknowledged as having roused his people by constitutional means from a state of political and social servitude and brought them to realise that they were an ancient and noble nation.[14]

The desire to be associated with the celebration of Catholic Emancipation led De Valera and Fianna Fáil to secure a prominent presence in the 1929 proceedings, accepting thereby the leading role of Cumann na nGaedhael and the governor general. The *Catholic Emancipation Centenary Record* later proclaimed:

> The presence of the governor-general, the president of the executive council, the leaders of the opposition and of the Labour Party, of outstanding Catholics from the North-East, indicated not indeed any weakening in political loyalties, but a strengthening of Catholic charity; the assuagement of bitterness born in civil strife, and the probability that a sad chapter in our history has been closed.[15]

The overall co-operation and organisation was outstanding. By 8 March 1929, the secretary of the Minister for Defence was able to inform members of the executive council that the celebrations for the centenary would run from 16-23 June, and that it was estimated that upwards of half-a-million people would be present for High Mass in the Fifteen Acres in the Phoenix Park, on Sunday 23 June, and that it was anticipated that 200,000 people would take part in a procession of the Most Blessed

Sacrament from the Phoenix Park to Watling Street Bridge where Benediction would be given. He added that the chief marshal for the celebrations on 23 June, the commissioner of the Garda Síochána, requested the Minister for Defence for 2,500 troops for duty in the Fifteen Acres.[16]

Four days later, 12 March, the cabinet agreed that arrangements should be made for the release of as many troops as possible for duty in the Fifteen Acres, and a stamp with a portrait of Daniel O'Connell was approved. In keeping with the celebrations it was also decided to seek for the adjournment of the Dáil on Friday 14th instant until Thursday 20th.

As the time drew near, householders and owners of premises responded to the appeal of the Centenary Committee to decorate their property appropriately. Dr Hackett, Bishop of Waterford and Lismore, observed that never in the memory of any living person in Dublin had the decorations for any purpose been so extensive; and again and again the outstanding displays by the poorer people in the city's back streets were remarked on. On the central day of celebration huge crowds came to the capital. Eighty trains arrived in Dublin, some leaving from midnight to get passengers to Dublin on time, and on arrival the travellers were able to buy 'ration bags'. The *Irish Independent* noted that the largest contingent came from Cork and Limerick; but there was also a large representation from the North of Ireland, and many returned emigrants from North America. In readiness for the great concourse at the special Mass in the Phoenix Park, which was to be the highlight of the week of celebration, Garda Commissioner Duffy gathered eight thousand stewards to marshal the expected crowds. These met in the Park to rehearse for the great event. He expressed to them his hope that they would carry out their duties in such a way as would reflect credit on themselves and on their great Catholic country.[18] Two thousand five hundred of the stewards were members of the Gaelic Athletic Association, but overall, as the *Irish News* observed, the stewards conveyed a new sense of national unity.

> One of the most noteworthy side-issues of the Emancipation Centenary arrangements has been the gathering together of thousands of stewards for the great Procession, and men are now standing shoulder to shoulder on the training ground who formerly served in the National Army, the IRA, and the British military and naval forces. What a triumph for the Faith.[19]

On 8 June, Edward Byrne addressed a letter to the clergy to be read in all the churches. It set the religious tone of the days of celebration. They were to impress upon the people that these celebrations were not to be a mere pageant to be witnessed, or a mere expression of national jubilation or pride. Our feelings and conduct should reflect a deep spirit of thankfulness to God for graces bestowed on our people and earnest prayerfulness for his blessings on ourselves and our country. In preparation for these days there should be in every church of the diocese, so far as possible, a General Holy Communion for women on Sunday, 9 June, for men on Sunday 18 June, and for children on Saturday, 22 June. Referring to the culmination of the celebrations in Dublin, he instructed: 'Catholic Dublin will outwardly honour its Eucharistic Lord by the reverence and recollection of its demeanour in the Phoenix Park at Holy Mass and during the Procession.' When those in the Procession were not singing hymns, they should reverently alternate with their neighbours in reciting the Rosary. They should not give dis-edification by unnecessary conversation.[20]

On 19 June, a significant arrival in Dublin was that of Archbishop Luigi Pisani, as papal envoy, bearing a special blessing from Pope Pius XI.

The Central Event

On the day of the Mass in the Phoenix Park, approximately half-a-million people[21] were reminded through one hundred loud-hailers that they should conduct themselves as they would in church, and that they should not smoke from the time they assembled in the Park to the conclusion of Benediction on Watling Street Bridge, the first bridge across the Liffey as they processed from the Phoenix Park. Participants were informed, however, that while they could not smoke, they could get a cup of tea in the marquees set up in the Park. To assist people in finding their locations in the vast crowds, maps were published in the newspapers outlining areas designated for men on the gospel side of the altar, and for women and children on the epistle side. The President of the Executive Council had a special place on the gospel side in front of the high altar.

One thousand two hundred troops lined the route to the Phoenix Park, and prior to, during and after Mass, the 8,000 stewards carried out their duties to Commissioner Duffy's satisfaction. The Mass was attended by 1200 priests, the papal envoy, all the archbishops and bishops of Ireland, the bishops of Southwark and Pella, the abbots of Mount Melleray, Roscrea and Welbech, President Cosgrave and members of the Free State government, with members of the Seanad and the Dáil, and representatives of the universities and public bodies.[22] Archbishop Byrne presided, and Archbishop Mac Rory was chief celebrant.

The altar in white and gold dominated the scene. The Celtic cross surmounting the lofty baldacchino, the Roman crosses on the slope of the roof, proclaimed the Irish and Catholic significance of the structure.[23] The *Irish Independent*'s reporter was moved to comment:

> There were moments yesterday when one felt how feeble words are to convey the thoughts that arise in the mind. One such moment was that which followed the Elevation at the Solemn Pontifical Mass of the Holy Trinity in the fifteen acres in the Phoenix Park.[24]

Following the Mass, the procession to Watling Street Bridge for Benediction began with the Minister for Justice, Fitzgerald-Kenney, and De Valera acting as canopy bearers for the Blessed Sacrament, the first of the various dignitaries who took turn in this role. The Blessed Sacrament was borne in turns by the Archbishops of Armagh, Dublin, Cashel, and Tuam.[25] The Procession was at times twenty-five people deep and was estimated to take three hours to pass any one point.

The *Catholic Emancipation Centenary Record* further observed that as far as the eye could reach citywards were long unbroken columns of men on either side of the river, under the most bounteous and brilliant display of flags and bunting that Dublin had seen in its long history of pageantry, only it was not just pageantry – 'it was prayer, and, mainly, the prayer of the poor and the lowly'.[26]

Once the Procession reached the bridge, only the Hierarchy, the Ministers, led by President Cosgrave, the representatives of the Irish Corporations in their brilliant robes, and the Guard of Honour of the National Army, were admitted behind the barriers erected both sides of the bridge. The altar on the bridge was a smaller replica of that at the Phoenix Park.[27]

The Impact

It was a week of celebration that evoked pride at the country's manifestation of discipline, unity and organisation, and pride in its Catholic history and identity. For the government it had the further dimension of assurance that their work to create stability and peace had enabled these days of celebration to be such a major success. The day after the Mass and Procession, President Cosgrave sent a note to the archbishop's secretary inquiring after his Grace's health and giving expression to deep emotion and satisfaction.

> Would you be good enough to let me know whether His Grace feels well after such a trying day. Personally it was the greatest day of my life. Everything was in order and passed off without a hitch. The people behaved splendidly. Their reverence, decorum, discipline and good humour attracted great praise from all the visitors from other countries.

He had been apprehensive that the traffic would account for accidents, but nothing serious happened. 'How are you after the day? The march down to Watling Street was tiring, but who would have missed it?'[28]

A number of the bishops, who had been sceptical about the possibility of managing the titanic organisation of a Eucharistic Congress, now felt much relieved. The hierarchy issued a joint statement of praise, congratulations and thanks for the success of the celebrations; but a relieved and joyous Archbishop of Dublin made his own personal statement to his people on 28 June 1929: 'Dublin's great day has come and gone. It has left behind it a memory of intense religious feeling that will long be an inspiration to our people.' To the Executive Committee and their many willing co-operators, he expressed his sincere gratitude, and then turned in praise to his beloved Dublin people for the manner in which they responded to the appeal made to them and especially to the poorer members, who, 'with that generous Catholic instinct which has always characterised them, led the way and set a standard for others'. Finally, he expressed his thanks to the rural parts of the archdiocese where every town and parish entered wholeheartedly into the spirit of those joyous days.[29]

Importantly for the bishops and for the destination of the Eucharistic Congress, the papal envoy, Luigi Pisani, was suitably impressed. The day after the celebration in the Phoenix Park, he informed the *Irish Independent* reporter that 'It was pious, it was grand, it was Irish.' Two days later, when Charles Bewley presented his credentials to the pope, as the first accredited representative of the Irish government, his words reflected the euphoria and new confidence generated by the week of intense, unified celebration. Careless of hyperbole, he addressed his Holiness with the rhetorical question:

> For is there, indeed, any nation in the world whose history can show greater devotion to the cause of Christianity, or is there any other nation whose history has been so determined in all its phases by its attachment to the Catholic faith and to the Holy See?[30]

Negotiating for Envoys to Rome and Ireland

The mention of Bewley, introduces the delicate issue of an exchange of envoys between Ireland and the Vatican. Bewley's appointment was part of the Cosgrave government's plan, kept secret from Archbishop Byrne, to have a mutual exchange of diplomatic representatives between Ireland and Rome. The Free State government had desired this for a number of years. An Irish envoy in the Vatican would allow the government to represent itself efficiently there, and would counter the anti-Cumman na nGaedhael bias emanating from the Irish College, while a nuncio in Dublin would enhance the standing of the Irish Free State, and might help the government to have more control over the bishops.

Early in 1929, the Cosgrave government quietly undertook to seek an exchange of envoys despite the known opposition of a number of the hierarchy, among whom the Archbishop of Dublin was believed to be the most intransigent. From his time as vice-rector in Rome, Edward Byrne remained suspicious of the Holy See's capacity to make independent judgements on Ireland, and he did not wish to have a nuncio, especially an Italian diplomat, living in his archdiocese, having a direct line to Rome, and placing him in an anomalous position. The Minister for External Affairs, the very able Patrick McGilligan, decided only to tell the archbishop of the *fait accompli* within twenty-four hours of publication.[31]

McGilligan and Joseph Walshe, the first secretary in the Department of Foreign Affairs, went to Rome to discuss the matter directly with the Holy See. On 18 April 1929, they had an interview with the Pope, and then entered into negotiations with the Secretary of State, Cardinal Pietro Gasparri. They hoped to be able to announce the appointment of a nuncio in time for the Catholic Centenary Celebrations. But Rome delayed its decision. The temporising appears to have been linked to the reported opposition of a number of bishops, and especially Dublin, to having a nuncio stationed in Ireland.

Meantime, Gasparri raised the question of an Irish cardinal. In Dublin, especially after the success of the Centenary Celebrations, there was a strong expectation that the cardinalate would go to Archbishop Byrne. On 8 July 1929, Charles Bewley was instructed by the government to put to the Vatican Secretary of State that the Free State government wished Dublin to get the cardinalate because: 1. Dublin was the real capital of Ireland, and the Emancipation Celebrations organised by the bishops brought out that fact; 2. The cardinalate always went to Dublin before Logue's time; 3. Maynooth, Ireland's great clerical university, was situated near Dublin; and 4. It would be regarded as a fitting gesture following the success of the Emancipation Celebrations. After meeting with Gasparri, however, and putting the case to him, Bewley had the impression that the 'red hat' would go to Armagh.[32]

The summer moved into autumn without any decision from Rome. Eventually, on 25 November 1929, Gasparri informed Bewley that Mgr Pascal Robinson OFM, would be appointed nuncio, and that Archbishop MacRory was to receive the 'red hat'. No public announcement was to be made for the present.

The Nuncio to Ireland

Robinson was born in Dublin in 1870. His family moved to New York. He embarked on a career as a journalist, and only after some years joined the Franciscans. He became a professor of medieval history, and was highly thought of in Rome, where he was 'consultor' to a number of congregations. When the appointment became known, Mgr Hagan presented Archbishop Byrne with an unflattering portrait of the incumbent. 'Briefly, he is one who has been on the make for the past thirty years, and who by his audacity, ready tongue … and his persistence in looking after No 1 has been able to forge his way step by step … for he has never done anything, never will do anything, and never thinks of doing anything.' It was a manoeuvre by the Vatican, and before long he would be replaced by an Italian.[33] Bewley, however, in his report to the first secretary in Foreign Affairs, on 25 November 1929, observed that it was entirely exceptional that a non-Italian should be appointed as nuncio. The appointment of Robinson was made only because the Holy See had been informed that an Italian would be entirely unacceptable.[34]

On 26 November, the Irish Executive Council approved the appointment of Robinson, and the following day Cosgrave instructed the secretary to the government, Michael McDunphy, to call on the archbishop to inform him of the papal decision. Doubtless, he expected a strong reaction from Dr Byrne at being excluded from all prior negotiations, but to his surprise, the archbishop assured McDunphy that he was very pleased with the appointment, and particularly pleased that the person selected was an Irishman. He believed that the appointment would be a popular one.[35]

He had not been taken in by Hagan's analysis of Pascal Robinson; and it is likely that he was assured by his friend, Bishop Fogarty, who knew Robinson personally and had come to like and esteem him highly. Fogarty informed Cosgrave on 30 November, that he felt Robinson would fill the office of nuncio without any unpleasant officiousness and that the appointment was a sign that the pope had made a special effort to gratify Ireland.[36]

Cardinal's hat and Dublin

In the absence of a public announcement about the cardinalate, many people in Dublin still hoped it would come to Dr Byrne. Sean T. O'Ceallaigh, indeed, in a letter to Hagan, surmised that the papal representative was part of a bargain for giving the hat to Dublin not Armagh.[37] Towards the end of the year, however, the truth was known. 'Dublin has fared badly in the distribution of honours with the hat going to Armagh', Bishop Fogarty commented to Hagan on 29 November 1929.[38]

The main factor against Archbishop Byrne appeared to have been his poor health. This was highlighted, it seems, at a papal audience, when his Italian appeared not sufficiently fluent to translate Pius XI's address to a group of pilgrims.[39] Cardinal Merry del Val expanded on this. He had heard from more than one clergymen in Rome that the Archbishop of Dublin on the occasion of his last visit gave the impression of being in a poor state of health and, in fact, in danger of a nervous breakdown. His belief was that the preference would be given to Armagh on personal grounds.[40] Again, when Bewley met with Pisani, who had been papal envoy at the Centenary Celebration, the latter observed that the Archbishop of Dublin did not seem at all strong, but he spoke with great cordiality of the Archbishop of Armagh.[41] Bewley confirmed the foregoing views in his report to the first secretary of the Department of Foreign Affairs on 25 November 1929. He was convinced that the matter had been a foregone conclusion, that the authorities in Rome had definitely decided that Dr Byrne was, for reasons of health, and possibly other considerations, not a suitable person to be raised to the position of Cardinal.[42]

Byrne once again accepted the decision calmly and with equanimity. He sent a telegram to Cardinal MacRory: 'Heartiest congratulations. Sincere good wishes. *Ad multos annos.*' The previous June, Dr Mageean, following his appointment as Bishop of Down and Connor, responded to a telegram from Byrne with the observation – 'what pleased me so much was its obvious sincerity'.[43] Evidently, Cardinal MacRory felt the same. Thanking his Grace for his kind and generous congratulations, he added: 'No others gave me more pleasure. The older see has got the preference in spite of the utter unworthiness of its occupant; but let me say that if it had been otherwise and the choice had fallen upon Your Grace, nobody would have congratulated you more warmly than I.'[44]

Edward Byrne was liked by his fellow bishops. There was a sincerity and an unassuming quality about him that attracted people. His illness and rather self-effacing nature helped him to become detached from ambition; and part of him, doubtless, was relieved at not having the added weight of cardinalate and its additional visits and correspondence with Rome. Besides, because of his progressive illness, he probably expected that the cardinalate would go to Armagh, and such regret as he was likely to have had would have been for the people of Dublin and his friends and supporters who would have felt honoured by his elevation.[45] Even his critics were beginning to realise that this unassuming man had unexpected depths. On 1 January 1930, the former Carmelite provincial, Peter Magennis, writing from

Dublin to Hagan, explained that he had visited the archbishop and was surprised at how well he looked. He added: 'He has taken the present situation magnificently, and seems not to care a 'd' how things have gone. He is bigger than ever we took him to be ... I left Drumcondra with the usual regrets as to "the might-have-been".'[46]

On 30 December 1929, Archbishop Byrne posted a letter to the new cardinal at Rome assuring him that his house would be most cordially at his disposal on his return and that his car would meet him at Dún Laoghaire.[47] Unfortunately, the letter did not reach the cardinal until 14 January, five days after he had returned to Ireland. The *Irish Catholic Directory* reported that Cardinal MacRory returned on 9 January and received enthusiastic receptions at Dún Laoghaire, Dublin, Drogheda, Dundalk, and Armagh. It added, however, that at Dún Laoghaire he was greeted by President Cosgrave and a very large and representative gathering of clergy and laity; and then, before he left Dublin by a special train, which was placed at his disposal, for Armagh, His Eminence visited His Grace, the Archbishop of Dublin, who cordially congratulated him on his new dignity.[48]

The Nuncio and the Archbishop

Meantime, Pascal Robinson had received 'a very nice wire' from Dr Byrne, and was anxious, according to a report from Bewley on 5 December 1929, that 'the bishops should be conciliated as much as possible, especially Dublin'. He requested that when preparations were being made for his reception, that the bishops, especially Dublin, should be asked to take part. He was clearly nervous about the possibility of a hostile reception in ecclesiastical circles.[49]

He need not have worried. Edward Byrne wrote to him to assure him that he was only too anxious to give His Excellency every honour and respect on his arrival, and he suggested that on his way to the civic reception in his honour he should stop at the Pro-Cathedral for a solemn *Te Deum*.[50] Robinson replied agreeing entirely with the proposal.[51] The government, to make up for ignoring Byrne in the appointment of the Nuncio, left the reception at the Pro-Cathedral entirely in his hands. J. P. Walshe, secretary to the Department of Foreign Affairs, assured Fr Dunne, 'Whatever the archbishop desires we shall do.'[52]

First Nuncio to a Free Ireland

All was worked out in detail for the historic arrival of a Papal Nuncio to an independent Irish state. When he arrived on 14 January 1930, the exuberance of the occasion was captured in newspaper headlines: 'DAZZLING CATHEDRAL SCENE. TRIUMPHANT RETURN OF A SON OF ERIN, CLIFFS ABLAZE WITH BEACONS. NEWORK OF ILLUMINATIONS.' The reporter, for the *Irish Independent*, Eldred Reeve, commented:

> Long before he stepped ashore the Papal Nuncio saw the first signs of welcome of the Irish people gazing from the cliffs of Wicklow and Dublin. Beacons flared into light on the hills along the curving bay that sweeps from Bray Head to Howth Head ...

'As the Nuncio stepped ashore, he was cheerfully greeted by the Archbishop of Dublin. "I welcome you most heartily on behalf of the people of Dublin and the Irish Free State", said Dr Byrne, and the Nuncio thanked him. The bond of the State to the Pope was sealed as President Cosgrave knelt before the Nuncio and kissed the Papal ring ... We watched silently, knowing that the moment was significant for the Catholic religion and for Ireland.'[53]

Towards the end of January, a letter from Bishop J. Dignan, of Clonfert, to Hagan, reported that Archbishop Byrne held a reception for the Nuncio in the Pro-Cathedral, to which he invited every bishop. The archbishop, Dignan understood, was favourably impressed by the personality of the Nuncio and was especially struck by his modesty. Deignan was concerned, however, that the appointment would have an adverse effect politically on the Irish church.[54] His fears proved unfounded. Pascal Robinson remained in Ireland until his death after the Second World War. A practised diplomat he was highly respected in the Vatican, and proved a wise and stable influence in the area of church and state relations.[55]

On 5 February 1930, Walshe informed Bewley that the Archbishop of Dublin has not only treated the Nuncio with the greatest possible cordiality, but he had been exceedingly amiable with the Department in everything concerning the arrangements.[56] This comment raises the question – how much of the archbishop's alleged intransigence was a projection of the Department of Foreign Affairs or of his vicars general and those close to him? His successor, Archbishop McQuaid, was to observe to a senior member of the managers of secondary schools that he was frequently amazed at the views attributed to him![57]

Fears of radical republicans
In a letter to Pascal Robinson on 14 May, Dr Byrne thanked him for his kindness in making sure that his (Byrne's) letter reached a certain cardinal in Rome. He went on to offer advice of a semi-political nature. His Excellency may have seen in the *Standard* newspaper the proposal to form an Irish Academy. The names associated with it were practically all strong Republican politicians mostly of the extreme sort. He trusted that the Holy Father would not be deceived into sending any mark of approval to these people who were not at all representative Catholics and were in times of trouble anything but loyal to the hierarchy.[58]

Concern about the activity of radical republicans had been felt for some time by members of the government. Already on 17 June 1929, at the start of the Centenary Celebrations, the attorney-general, James Fitzgerald Kenny, called for a denunciation by the entire bench of bishops of the recent spate of murders, including that of Guard O'Sullivan in Co Clare. From captured documents he was aware that other murders were contemplated by these men.[59] The archbishop's reaction was expressed in a note written on the letter: 'At present, in times of such national joy and religious fervour, it would come badly from the bishops.' On 1 July 1929, the office of the president informed the Minister for Defence of a memorandum from the Department of Justice concerning arms and ammunition found in Lower Camden Street, an arms dump in the metropolitan area, a split in the reunited IRA Association, and the formation of a Workers' Defence Corps in Dublin. It went on to name some IRA men and a representative of the Irish Class War Prisoners' Aid, from Belfast, as active members of the Communist and Irregular organisations. On 5 July, the office of the president provided further information from the Department of Justice, that a party of Irregulars had been captured at Cherryfield, Ballymun, Glasnevin, Co Dublin on 30 June.[60]

Representation recalling Civil War days
Later in the year, Archbishop Byrne was approached on behalf of two republican prisoners, Aidan Sweeney and Patrick

McGuinness, who were said to be in solitary confinement and cut off from other prisoners. He made representation to the president. Mr Cosgrave replied on 20 December 1929. Sweeney and McGuinness were in Mountjoy prison and sentenced to two years imprisonment for the unlawful possession of firearms and ammunition. They refused to recognise the court and styled themselves 'political prisoners', and wanted to be allowed to exercise separately from other prisoners. When this was not permitted, they declined to exercise and to work, and hence remained in their cells. They were fundamentally 'Irregulars' and in view of the very serious crimes, including murder, committed by the 'Irregular' organisation, they could not obviously be permitted to carry on their campaign of defiance against authority in the prison itself. A lot of lying propaganda had been spread about concerning these prisoners and pictures had been drawn of them languishing in solitary confinement. The position was, Cosgrave insisted, that they had behaved unreasonably and in a spirit of sulk had abstained voluntarily from work and exercise both of which were available to them on any day they decided to submit to the ordinary prison discipline to which they were subject as a result of the crimes for which they were found guilty. He explained in conclusion that prisoners nowadays were allowed a certain amount of conversation while at exercise or at work so that if these prisoners went to exercise and work they could enjoy automatically what Dr Byrne has been asked to secure for them.[61]

Dublin chosen for International Eucharistic Congress

On 20 November, a crown on the Centenary Celebrations was announced in an unofficial message from Rome. Dublin had been selected as the meeting place of the International Eucharistic Congress to be held in 1932. Consequently, the spiritual significance of the Eucharistic Congress was the archbishop's message in his Lenten pastoral letter of 1930. He concluded by calling on all his people, even at this distance from the event, to prepare for it spiritually by prayers for the success of the Congress, accompanied by an earnest effort on the part of each one 'to come nearer to Our Eucharistic Lord, to know Him better and to love Him more, and to receive more fervently the Bread of Angels'.[62]

A Cathedral for Dublin

The item that made most news concerning the archbishop during 1930, however, was his announcement that he had acquired a site for a cathedral in Merrion Square, Dublin. Mindful of Archbishop Walsh's efforts to purchase a site and of his dictum that an archbishop and archdiocese without a cathedral was like an admiral without a flagship, he had carried on the quest. The headings in the *Irish Independent* for 14 July 1930 gave the result of his efforts:

> CATHEDRAL FOR DUBLIN IN MERRION SQUARE. 'A NOBLE SITE', says MOST REV DR BYRNE. AGREEMENT SIGNED BY HIS GRACE AND LORD PEMBROKE. PURCHASE PRICE £10,000. DIOCESE WILL NOT ENTER INTO POSSESSION UNTIL 1938. CITY'S MOST BEAUTIFUL SQUARE.

This information was drawn from a letter of the archbishop read in the Pro-Cathedral on 12 July. It also announced that for years the Catholic people of Dublin had felt that the Pro-Cathedral was unworthy as a cathedral of the capital of this Catholic nation. After visiting several sites over a period of time, the site in Merrion Square was chosen and bought.

A number of newspapers in Ireland and Britain displayed an interest in the new cathedral and its design. Writers of letters to the press stressed the importance of having a Celtic design, and a trade union representative called for Irish materials in its construction. It was assumed that there would be a competition for the best architectural design. The *Irish Independent* assured the archbishop that the whole nation would deem it a duty and a privilege to participate in the project, and went on to pay a tribute to him:

> Archbishop Byrne's activities in the city and archdiocese of Dublin have already stamped him as one of the most untiring and zealous of builders; for during the last ten years more churches and schools have been built or renovated under his guidance than, perhaps, in any previous decade. His crowning achievement in this direction is the purchase of Merrion Square.[63]

The archbishop, in an undated draft of a letter to President Cosgrave, informed him of the purchase of the site and added that it was his kindly interest in the securing of the square for Dublin Catholics, and the help he was always ready to give him, that made the happy consummation at all possible. He concluded with a wish that reflected the reality of his own uncertain future: 'God grant that you may see the glorious Cathedral of the future nearing completion. I should sing my *Nunc Dimmitis* if I saw a few stones above the foundation.'[64]

In his letter read in the Pro-Cathedral, Dr Byrne explained that it would not be necessary for some time to face the question of raising the large sum required for the erection of the cathedral, and he added that the commonly held idea that he had the vast sum of £25,000 at his disposal was completely groundless. The total available was approximately £2,500. 'In any case', he emphasised, 'until 1932 all our energies will be concentrated on the preparations for the great International Eucharistic Congress, which has first claim on our resources.'[65]

The preparations, indeed, occupied much of his attention from this point onwards. He participated in the joint pastoral letter from the bishops, on 23 November 1930, which looked to the combined celebration in 1932 of the International Eucharistic Congress and the fifteenth centenary of St Patrick's coming to Ireland. They estimated that the cost of the celebrations would come to at least £80,000, but knowing the generosity of the Irish people they trusted that this would stimulate rather than appal them. The first Sunday of Advent was appointed for a special collection for the Eucharistic Congress Fund to be made in every parish in the country.[66]

Educational developments. The minister and the bishop
During 1930, Archbishop Byrne, among his other duties, was necessarily concerned with educational issues. His responsibility extended into every branch of education which, as indicated, was undergoing extensive development under a native government. Despite limited resources, the respective ministers for education between 1923 and 1932, Eoin MacNeill and John Marcus O'Sullivan, brought about significant initiatives. The Department of Education was created and its procedures were established. 'Systematic investigations were launched into various issues, a new secondary examination and curricular structure was devised, a primary certificate was introduced, a network of preparatory colleges was established, and legislation was suc-

cessfully promoted in the late twenties on school attendance, the universities and vocational education.' A model had been established that was to be followed for almost forty years.[67]

In the course of 1930, the issues requiring Dr Byrne's attention included the appointment of teachers to Catholic training colleges; the problems relating to training colleges in the Gaeltacht and transferring students to Talbot Street, Dublin, under his Grace's jurisdiction; the appointment of principals in primary schools; the training of nuns for teaching in primary schools; the training of teachers in the Irish language; fears relating to the Model schools; and objections to the new Vocational Education Act. The last two issues demonstrate how carefully the Department of Education dealt with matters involving the bishops.

Joseph O'Neill, secretary of the Department, replied on 13 October 1930 to a letter of the archbishop, dated 23 July, which raised the manner of appointment of teachers to Model schools under the proposed system of joint management involving the Department and the local bishop. He had been directed by the minister to suggest certain arrangements for consideration. These made it clear that the archbishop, or his representative, would have a decisive say in the appointment of teachers.[68]

With regard to the Vocational Education Bill, Minister for Education, John Marcus O'Sullivan, showed himself eager to assure Mgr Waters, acting for the archbishop, and then the archbishop himself, that there was nothing objectionable in the Bill. Writing at some length to Mgr Waters on 12 August 1930, he dealt with criticisms of the proposed Act that had appeared in articles in Catholic publications and were being emphasised by the opposition political parties, and assured him that no new principles were being introduced which were opposed to Catholic practice in educational matters in this country.[69] Following further public criticism, the Minister endeavoured to get in touch directly with the archbishop, and was left wondering whether Mgr Waters had been in communication at all with Dr Byrne. He sent the archbishop a copy of his letter to Mgr Waters and a copy of the debate in the Dáil on the second reading, adding that after a perusal of these, he felt confident that His Grace would be convinced that his intention that no new principle in regard to the control of education had been introduced would be borne out.[70]

Church and State

A further instance of church-state relations was evident on Christmas Day 1930 at the Pro-Cathedral, when a time-honoured practice was revived. The Lord Mayor of Dublin and the members of the Corporation attended at High Mass. The archbishop presided and, after the Mass, the Lord Mayor, Senator Alfred Byrne, presented the members of the corporation to Dr Byrne: an instance not of the unity of church and state, but of the Catholic nature of contemporary Irish society, of the fact that many people in public life were devout Catholics, while retaining independence in matters of political allegiance and political policy.

CHAPTER ELEVEN

1931- 1933

*Insights and Alarms. The International Eucharistic Congress
– and a country transformed*

Prelude
The years 1931-1933 were highly significant for the young Irish
state. The huge success of the International Eucharistic Congress
was of vast importance at home and in the estimation of Catholics
overseas, but these years also witnessed concerns about communist activities, the resurgence of IRA violence, and a change
of government that seemed almost impossible seven or eight
years previously. All these played a larger or lesser part in
Edward Byrne's life, but what he brought to them in terms of his
style of government and certain qualities of personality and
spirit also merit attention. This chapter, as a consequence, is divided into two sections. Section One will consider most of the
foregoing, beginning with the archbishop's style of government,
while Section Two will concentrate on the Eucharistic Congress,
in its preparations, manifestation, and immediate aftermath.

SECTION I

ASPECTS OF DIOCESAN GOVERNMENT

Edward Byrne, as indicated earlier, tended to govern collectively.
He showed little desire to focus power in his own hands. Every
week he met with his council – vicars-general John Waters,
Francis Wall, James J. Dunne, Patrick J. Walsh, Michael Cronin –
who, together with him and his secretaries, Tom O'Donnell and
Patrick Dunne, ran the archdiocese. From the file on vicars-general
in the archbishop's papers it is evident that they were involved in
decisions about the appointment of clergy to parishes, about male
and female religious who were subjects of the archbishop or
who were seeking a foundation or questing for vocations in the
archdiocese, about church repairs, special faculties, particular
parish requests and needs. Frequently, His Grace delegated special
tasks to his vicars general, as previously noted with respect to
diocesan censorship; and he virtually handed over the diocese
to them when he went on vacation.[1] The secretaries and the vicars

general were protective of the archbishop because of his poor health, and in some instances were more than ready to take on roles of authority and influence.[2]

The archbishop felt comfortable in this situation of support from an inner council of vicars-general and others, a number of whom had been fellow students with him at Clonliffe and/or friends. It seems to have created resentment, however, not only among some older clergy but also among some priests who served in the archdiocese but had not been educated at Clonliffe and had come, perhaps, from outside Dublin.

Characteristics of his administration and personality
Edward Byrne and his counsellors, as has been seen, were part-icularly supportive of the various works and organisations linked to the St Vincent de Paul Society, not least its care of the homeless men in its night shelter, Back Lane, Dublin. He had contributed to it regularly from soon after his consecration.[3]

It was said of him, after his death, that he was noted not only for his concern for the poor but also for the spiritual care of his people. This last reflected his own deep spirituality. He was al-ways the man of God, his panegyrist remarked, yet always kindly and human and with 'a wide understanding and toler-ance for the shortcomings, follies and failings of others, even in spiritual matters. But where there was question of any import-ant point of church discipline, principle, or right, he was inex-orable'. His judgement, however, was calm and sound and he avoided hasty judgements.[4] His deep spirituality was remarked on by Fr Michael Browne SJ, himself known for his prayerful-ness and austerity, and was evident at various times in his life. Many, as previously noted, referred to his kindness and grac-iousness. One such, the Jesuit provincial, John Fahy, a person with a similar quality of heart, informed the archbishop on 2 January 1931 that he was being replaced as provincial and being sent to the Irish Jesuit mission in Australia. As he retired from office, he wished to thank His Grace for his constant kindnesses, adding that 'kindliness and grace mark your administration as they marked your life before your elevation to the See of Dublin.'[5]

Another friend who experienced his Grace's kindly humanity died in Dublin on 26 March 1931. Timothy Michael Healy, for-mer Governor General, and the archbishop, as has been seen,

enjoyed each other's company. Edward Byrne, no less than
Shane Leslie, would have enjoyed the irony on the occasion of a
Requiem Mass for Tim Healy in Westminster Cathedral on 11
April 1931. 'The wheel has come full circle', Leslie observed.
'The cardinal gave absolution over a catafalque draped with the
Irish Tricolour ...'[6]

The Cause of Matt Talbot

The archbishop's concern for the spiritual well-being of his people and the exaltation of the poor was manifested in his respect
and regard for a working man, whom he would have known
from his years in the Pro-Cathedral. Matt Talbot died on 7 June
1925. His reputation for holiness soon spread beyond the shores
of Ireland. On 8 November 1931, a pastoral from Dr Byrne letter
was read in all the churches in Dublin. He announced that because of his own personal admiration for Matt Talbot's virtues
and life and the petitions of others, he had decided to open what
was known as 'the Ordinary or Informative Enquiry into the
reputation for sanctity of the Servant of God, Matt Talbot'. This
enquiry would also cover whatever miracles might be attributed to him. The archbishop reminded his readers and listeners
that this was the first step of a long process. He urged all who
had knowledge of Matt's life to come forward with evidence,
and he asked the prayers of all for the guidance of the Holy
Spirit.[7]

To encourage people to pray that God might show forth the
intercessory power of his servant, Matt Talbot, the archbishop
had a special prayer printed and widely distributed not only in
Ireland but throughout the world. He also commissioned Sir
Joseph Glynn to write a biography. A further work of this nature
was to be written in 1954: a scholarly book by Mary Purcell entitled *Matt Talbot and His Times* (Dublin 1954). The process towards beatification proved slower than expected. In 1973 Matt
was raised to the title of 'Venerable', but there were no further
major development over the next thirty or more years.

Pressing considerations

The Eucharistic Congress was to be the over-riding consideration
of the body of bishops during 1932, and preparations for it during 1931 took up a great deal of their time. Archbishop Byrne
was filmed cutting the first sod on the site of the great altar to be

constructed in the Phoenix Park. He is rather bowed, but he used the spade effectively. In blessing the site, however, the tremble in his left hand is clearly visible.

Another important consideration, however, weighed on the hierarchy in those years, namely the re-emergence of a violent IRA, which was prepared to kill policemen and intimidate juries, and which had links with Moscow-instructed communists. Both groups came together in an organisation called Saor Éire.

Danger of revolution?

In 1929 the government, through the attorney-general, had appealed unsuccessfully to the bishops for a pronouncement against this new violent IRA. Now Cosgrave made the appeal in person. First he contacted the cardinal, and then on 17 September 1931 he wrote to Archbishop Byrne assuring him that there existed 'a situation without parallel as a threat to the foundations of all authority',[8] and enclosed for his perusal three documents: A report to the government from the Department of Justice on the 'Alliance between Irish Republican Army and Communists'; a memorandum on certain organisations showing 'the Existence of a Conspiracy for the Overthrow by Violence of State Institutions'; and an extract from the *Daily Express* of an interview with Frank Ryan and others leaders of the IRA on their aims and actions. The extensive report from the Department of Justice gave details of IRA and communist activities, the names of people involved, and their avowed aims. A similar letter and enclosures went to each bishop. The hierarchy responded at their October meeting in Maynooth. They delivered a pastoral letter on the situation, which was given extensive coverage in the press on 19 October 1931.

'Deeply conscious of our responsibility for the Faith and Morals of our people', the letter commenced, 'we cannot remain silent in face of growing evidence of a campaign of Revolution and Communism, which, if allowed to run its course unchecked, must end in the ruin of Ireland, both soul and body.' The document then outlined the actions of 'a society of militant character, whose avowed objective was to overthrow the state by force of arms'. Its 'methods and principles of action' were 'in direct opposition to the Law of God'. Side by side with it was a new organisation entitled 'Saor Éire' which was 'frankly communistic in its aims'. 'No Catholic can lawfully be a member' of either organisation, the bishops concluded. Conscious, however, of the country's social and economic problems and needs, and how violence could grow from such conditions, they emphatically appealed to all parties 'to forget their differences for the time being, and to join their forces to find a solution ...' that would be 'in accordance with the traditions of Catholic Ireland'.

On 17 October, the day before the issue of the joint pastoral, which condemned the IRA implicitly and 'Saor Éire' explicitly, the government introduced the Constitution (amendment No 17) Act, which established a military tribunal to try cases of sedition, illegal drilling and membership of illegal organisations. Two days after the pastoral, the IRA, 'Saor Éire', Cumann na mBan, Friends of the Soviet Union, the Workers' Revolutionary Party, and seven other associations were declared unlawful in the Irish Free State.

There were hundreds of arrests, meetings were prescribed, and the republican paper, *An Phoblacht*, was suspended. Republican activity was reduced to subsistence level. It was a similar story with the influential Revolutionary Workers' Groups. Even lorry drivers and commercial travellers for Russian Oil Products were stopped and searched. By December, the Revolutionary Workers' Groups were obliged to suspend their newspaper, the *Workers' Voice*. (9) The combined effort of state and church brought temporary stability.

In the background to their joint activity, without churchmen approving government policy such as the establishment of a military tribunal, was a joint concern for a peaceful Eucharistic Congress, when Ireland would be the centre of considerable world attention. *An Phoblacht*, for 11 April 1931, gave grounds for such concern. In its editorial, under a section headed 'Prepare for Coercion', it reminded its readers:

Next year the colossal influx of visitors to the Eucharistic Congress will afford the most unique opportunity in our history to expose the tyranny of British rule in Ireland ... and to shatter the lie that Irish people are freeman ...The fullest advantage must be taken of this opportunity ...

The thousands of visitors must be provided with information that Ireland is not free but 'is divided into two British dependences' in which 'Irishmen are incarcerated for Irish patriotism'. This information, and many other extracts from *An*

Phoblacht, were sent to Archbishop Byrne, and, it may be assumed, to the other archbishops and bishops.[10]

Reactions to the bishops and to the government
There was a sense of outrage among many republicans at the bishops' pastoral and at government policy. Already on 10 October 1931, Count Plunkett sent to Archbishop Byrne a protest from the Army Council of Óglaigh na hÉireann against church pronouncements, and he added his own protest against the government's intention to set up court-martial courts. On 2 November he objected to the announcement at Masses in the Sacred Heart Church, Donnybrook, of a triduum of prayer in reparation for the crimes committed by the two organisations mentioned in the bishops' pastoral. He wanted these announcements to be publicly withdrawn, and pointed out that only one organisation was mentioned by name in the pastoral. His protests did not deter him, however, from requesting Dr Byrne, on 22 October and 20 November, to intervene to save George and Charles Gilmore from being shot as a result of trial by court-martial. They had not been found guilty in the civil courts. On 27 November, he complained that Mrs Gilmore had not been allowed access to her two sons and was refused all information about them.

In addition, the archbishop received many requests to intervene in connection with the alleged conditions under which republican prisoners were detained in Mountjoy prison, especially those on hunger strike. These requests frequently came from women. Earlier on 10 June 1931, Maud Gonne MacBride, on behalf of the Women's Prisoners' Defence League, had requested him to use his great influence to end these prison scandals.[11]

The archbishop, as noted many times, had a record of responding to such appeals and bringing the matter to the government's attention, often with little effect. In 1932 he also responded to representations on behalf of Mrs Jane O'Brien, under sentence of death for murder, by signing a petition that the death sentence be commuted.[12]

One also notes around this time, and in subsequent years, that a number of people with problems, even within the Dublin archdiocese, by-passed the archbishop and wrote directly to Cardinal MacRory. While some of these may have been out of awareness that Dr Byrne was very busy before, during, and in the aftermath of the Eucharistic Congress, or out of concern for his health, other reasons may have been tardiness in decision making in Dublin or/and a dislike of the corporative type of government in the archdiocese and of the people involved.[13]

The bishops' request for a giant effort by the political parties to solve the social and economic problems met with an ambivalent response from the main opposition party. Frank Aiken of Fianna Fáil claimed to be appalled by the pastoral letter and the threatened excommunication of the IRA, and he urged Cardinal MacRory to enter into negotiation with the IRA and Saor Éire.[14] The party newspaper, the *Irish Press*, on 19 October 1931, however, made it clear, in its editorial, that when it came to communism Fianna Fáil stood by the social teaching of Popes Leo XIII and Pius XI. Generally, the bishops appeal to political parties 'to forget their differences for the time being' and join together to find a solution for the social and economic problems, proved unable to move the parties to set aside their differences and their political ambitions. The appeal, indeed, had little chance of success. Divisions were still deep, and Fianna Fáil, understandably, was not prepared to weaken its political surge towards government by a temporary alliance with Cumann na nGaedheal and other parties.

The 'Red Scare'?
Concern about communism was palpable during these years. In retrospect it has often been dismissed as a 'red scare'. It is pointed out that there was only a small minority who were communists, and that the country was unlikely to stand for another civil war. But at the time it was freely argued that Lenin brought down the government of Kerensky with a handful of supporters, and the memory was fresh of the Soviet revolution and of further attempts at soviet style revolution in European countries. Besides, a number of young Irishmen had been trained in Moscow, and Moscow was taking an active part in fomenting rebellion and expanding membership in Ireland. In practice, Moscow proved too ideological and rigid in its instructions to Irish communists and occasioned divisions and confusion,[15] but this was not fully known to the government and other interested observers. Cosgrave and many of his ministers clearly believed in the red peril, as did the former leader of the Labour Party, Tom Johnson,[16] and the shrewd, well-informed, Bill O'Brien, general secretary of the

Irish Transport and General Workers' Union and a founding member of the Labour Party.[17]

A factor promoting a spirit of vigilance against Soviet Communism and support for a more just society was the appearance of two encyclicals by Pius XI: *Quadragesimo Anno* (forty years after the appearance of *Rerum Novarum*) with its celebrated, but misleading dictum that 'no one can be at the same time a sincere Catholic and a true socialist', and its promotion of a form of corporatism to solve the problems caused by the collapse of capitalism; and *Non Abbiamo Bisogno* on Catholic Action. Both gave rise to numerous pamphlets, articles, conferences, and created a further sense of urgency.

Diplomatic triumph and Election disaster

On 11 December, an important victory was achieved by the government with the passing of the Statute of Westminster Act, 1931, which provided that no law of a dominion parliament shall be inoperative on ground of repugnancy to British law; and any dominion parliament is empowered to repeal or amend any act of the United Kingdom parliament in so far as it is part of dominion law. It was an achievement that owed a great deal first to the skill of Kevin O'Higgins and then to that of Patrick McGilligan in their negotiations with other dominion countries.

The achievement, however, carried little weight with the general public following a supplementary budget in November, which pushed the price of petrol up by four pence a gallon, and income tax by sixpence in the pound, and reduced the wages of teachers and the Garda Síochána. Deeming the adverse effect of such measures on the electorate as an unworthy partisan political consideration at a time of adverse economic circumstances, and confident that his government's record in securing law and order was a decisive factor, Mr Cosgrave called a general election on 29 January 1932. The result took him by surprise. Even his reliable Church of Ireland support had been weakened by the censorship involved in the Immoral Literature Bill and by the prolonged controversy over the appointment of a Protestant librarian in Co Mayo.

This last centred on the appointment of Miss Dunbar-Harrison, a graduate of Dublin University, by the Local Appointments Commission, and the opposition to the appointment by Mayo County Council and by the Catholic Archbishop of Tuam, Thomas Gilmartin. All sorts of fears were raised about the adverse effect of a Trinity College graduate on young children using the library, on the kind of books she was likely to introduce and so on. The government supported her appointment, many clergy and extreme Catholic journals opposed it, and De Valera opposed it on the grounds that Miss Dunbar-Harrison did not speak Irish. A clash between church and state seemed imminent, and there were divisions in the cabinet. Cosgrave sought a meeting with the cardinal. In the aftermath, Archbishop Gilmartin was placed on the defensive and suggested as a compromise that the librarian be transferred to another position at a suitable time. Cosgrave agreed to this. The extended controversy, however, provided further grounds for dissatisfaction with the government among sections of the Catholic and Protestant population. The Archbishop of Dublin took an independent line that put pressure on Archbishop Gilmartin to pull back from his intransigent position. On 3 April 1931, as he was about to go to Rome in preparation for the Eucharistic Congress, he warned Cardinal McRory against any public pronouncement regarding the Mayo librarian. 'Outside the Mayo diocese we have no direct interest in the matter', he declared, and he had been reliably informed that if a pronouncement were made the president and the minister for education would resign rather than engage in controversy with the church, and this 'would break up the government and be the beginning of chaos'.[18] Subsequently, while in Rome, Dr Byrne, interviewed by Charles Bewley, the Irish government representative to the Holy See, remarked that in his opinion the agitation was worked up for reasons which had nothing to do with religion, and that nobody in County Mayo was likely to be influenced by the religious convictions of the librarian. He agreed with Bewley that the books in the library were first selected by a committee and the librarian could only distribute the literature already selected. He had no sympathy with the campaign, and was glad that Fianna Fáil had not been able to make much use of the incident, and that they put their protest on grounds of the Irish language and not on religion.[19]

The election was hard fought and intense, with violent incidents. The result gave Fianna Fáil 72 seats, and Cumann na nGaedheal 57. The Labour party was down from 13 to 7 seats, and two members of the breakaway Independent Labour were elected. Fianna Fáil was five short of an overall majority. It joined with Labour, whose members were in broad agreement with De Valera's social programme. On 9 March 1932, as a result, Éamon de Valera took office as President of the Executive Council of the Irish Free State. There had been a peaceful transfer of power – a testimony to the firm democratic foundation maintained by the Cumann na nGaedheal government during their turbulent ten years in office; and in external affairs they had secured a freedom of movement that De Valera was to exercise with vigour.

The leader of Fianna Fáil had received strong support among the younger clergy and from some bishops; and also in convents if one were to judge from the reaction to the election result of Sr M. Columba, the Convent, Ballingarry. Writing to Mrs Sheehy Skeffington, on 14 March 1932, she exclaimed:

Is it not glorious to have Mr de Valera at the helm again! ... It has thrown thirty years off my life! God be thanked for everything, we can put our whole heart now into our prayers for the rulers of our country.[20]

The new government and the Eucharistic Congress?
Where did the new development leave Archbishop Edward Byrne and his well-advanced plans for the 31st International Eucharistic Congress? Cosgrave was said to have called the general election early in the year to avoid 'politicising' the Congress, which was to be held in June.[21] Byrne trusted Cosgrave, he could depend on his support and that of the government. What was to be expected of the new government, whose members had formerly been condemned by the bishops? Fears, however, were soon allayed. The Eucharistic Congress provided an opportunity for members of the new cabinet to establish their reputation as devout Catholics, and to make a favourable impact on the thousands of visitors from numerous countries. Besides, as a devout Catholic, De Valera wished the occasion to be a great success for the church and the country, and similar views were held by his ministers and close colleagues, many of whom had clergy or religious as relatives or friends.

SECTION II

THE 31ST INTERNATIONAL EUCARISTIC CONGRESS

Preparations and frank talking

As noted above, the preparations for the Eucharistic Congress required Dr Byrne to go to Rome in April 1931. Charles Bewley reported to the First Secretary in Foreign Affairs, on 14 April 1931, that His Grace of Dublin arrived in Rome the previous week. He had shown himself extremely friendly,[22] and the Irish College was much more friendly since the death of Mgr Hagan.[23] Bewley found the archbishop very frank about certain church matters. He informed him, *inter alia*, that Monsignor Pisani was not at all *persona grata* (Dr Byrne's expression) with the Irish episcopate, and that they considered him an inquisitive person, who even in his short stay at the time of the Catholic Emancipation Celebrations spent his time enquiring into matters which were no business of his. He also said that, although Monsignor Pisani now professed great esteem and affection for Ireland, his attitude was very different when he was in India. Bewley gathered from the trend of Dr Byrne's conversation that he was anxious to guard against Mgr Pisani being sent to Ireland. Dr Byrne also confided that at his audience with the Holy Father and with the Secretary of State, Cardinal Pacelli, he had taken the opportunity of praising the Nuncio, Mgr Robinson, and expressed the satisfaction of the general episcopate at his presence in Ireland.[24]

Celebrating St Patrick

In conjunction with the Eucharistic Congress it was planned to celebrate also the fifteen-hundredth centenary of St Patrick bringing Christianity to Ireland. The first fanfare to the patrician celebration was a gathering on Station Island, Lough Derg, Co Donegal, a place of penitential pilgrimage for centuries known as 'St Patrick's Purgatory'. The occasion was the consecration of a new basilica by the Papal Nuncio, Mgr Pascal Robinson, on 17 May 1931, and, significantly, among those attending were President Cosgrave and Mr de Valera.

During 1931, presumably with the demands of the Eucharistic Congress in mind, Mgr Francis Wall was made Auxiliary Bishop of Dublin, with the title Bishop of Thasos.

Co-operation of government and committees in the preparations
In a letter to Cardinal MacRory, on 12 March 1932, Edward Byrne told him that Congress arrangements were going well, that the various committees were getting immense labour and earnestness into different branches of the organisation, and that the new government seemed to be even more anxious than their predecessor to put religion to the front, to display more, as to the underlying intention, *Ecclesia de intentione non judicat.*[25]

The committees and sub-committees referred to were under the same management and co-ordination as in 1929. Frank O'Reilly of the CTSI, and the leaders of the Vincent de Paul Society and the Catholic Young Men's Association were the key figures, but in fact every parish throughout the country and virtually every Catholic organisation was involved. In Dublin, particular attention was paid to involving people in the poorer areas.

A Pastoral to inspire his people
On 5 June 1932, a long pastoral letter from Archbishop Byrne was read in all the churches of the archdiocese to ensure that the spiritual nature of the entire celebration was kept strongly to the fore. He linked devotion to the Blessed Sacrament with aspects of Irish history, with the readiness of their ancestors to risk life and property in Penal times in order to attend Mass. He urged that all members of the diocese join in an octave of prayer and reparation coming up to the feast of the Sacred Heart of Jesus, that those days be days of mortification and prayer, and that those who were in easier circumstances might voluntarily practice some renunciation and bestow on the poor the proceeds of retrenchment.[26]

Across the country spiritual retreats of various kinds prepared the hearts and minds of the people for a time of spiritual exaltation and blessing.

Arrival of Papal Legate
On 15 June, his Eminence Cardinal Lorenzo Lauri, the papal delegate to the Eucharistic Congress, began his journey to Dublin. He arrived at Dún Laoghaire on 20 June to a tumultuous welcome. Hundreds began to assemble at Carlisle Pier for hours before the arrival of the boat. Shortly before 3 o'clock the crowds had swelled to an estimated 50,000. Despite the congestion,

decorum was maintained. 'An outbreak of applause greeted his Grace the Archbishop of Dublin, Most Rev Dr Byrne, as he walked with his secretary from Croft Road to the pier. At 2.55 the boom of a gun announced to the waiting throngs at Dún Laoghaire that the *S.S. Cambria* was in sight. Thereafter the guns boomed at regular intervals until, with planes in cross formation whirring overhead and the canon booming the Royal Salute, the ship entered the harbour.'[27]

In the lead up to this historic moment, the archbishop had to deal with two minor crises, one of which involved a possible clash between church and state, the other a question of ecclesiastical precedence. This last was between Cardinal Mac Rory and himself.

An issue of ecclesiastical precedence
The archbishop phoned his Eminence to inform him that, on instruction from Rome, all the cardinals were to await the Legate's arrival in the Pro-Cathedral. On 8 June, Cardinal MacRory wrote that he thought Rome would expect him to be present at the pier to greet the Legate, and it would be 'a very serious slight to the Legate' if he were not present when he was expected to be. He suggested that Dr Byrne write to Rome to confirm where his duty lay.[28] Dr Byrne responded with a mixture of diplomacy and humility, and with information on his relations with De Valera. 'Of course, I have no objection in the world to your coming to Dún Laoghaire as the chief of the Irish hierarchy; but it is scarcely my place to write to Rome to know what Your Eminence should do.' He continued:

> It has been arranged that I should travel to town in the carriage with the Legate and President de Valera. I may say that I have had considerable trouble with the President. His claims amount to excluding me altogether from the Legate's car. It was at first suggested, by the Ministry for External Affairs, that I as Sponsor of the Congress and the Legate's host, should accompany the Legate, and that Your Eminence should be accompanied by the President. This was superseded by the extraordinary proposal that the President alone should accompany the Legate.

The archbishop concluded: 'If Your Eminence comes to Dún Laoghaire it would be altogether unfitting that anyone else but yourself should take the first place with the Legate and the President. After welcoming the Legate, I can go to the Pro-Cathedral and await your arrival there. I should be glad to do so.'[29]

The cardinal decided to write to Rome himself. On 16 June, he informed the archbishop that he had had a reply from Rome which announced that he was 'expected to do as the other cardinals'. He declared himself satisfied with this.[30]

The Archbishop and De Valera: A clash on right of precedence
There remained the more important issue, who was to be first to greet the Papal Legate, the archbishop or the president? The original arrangement with the Cosgrave government was that the Archbishop of Dublin would be the first to enter the ship and welcome the Legate in the saloon area. He would be followed by the president of the executive council, by members of the executive council, and by various ecclesiastical and civil dignitaries. When Mr de Valera was elected, however, he soon made it clear that he contemplated changes in some of the arrangements for the Congress. He let it be known publicly that the governor general would not be invited to the state reception for the Legate in Dublin Castle, and that he and his ministers would not wear morning suits and top hats when attending events. Privately, he contacted the archbishop's secretary to state that arrangements for receiving the Papal Legate must also be changed. He was, he announced, the elected Catholic leader of a Catholic country, and he must be the first person to welcome the Pope's representative to Ireland. He also indicated that he and the Legate should sit in the leading car in the cortege, while the archbishop should ride in the following automobile. The archbishop insisted that he travel in the same car as the Legate, and won his point; and he remained determined to be the first to greet the Legate. The latter would expect to be greeted first by the Archbishop of Dublin, who would then introduce him to the other dignitaries. The last thing Byrne wanted, however, was to have a public confrontation with the newly established president of the state, who seemed willful and uncompromising. He had released 20 political prisoners on 10 March, the day after his election as president; he had made it clear that he planned to suspend the Land Act and was at present in open defiance of the British government over land annuities. The

archbishop and his colleagues explored ways of finding a non-conflictual solution.

A quiet diplomatic coup

The solution came through the influence of His Grace's former secretary, Mgr Patrick Walsh, parish priest of Glasthule close by Dún Laoghaire. Walsh was a year-round swimmer and had come to know the captains of the ships on the Holyhead-Dún Laoghaire line. He called on Captain Copeland, skipper of the *Cambria* that was to bring the Legate to Dún Laoghaire, explained the dilemma and asked his help. The captain, who was a Protestant, came up with a ready remedy. When the steamer docked, the welcoming party would be gathered at the point at which the gangway to the first class or saloon section of the ship would be lowered. His sailors would make much fuss about their work and the lowering of the gangway would be delayed. Meanwhile, the archbishop could make his way quietly along the pier towards the aft of the ship. There, a gangway would be quickly lowered and His Grace could unobtrusively board the ship and make his way unnoticed to the saloon in which the Papal Legate waited. Greetings would be exchanged. Then, and only then, would the saloon gangway be lowered, the red carpet laid down, and Mr de Valera could lead his executive council up the gangway. To the waiting crowd it would seem that the Legate was greeted first by 'the elected Catholic leader of a Catholic people'.

The archbishop reached the saloon, greeted the Legate, and then moved to a seat at the side. Mr de Valera entered and was introduced to the Legate not by the archbishop but by Mgr Walsh who, presumably, had entered with his Grace. Mr de Valera then introduced the members of the executive council. A photograph was taken to mark the occasion: Mr de Valera and Mr O'Kelly stand on either side of the papal representative, their trilby hats on their hearts. The archbishop may be glimpsed in the second row.[31]

On to the Pro-Cathedral

The party descended to the pier, where the Legate inspected a Guard of Honour. President de Valera accompanied him on his right, Archbishop Byrne on his left. The Legate, his assistant priest, the archbishop and De Valera then took their seats in a waiting car. The ten immediately following cars each carried a member of the executive council. At Merrion Gates, the boundary of the city of Dublin, there was a further reception party. The Legate sat while the Lord Mayor, Alfred A. Byrne, read an address of welcome. The photograph in the *Irish Independent* shows De Valera standing on the Legate's right. The archbishop is not to be seen.

The cortege continued to the Pro-Cathedral, where the Papal Legate was welcomed by enthusiastic crowds. In a building across the road from the Pro-Cathedral, the cardinals and bishops from different parts of the world robed and then, led by the Legate, processed to a fanfare of trumpets to the entrance of the Pro-Cathedral, at which they were received by the Archbishop of Dublin. The procession then proceeded into the packed church, where the Papal Legate met the cardinals and other church dignitaries. The president occupied a special place and prie-dieu, and the ceremony was conducted with appropriate solemnity. Afterwards, thousands of people crowded the sidewalks, doorsteps and windows, and cheered a welcome as the car bearing the Cardinal Legate, Lorenzo Lauri, and the Archbishop of Dublin moved slowly behind their cavalry escort through the streets leading to the archbishop's palace in Drumcondra. The Papal Legate seemed greatly surprised and pleased at the vast welcoming crowds and at the great wealth of decorations that adorned every street and house.[32]

In Blackrock and Dublin Castle

On 21 July, the day after the arrival of his Eminence Cardinal Lorenzo Lauri, two social functions were held in his honour: a garden party at Blackrock College, and a State Reception at Dublin Castle.

The former event was hosted by the hierarchy. Some 20,000 people attended, as the sun shone on dignitaries from all parts of the world, including the Governor-General and Mrs MacNeill, De Valera and his ministers, and citizens from every walk of life. His Eminence, the Cardinal Legate, accompanied by His Grace, the Archbishop of Dublin, arrived at 4 o'clock, and were met at the college door by Very Rev J. C. McQuaid, rector of the college, who escorted them into the college, where the Legate was received by Cardinal MacRory and the archbishops and bishops of Ireland. Afterwards, he came onto the balcony overlooking the grounds and was enthusiastically applauded. He bestowed his blessing on the gathered thousands, some of whom began to sing and soon all were singing in unison: 'Faith of our Fathers, Holy Faith'. Marquees and little tables were all around the grounds attended by girl guides, and music was rendered by the No 1 Army Band, the Band of the Metropolitan Garda Síochána, and St James's Pipe and Reed Band. President de Valera expressed his appreciation to his friend Dr McQuaid, subsequently, for managing to ensure that his and the Governor General's paths did not cross!

The State reception was held in St Patrick's Hall, Dublin Castle. There was an attendance of about 4,000 guests. The President and Mrs de Valera received the guests as they entered the hall. Subsequently, they were presented individually to the Legate. They filed past for some hours. After this, the cardinal was escorted to the seat of honour on the dais to the accompaniment of a fanfare of trumpets. Flanking him on the dais were Cardinal MacRory, Primate of all-Ireland, Cardinal Verdier, Archbishop of Paris, Cardinal Lavitrano of Palermo, Cardinal Bourne of Westminster, Cardinal Dougherty of Philadelphia, and His Grace, Most Rev Dr Byrne, Archbishop of Dublin. President de Valera, speaking first in Irish and then in Latin, welcomed his Eminence to Saorstat Éireann. In the course of his address, he observed:

> With all veneration, respect, and rejoicing do we, the Government of Ireland, welcome your Eminence. By reason of our public office and its duties, it is most fitting that the Irish Government should not only assist in this way the great and solemn function of the Eucharistic Congress here in Ireland, but should also take their due part … in its proceedings.

Recalling Ireland's long tradition of fidelity to Rome, the president commented: 'Who can fail on this day to recall to mind the utterance of our Apostle, recorded of old in the Book of Armagh, "Even as you are children of Christ, be you also children of Rome".'

His Eminence, in his reply, paid tribute to the fidelity of the Irish people from the days of St Patrick, and assured his listeners that the Holy Father, Pius XI, loved Ireland, and sent to all its inhabitants and visitors a great and all-embracing Apostolic Blessing.

When his Eminence and his party left Dublin Castle at 11.00 pm, they found the streets thronged with people. Their cars slowly made their way through cheering crowds in floodlit streets.

Formal Opening and Progress
In such a blend of solemnity and rejoicing was the scene set for the formal opening of the 31st International Eucharistic Congress at the Pro-Cathedral on 22 June. Again the church was packed well before the ceremony commenced. At 3.20 pm the Cardinal Legate arrived, followed by the Archbishop of Dublin. They knelt in prayer. Then Mgr Walsh, chancellor of the Metropolitan Chapter, entered the pulpit and read the Latin-written Pontifical Letter opening the Congress. He was followed by Mgr Spellman, of the cardinal's suite, who read a translation in English. The Letter referred to the Irish people's transmission of their faith across the English-speaking world, their fortitude and fidelity under persecution, their loyalty to Rome, and their devotion to the Mass and the Holy Eucharist. The Pontiff bestowed the Apostolic Blessing on all.[33]

His Grace of Dublin then spoke on behalf of the hierarchy, and of the whole Irish nation who had co-operated so magnificently, by means both spiritual and temporal, in the manifold preparations that had been made. Then after further words on Ireland's historical devotion to the Eucharist and to Rome, he announced that the preparations had been successfully concluded and everything seemed in readiness for the opening of the Congress. Wherefore, he requested the Most Eminent Lord Cardinal, in God's name and for his greater glory, to inaugurate this Thirty-first International Eucharistic Congress.[34]

Archbishop Byrne's confidence that all the preparations had 'been successfully concluded' was shown to be justified. Thousands attended Mass and devotions daily in the archdiocese until 26 June, when over a million people, from all parts of the country and from different parts of the world, attended the Pontifical Mass in the Phoenix Park, and afterwards, in their thousands, processed in four great sections to Benediction on O'Connell Bridge. All was conducted with exemplary organisation.[35]

One Man's graphic account of the culminating ceremonies
The events of that day have often been described. An account of
special interest is that of the then Minister for Posts and
Telegraphs, Senator Joseph Connolly:

> In June 1932 Ireland had the great honour and privilege of
> holding the Eucharistic Congress. I say Ireland because, al-
> though Dublin was the selected centre for the Congress, all
> Ireland, from Murlough Bay (Co Antrim) to the Cobh of
> Cork, was united in the greatest manifestation of religious
> joy and devotion that has ever been known in the country.
>
> The preparations for the great event had gone on for
> months. It was as if the homes in the country had been sub-
> jected to a vast spring-cleaning and redecoration, and this
> applied to the poorest slum areas in Belfast and Dublin, as
> well as to the suburban villas, the mansions and the remote
> farm houses. There were of course the vast imposing
> schemes of decoration and illumination that had been
> planned and carried out by the organising committees, but
> even more impressive were the small shrines and the blaze of
> colour and light that expressed the spirit of Catholic devo-
> tion in every side street in every town in Ireland.

G. K. Chesterton, who was a welcome guest for that week,
aptly described this feature of the Dublin scene when he wrote:
'Instead of the main stream of colour flowing down the main
streets of commerce and overflowing into the crooked and neglected slums, it was exactly other way; it was the slums that
were the springs. These were the furnaces of colour; these were
the fountains of light.'
In Dublin, evening after evening, as the different groups
made their way to the Phoenix Park, men one night, women another, and children having their own special occasions, there
was the quiet atmosphere that accompanies prayerful devotion
… So the week progressed in perfect June weather until the culminating event on the closing Sunday morning when it was
estimated that upwards of a million people assembled on the
'fifteen acres' section of the Phoenix Park for High Mass.

> It was an unforgettable scene. The magnificent high altar, the
> gorgeous vestments of the cardinals and prelates of the
> church, the sea of white surplices and the vast assembly of a
> whole population kneeling in quiet devotion as Count John

McCormack's beautiful voice floated over their heads in the *Panis Angelicus*.

Connolly was pleased to record his own contribution as Minister for Posts and Telegraphs, when his engineers, with the co-operation of the Board of Works, made it possible for the voice of his Holiness, Pope Pius XI, to sound over the Park imparting the Papal Blessing to the vast audience.

In the afternoon Solemn Benediction of the Blessed Sacrament was given from an altar erected on O'Connell Bridge, while hundreds of thousands of worshippers filled the four long quays as well as the main approaches to the bridge. 'Those responsible for the marshalling and stewarding of the vast multitude', Connolly continued, 'did a wonderful job, and the discipline and co-operation of the people secured perfect order. It was, of course, above all else, the sacred ceremonies that ensured this. Dublin for that day had become a vast open-air cathedral, where all Ireland was meeting in prayer and devotion and where the dignitaries of the Catholic Church from all ends of the Christian world had come to join them.

'It was the final act of the Congress, completing what must have been for all those privileged to participate, the most memorable week that Dublin and Ireland had ever known.'[36]

Public involvement
A year later, the then well-known author, Alice Curtayne, writing in the *Capuchin Annual* on 'The Story of the Eucharistic Congress', remarked on the overall sense of public involvement: 'One glimpse of this we had in the mere matter of wearing the Congress badge, which was displayed by postmen, tramwaymen, Civic Guards, jarveys, crossing sweepers and, in short, by everyone imaginable. But they did not merely wear the badge; they carried out the Congress ... Visitors from overseas, especially those who had attended previous Congresses, at Carthage, Sydney, or Chicago, were loud in their emphasis on the difference: the miraculous unanimity of a people behind the Congress Committee ... Other Congresses were like the dramas played before a great concourse of onlookers, but that the Congress in Dublin was like a drama in which everyone was an actor, down to the smallest child in the darkest back alley of the city.'

Byrne for Cardinal?

It was the highlight of Edward Byrne's time as archbishop. Congratulations poured in from fellow prelates, and the *Irish Times* noted on 27 June 1932: 'Possible new cardinal – Dr Byrne's name suggested. A Roman Catholic dignitary, when questioned, told a London newspaper that he heard no news of any possible appointment' but 'for there to be two cardinals in Ireland would be a good thing for Ireland and a source of great encouragement. Dr Byrne's work in connection with the Congress has been appreciated by all Catholics, high and low, who have visited Dublin. It has entailed an enormous amount of work for him and his associates.'

It was as far as the possible appointment went. There was, however, a personal tribute from the Pope. He praised the thoroughness of the organisation, the splendour and magnificence of the material preparations, and the spiritual preparation of the people. The unity of all classes 'partaking of the one heavenly food, proud of one thing only, namely, that they were Irish Catholics, that is to say, devoted children of the church, who through great sorrows, losses, and martyrdoms had, with steadfast constancy, preserved the Faith of their fathers ever fresh and vigorous'. And turning to the archbishop, he declared:

> For all that was accomplished, from the first beginning until the signally successful ending of the Congress, the Holy Father gives well-merited praise to you who spent yourself wholly and unreservedly in arranging and carrying out everything so wisely and so effectively, to the civic authorities, the clergy and the people.[37]

Not surprisingly, when, in September, His Grace blessed the foundation stone of the first church in Dublin to be dedicated to Christ the King, it was viewed as a monument to the Eucharistic Congress. Large crowds flocked to Cabra, on the outskirts of Dublin, for the occasion, and the archbishop was greeted with 'intense enthusiasm'.[38]

Aspect of the impact of the Congress

The Eucharistic Congress added further to the healing process that was advanced by the centenary celebrations in 1929. It manifested a people's pride in the conjunction of faith and fatherland, in the virtual identification of Irish and Catholic. De Valera and his ministers were major recipients of this. Any doubts about their Catholic observance were removed. De Valera went out of his way to link national identity to allegiance to Rome; a conjunction that also served to differentiate Ireland from Britain, to assert its uniqueness, and to be called on in subsequent years when his policies nearly impoverished and split the country.

International tension and fear of Communism
These years in the 1930s were years of great international uncertainty. The fear of communism had provoked national movements in Italy and Germany, and disquiet in other countries. America's financial crisis had widespread repercussions and raised questions about the future. Not surprisingly, an article Archbishop Byrne was reading during 1932 was entitled 'What will America do now?'[39]

Fear of communism was evident among the Irish hierarchy as 1933 commenced. Social protest over wages and conditions, as among the miners in Castlecomer, led readily to accusations of communism, and Dr Collier, Bishop of Ossory, issued a pastoral that placed the entire communist organisation and programme in his diocese under a ban. Lenten pastorals emphasised the danger from the agents of Moscow, and on 17 March Cardinal MacRory called for 'a solid Irish Catholic front against the menace of communism.' As if in response, on 2 April 1933, some 1,000 men and women marched in an anti-communist demonstration in the streets of Dublin. The demonstration was said to have been organised by St Patrick's Catholic Anti-Communist League.[40]

The committee of the League requested a meeting with the Archbishop of Dublin 'to discuss matters pertaining to the League'. They enclosed the objectives of their organisation, the first of which seemed appropriate for the time: 'To expose and combat the menace of communism by propagating the teaching of the Catholic Church particularly on social questions.' They also emphasised that in carrying out their objectives 'the League shall be strictly non-political'. The archbishop, however, seemed to view such enthusiasts with less than enthusiasm. He had his secretary reply: 'The Archbishop would prefer to discuss the matters referred to in writing ... Should His Grace then consider an interview advisable, he will let you know.' Other communications came from the League on 21 June, 18 September, and 14

October. It is not clear that Dr Byrne ever met the League's representatives.

He was careful about giving approval to untried Catholic lay organisations and, to judge from his Lenten pastoral, his main emphasis was not on the danger of communism but on a pastoral issue, namely, that the Pope wished 1933 to be commemorated as the nineteenth centenary of the passion and death of Christ and had announced a Holy Year to begin on Passion Sunday.[41]

Being neutral amidst political tensions

Apart from communists, there were enough grounds for concern among the native political parties. De Valera had dissolved the Dáil on 2 January 1933 and, after a tense and troubled election campaign, managed to emerge on 24 January with an overall majority. He obtained 77 seats to 48 for Cumann na nGaedheal the nearest contender. With his new majority, he dismissed Eoin O'Duffy, chief commissioner of the Garda Síochána, on 22 February. Meantime, an Army Comrades Association had been formed to defend Cumann na nGaedheal platform speakers from the violence of the IRA during the general election. In March, the national executive of the Army Comrades Association adopted blue shirts and black berets as distinctive dress of association, reminiscent of the black shirts of Mussolini's Italy and the brown shirts of Hitler's movement. On 20 July, O'Duffy was elected leader of the Army Comrades, and the political atmosphere grew palpably strained.

Edward Byrne considered Cosgrave a friend, but he was careful to show no political preference as archbishop. Whatever political differences there were, his responsibility was to the vast majority of Dáil members, who were committed Catholics, and he was dedicated to strengthening their commitment. He drew attention to the practice of having a solemn votive Mass of the Holy Spirit for members of the Oireachtas; and in the Pro-Cathedral, on 8 February 1933, he presided at the Mass and implored the Divine guidance on the deliberations of the Oireachtas and the blessing of God on its work. It was attended by deputies, senators, and members of the judiciary, civil service, army, and Garda Síochána.

Unexpectedly, after the Mass, President de Valera and the members of the Executive Council visited the presbytery, where the president presented his colleagues to the archbishop.[42]

On 17 March, De Valera and his ministers attended Mass in state at the Pro-Cathedral and were accompanied from Government Buildings by a cavalry escort wearing full-dress uniform of blue and gold – the same as worn by the escort which accompanied the Papal Legate at the Eucharistic Congress.[43] The display was no doubt a mark of religious respect to the feast day of the national apostle, but it was also, perhaps unconsciously, a sign of the new culture of public display, the era of strong authoritarian leaders, who signified their power and authority by distinctive dress, symbols and other trappings of power.

And as if to silence all doubts about the religious observance of members of the Oireachtas, there was the striking manifestation on 6 April, when the Dáil almost emptied as several parties paired to allow deputies attend the Holy Hour ceremonies requested by the Pope, and again on 22 June, when it was arranged that no division would take place in the Dáil between 7 and 9.30 pm to permit members to take part in the opening of three days of prayer in honour of the anniversary of the International Eucharistic Congress.[44]

Other international events

During 1933, the archbishop was once more linked to international occasions. In June, Dublin was the venue for the British Medical Association. Dr Byrne, as patron and chairperson of a number of Catholic hospitals, found himself in the role of host. With the great success of the garden party for the Papal Legate in mind, he thought of Blackrock as the venue to host a reception for the Medical Association. He had good relations with the Holy Ghost Fathers, and particularly with Fr John Charles McQuaid. His choice of Blackrock met with a ready response.

President de Valera and his entire cabinet attended the reception. The archbishop seems to have received a setback in his health just before the event, but he insisted on attending. A photograph of the occasion shows President de Valera and Fr McQuaid escorting a frail looking Archbishop Byrne to a central area. Subsequently, the archbishop thanked John McQuaid for his 'courteous and tactful assistance'.[51]

However disabled he felt on this occasion, Edward Byrne responded positively a month later to the Fifth Biennial Conference of the World Federation of Education Associations, held in Dublin from 29 July to 4 August 1933. An invitation the previous March from T. J. O'Connell, of the Irish National Teachers' Organisation, was difficult to refuse. As director and organising secretary of the event, he informed Dr Byrne that he and his committee were 'firmly of the opinion that in an international conference of this kind, which will be attended by prominent educationists from all parts of the world, the religious character of our Irish educational systems and their close association with the church should be strongly emphasised, and we believe that this can be most effectively done by having Your Grace's name prominently associated with the conference.' He requested that the archbishop allow his name to appear on the programme and handbook, as patron of the conference.[46] Dr Byrne consented, and T. J. O'Connell was also happy to note on 13 July 'that His Grace will preside at the special conference High Mass on 31 July'.[47]

The widespread sense of closeness between clergy and people that was so marked during the Eucharistic Congress, continued during the remainder of Edward Byrne's episcopate.

Special Tributes
The memory and impact of the great week of nationwide prayer and community, which was reflected in the response of the members of the Dáil a year later, was heightened for the archbishop during 1933 by two further tributes from Pope Pius XI, and by a spontaneous expression of regard from the men of the Pro-Cathedral parish. The Pope, replying to Archbishop Byrne's gift of the *Pictorial Record of the Eucharistic Congress*, expressed thanks and paid tribute to those who contributed to the success of the congress, in particular to the bishops, the priests, the laymen, especially those in high position, but above all to Archbishop Byrne himself, 'who in work, vigilance and direction were the leader and author of all'.[48]

In further commendation, 'those in high position' in the state received also special recognition. President de Valera was received by his Holiness in private audience on 26 May, accorded all the honours due to his position, and was conferred by the Pope with 'the Grand Cross of the Order of Pius in recognition of his work for the Eucharistic Congress'.[49]

Meantime, on 2 April, the archbishop had attended the close of a fortnight's mission for men at the Pro-Cathedral, which was given by the Redemptorist Fathers. 'At the lowest calculation

10,000 men had assembled' during different sessions during the mission. Immediately after the ceremonies, on 2 April,

> The men in their thousands assembled outside the Presbytery to await his Grace, the Archbishop, whose appearance was greeted with loud and prolonged cheering, and amid scenes reminiscent of the great Congress they accompanied his Grace to the Archbishop's House.[50]

As he faced once again years of increasing debility and uncertainty, Archbishop Edward Byrne was warmed by the afterglow of a unique occasion and accomplishment, which built on the great centenary celebration of 1929 and had united the great majority of the Irish people in a common devotion that, for a time, superseded all barriers of history and politics, and in a religious commitment that was to last well beyond his lifetime.

PART III

1934-1940

'A saint is cheerful when it is hard to be cheerful: patient
when it is hard to be patient: he pushes on when he wishes
to stand still: he keeps silent when he wishes to talk: he is
agreeable when he wishes to be disagreeable.'
— *John of London Weekly*, 15 May 1930,
cited in Edward Byrne's notebook of quotations

CHAPTER TWELVE

1934-1935

Hospitals, Education, and Fr J. C. McQuaid.
Social Action, and the Legion of Mary

ADVOCATE FOR CATHOLIC HOSPITALS

At this stage it is appropriate to devote attention to one of Edward Byrne's major concerns, the progress and well-being of Catholic hospitals. This was a concern throughout his episcopate, but especially during the last decade of his life.

A centenary celebration
As Patron, and by charter Chairman, of the boards of Dublin's Catholic hospitals, he presided, on 25 January 1934, at the centenary celebrations of St Vincent's Hospital, 'Ireland's first Catholic hospital', and the first in Ireland to have a children's ward.[1] A telegram was received from Cardinal Pacelli, Vatican Secretary of State, conveying His Holiness's blessing on the Irish Sisters of Charity, the medical staff, nurses, attendants, friends and benefactors of the hospital.

The hospital chapel was filled to capacity for High Mass, presided over by the archbishop, and afterwards the visitors were conducted on an extensive tour of the hospital. The reception to mark the occasion was attended by 1,400 guests, including President de Valera and the Lord Mayor, Alderman Alfred Byrne. A special photograph recording the occasion shows a smiling archbishop standing among the medical staff but looking stooped and frail. The following day, the *Irish Press* paid the following tribute to the hospital:

> The celebration of the centenary of St Vincent's Hospital is one in which the whole nation joins. Not only is the order under whose charge this famous centre of healing is conducted, venerated by the Irish people for its innumerable works of charity, but the institution itself has won the gratitude of every class in the capital, and outside it, the city's poor most of all. Some five per cent of the patients whom it

has relieved and restored to health have been treated without charge.[2]

Appropriately, on the following day, and doubtless with the archbishop's approval, a large number of working class people were entertained to tea in the extensive out-patients department. On the Sunday, 28 January, 'one hundred poor families from the district had a conducted tour of the hospital with its decorations of fairy lights, gigantic palms and silver hangings. They were also entertained to a meal in the out-patients department ..., the menu consisting of beef, ham, mashed potatoes, greens and celery. Music was provided by the Irish Transport Union's Reed and Drum Band.'[3]

The Hollis Street Intervention
The archbishop, by reasons of health or / and inclination, was not a regular attender at hospital board meetings. He usually delegated a senior clergyman to substitute for him. He acknowledged his frequent absence on a memorable occasion in 1931 in relation to Hollis Street Maternity Hospital. A new Master of the hospital was about to be elected. The likely candidate, Andrew Horne, who had been Assistant-Master in 1924-26, was a past student of Belvedere College but, like his father before him, he had taken his medical training at Trinity College, seemingly with encouragement from some of the priests in Belvedere. On 25 July, however, the archbishop, intervened in the selection process.

In a letter to Dr Denis Coffey, President of University College Dublin, who chaired the sub-committee responsible for defining the terms and conditions of the mastership, Dr Byrne wrote:

It has, I believe, been stated in several quarters that I am not at all interested in the affairs of Hollis Street Hospital. This is a strange distortion of the real facts. It is not so long ago as to be out of memory that I gave very substantial financial proof of my interest in the hospital. [In 1927 he gave £1,000 to the building fund] By charter I am chairman of the Board of Governors. It is true that I do not attend ordinary meetings of the Board, composed as it is of members quite competent to manage the affairs of the hospital. I should not intervene now if an important principle were not at stake.

He went on to point out that the bishops of Ireland had over and over again warned parents that in allowing their children to attend Trinity College they were endangering their faith. 'Trinity College is now, as it always has been, Protestant in government, tradition and atmosphere.' 'Even so lately as last Lent', he continued, 'I repeated the warning and called attention to the encyclical of the Holy Father on Catholic Education', and 'now I understand that I am represented as being prepared to nullify my own episcopal admonition by lending my countenance to the elevation of a graduate of Trinity College as Master of Hollis Street.' He could not be indifferent in the matter and had to put aside personal feelings before his strict duty as archbishop of the diocese. Hence, it would be little short of scandal, in his view, if he kept silent in the circumstance and allowed it to be rumoured about, as he understood it had been rumoured, that he was prepared for personal reasons to connive at the election of a Trinity man when there are so many qualified National University men to be found.

Shortly after this, Andrew Horne withdrew his application and one of his staunchest supporters, the secretary to the Board of Governors, Henry Lynch, resigned. Fortunately for the hospital, the candidate subsequently chosen as the new Master, Dr John Cunningham, proved to be an outstanding choice. 'His mastership, which was extended by a special Act of the Oireachtas to ten years, was to prove one of the turning points in the development of the modern hospital.'[4]

As the author of the centenary history of the hospital observed, the archbishop felt the pull of 'personal feelings' and 'personal reasons' but was forced to take sides by 'larger issues of ecclesiastical and educated politics'.[5]

Primacy of religious issues and children's hospitals
Rivalry between Trinity College and University College Dublin, especially in the medical field, was still very strong in the 1930s, and was linked to both religion and culture. Trinity was still seen as the bastion of Protestantism and the bearer of a unionist tradition. The memory and fear of proselytism was an abiding presence among Dublin's Catholic clergy, and it strongly influenced Archbishop Byrne's attitude towards Trinity College and, indeed, to any question of amalgamation where he considered the religious faith of Catholics likely to be endangered.

A conspicuous example of this outlook appeared in December 1935 in relation to a proposed amalgamation of St Ultan's

Children's Hospital with the National Children's Hospital, Harcourt Street, Dublin.

Learning of his opposition 'on Catholic grounds', the board of St Ultan's requested an interview with him.[6] He met the deputation from the board, and presented them with a typed presentation of the grounds of his opposition. This provided a clear and trenchant indication of his views. 'I oppose this amalgamation on religious principles solely. I consider that in such a united institution the Faith of Catholic children (99% of the total treated) would not be safe. The Faith of Catholic children is of more importance in the eyes of the Catholic Church than any other thing in the world.' The amalgamation would create a virtual monopoly in the medical treatment of children in the South side of the city. This monopoly was to be conceded to a body whose attitude to the Catholic viewpoint would be at least suspect and he would fear even hostile. Then, having given examples of hostility in the past, and the many grounds for disagreement on moral issues, he insisted: 'Clearly, the atmosphere of the amalgamated institution would be overwhelmingly non-Catholic and in such an institution Catholic children (who would form 99% of the patients) would find themselves in a predominantly non-Catholic atmosphere. To this I will never consent.'[7]

Crumlin Children's Hospital
The archbishop thanked the Board of St Ultans for their communications, but remained adamant. He was convinced of the need for an independent Catholic hospital for children, and was concerned at the government's tendency to amalgamate hospitals irrespective of religion. In 1937 he bought 15 acres in Crumlin as a site for the proposed hospital; and on 22 January 1938 he wrote to the city manager, Mr Heman, on the importance of having a children's hospital for Catholics residing on the South side of the city. 'This grievance will become increasingly greater as time passes by reason of the vast areas taken over by the corporation for housing purposes.'[8] The city manager was well disposed to the proposal and suggested that His Grace send for the Lord Mayor and explain to him the need for a children's hospital.[9] By 21 January 1938, Fr John McQuaid was able to inform the archbishop that the Housing Sub-Committee of the Corporation had accepted and recommended to the General Council of the

Corporation for final acceptance, the Crumlin site of 15 acres.[10] Very wisely, Dr Byrne had delegated negotiating powers to a very able committee consisting of Fr John Charles McQuaid, from Blackrock College, Dr Stafford-Johnson (Master of the Irish Medical Guild of St Luke), and Mgr Michael Cronin, ably assisted by solicitor Arthur Cox. McQuaid seems to have been the chairman. He and Cronin reported back regularly to the archbishop, who took an active interest in all developments. The commitment of the committee resulted in McQuaid informing the archbishop on 14 March 1939 that 'I have just been notified by Mr Doran (the Minister's secretary) that the Minister (Sean T. Ó Ceallaigh) had given formal sanction for the Catholic Children's Hospital of 125 beds.[11] Even in his final illness, Edward Byrne responded to the need of his negotiating committee. On 16 January 1940, McQuaid wrote to him that he was pleased to learn from Fr O'Donnell that his strength was maintaining itself, and he then explained that the situation about the Children's Hospital was favourable. Mr de Valera was keen for the building to begin soon. He, McQuaid, believed that the best way to expedite matters was that the four trustees, in whose names the ground had been purchased, should now act as the authorised body with whom an agreement can be made. Two days later he acknowledged a letter from Fr Dunne notifying him 'of His Grace's assent to his proposal'.[12]

Struggle for independence

The archbishop fought strongly throughout the 1930s for the Catholic hospitals, using his quiet influence to obtain fair play for them in the distribution of funds from the Irish Hospitals Sweepstakes and in relation to the Irish Hospitals Commission and a hospitals system that was two-thirds controlled by non-Catholics.[13] Convinced of the greater efficiency, economy and flexibility of hospitals under the management of religious communities, he insisted on independence of state control in the running of the hospitals. This last involved him in a long struggle with the government on behalf of St Vincent's Hospital.

In 1934, Rev Mother Ricci O'Connor, the Superior General of the Sisters of Charity, wrote to the archbishop regarding plans for a new, more extensive St Vincent's Hospital. She sought his permission to use the congregation's funds to purchase land at Elm Park for the purpose. The development was encouraged by the Hospital Sweeps Committee. On 9 July 1934, she thanked him for his 'whole-hearted permission for the scheme of our new hospital and his blessings on it, which gave us great courage and confidence in the undertaking'.[14] Subsequently, in connection with the Sisters' projected private and general hospital at Elm Park, there were difficulties with the Department of Local Government and Public Health as regards inspection and control. The Sisters had no difficulty about inspection, but they sought independence in management such as they enjoyed in Linden Nursing Home and Hospital, Rathdrum, Stillorgan, Co Dublin.

On 2 May 1939, Archbishop Byrne sent an instruction to next Superior General, Rev Mother Mary Bernard Carew:

> It has struck me that it is essential that the Sisters of Charity should not begin to build their new Hospital until the question of inspection and control is satisfactorily settled. I have every confidence that Mr O'Kelly, the Minister, will re-consider the viewpoint of the Nuns and will finally come to a settlement of the question on the lines of what we call the Linden agreement. In the meantime, I believe that you ought not begin to build at Elm Park.[15]

Mr O'Kelly was replaced, however, by Mr P. J. Ruttledge, who, influenced by his department, officials referred to 'the unreasonable attitude of the nuns'. By 17 November, Arthur Cox thought that he had succeeded in getting the minister to see that the nuns were 'not so unreasonable as he had at first thought', but he feared that his officials might still succeed in enforcing their point of view upon him.[16]

The stalemate continued after Dr Byrne's lifetime

A further management issue arose in respect of the establishment of a 'Bed Bureau' by the government. Writing to Bishop Wall, on 27 April 1940, after the archbishop's death, Mother Carew explained: 'The proposed new St Vincent's Hospital scheme has been held up under the direction of the late Archbishop until an agreement was signed that there would be no interference in the control and management of the Hospital. I enclose a copy of a letter on this subject received from His Grace a year ago'. Continuing, she referred to the government Bill relating to 'Bed Bureaus'. All the hospitals, she explained, were in

full agreement that there was need for the establishment of a
Bed Bureau. They had proposed a scheme to meet the need, but
it had been ignored. Instead, a special Bill had been introduced,
the main point of which was highly controversial, and in its
present form, sought to bring practically all hospitals under
complete governmental control.

'While this scheme was being discussed', the Mother General
insisted, 'His Grace, the late Most Reverend Dr Byrne, was actively interested and was particularly anxious that any scheme
evolved should not in anyway interfere with our management
and control of our Catholic hospitals.'[17]

Archbishop Byrne's concerns extended also to smaller hospitals, such as St Anne's Hospital, Northbrook Road, which
catered for skin and cancer patients. This was run by the
Daughters of Charity. Feeling in danger, in 1926, of being placed
under lay management by the Hospitals Commission, they appealed to the archbishop. Subsequently, on 2 December 1927,
they expressed sincere gratitude for the great interest he had
taken in their hospital since its foundation, and especially for
the efforts he had successfully made to save it from the recent
danger that threatened it.[18]

Despite his strong stance for Catholic hospitals, the archbishop
maintained urbane relations with representatives of non-
Catholic institutions, and his papers indicate appreciative
recognition from such bodies. He readily encouraged the
Catholic hospitals to make common cause with all other hospitals when issues of independence, such as that of the 'Bed
Bureaus', were involved. Given his precarious health, he relied
increasingly during the 1930s on the special committee, led by
John Charles McQuaid.

The Co-operation of Fr McQuaid

Fr McQuaid, a member of the Holy Ghost Congregation, combined seemingly endless energy with very considerable ability,
zeal, charm and ambition. As well as being headmaster of
Blackrock College and chairman of the Catholic Headmasters'
Association, he established links with key figures in various
Catholic Action organisations, was interested in better housing
conditions for the poor, opposed to any advance in Protestant
influence, and was an adviser to prominent members of the
medical professions and friendly with officials of the National

Teachers Organisation and of the Association of Secondary Teachers. He sought to achieve the greater good by establishing a rapport with people in influential positions. This was obvious in his cultivation of the friendship of leaders of the state, Mr de Valera, and of the church, Dr Byrne. To this end he was prepared to devote time, skill and energy; and was also ready, it would seem, to disclose to De Valera matters concerning the archbishop's business. His friendship with the head of government was sufficiently close to allow him to make numerous suggestions on a wide range of issues, including medical matters; and also to his disclosing, in late 1934, confidential documents – 'for your own eyes' – on pending negotiations between Archbishop Byrne and Minister Sean T. Ó Ceallaigh following 'a very secret breakthrough' in attempts to get St Vincent's and the Mater hospitals to form 'a proper' – that is Catholic – medical teaching school with Hollis Street, in conjunction with University College Dublin's medical school.[19]

Fr McQuaid in educational matters
In educational matters, John McQuaid was very industrious on behalf of the archbishop. When Dr Byrne was invited, on 9 March 1934, by T. J. O'Connell, director and organising secretary of the World Federation of Education, to allow his name appear as patron of the international conference of the Federation to be held in Dublin, and subsequently to preside at High Mass on 31 July, he contacted Fr McQuaid and asked him to examine the history and philosophy of the Federation. McQuaid did so, and also contacted O'Connell and Joseph O'Neill, secretary of the Department of Education, with reference to any 'possible danger'. Subsequently, he was able to assure the archbishop that there was little fear of anti-Catholic views being propounded. The World Federation Conference proved a success, and Dr Byrne was happy to preside at the special High Mass.

Earlier, McQuaid had been in communication with Edward Byrne on a more important matter. In October 1933, the executive of the National Teachers Organisation issued an invitation to several educational associations with a view to forming a federation or joint council that would serve as an advisory body to the Minister for Education. One of the bodies invited was the Catholic Headmasters' Association, of which McQuaid was chairman. He perceived objections to the proposed council: that it was too unwieldy, that two successive ministers for education had rejected the idea of a council, that it gave too much power to undenominational lay organisations and, as he informed the archbishop in a memorandum, there was 'a certain danger of the commanding position being seized by these lay organisations at least in the eye of the public, with consequent division and misrepresentation'.[20] The papal and episcopal attitude in the 1920s and 1930s, it will be recalled, was to be chary of lay organisations that did not have a mandate from the local bishop.

On discussing the matter with Dr Byrne, the archbishop suggested that he contact Francis O'Reilly of the CTSI. The latter recommended that he visit the Archbishop of Cashel, John Harty, and his Eminence Cardinal Joseph MacRory. The cardinal approved the scheme he had devised and asked him to prepare a memorandum for the hierarchy. His Grace of Cashel also approved. On 16 June 1934, McQuaid wrote to Archbishop Byrne thanking him 'very gratefully for the encouragement and assistance' which enabled him 'to deal with the proposed federation' or council.[21] His scheme proved effective. He managed to persuade the secretary of ASTI, T. J. Burke, and T. J. O'Connell of the INTO, that it was better not to proceed with the federation, and he did so without alienating the respective bodies.[22]

By October 1934, the 'danger' was past. At the October meeting of the hierarchy, Archbishop Byrne praised Fr J. C. McQuaid for handling 'a very difficult situation with great tact and skill'. Cardinal MacRory expressed the hope that the hierarchy would hear no more about the federation.[23]

John McQuaid always displayed deference to the archbishop and was careful to express thanks for any favours granted him. Thus, on 5 April 1934, while informing Dr Byrne about the great success of the Blackrock Boys Holy Year pilgrimage to Rome, he added: 'I feel I owe Your Grace a special word of thanks for the extraordinary help that the letter of recommendation afforded. The first thing the Holy Father mentioned was the Garden Party of the Congress, on which Your Grace had laid stress in your letter. The entire community joins with me in returning heartfelt thanks to Your Grace.'[24]

Effects of Illness and some public functions
Early in 1934, Edward Byrne offered some indication of how his illness affected him. Bishop Mageean, Down and Connor, wrote

to him on 4 and 8 February expressing high regard and inviting him to preside at the CTSI conference in Belfast on 24- 26 June. The draft reply from the archbishop, on 16 February, expressed his regrets. He was sorry that he would not be able to do what was asked. He did not feel able for what would be a trial to him. 'My health is all right usually, and until some engagement turns up I am quite well. But when I look forward to anything in particular to do I am nearly always knocked up. I know you will understand and forgive my absence from your grand ceremonial.'

Dr Mageean thanked him for his kind letter, which reconciled him to His Grace's absence. He fully appreciated his reasons for not coming.[25]

Attending many functions
Edward Byrne, nevertheless, proved able to fulfill a spread of familiar public duties within his own archdiocese. His Lenten pastoral appeared with the other pastoral letters on 4 February. He emphasised the evil of intemperance and its increase among young people of both sexes. He deplored the custom of bringing alcoholic drink into dance halls and observed that 'pleasure' had become as a god before which every knee must bend; and in reference to communism, he quoted the Pope's encyclical on Social Order which declared communism to be 'blasphemously atheistic'. He attended the diocesan priests' retreat, and was pleased to be able to congratulate his clergy on the whole-hearted way they had taken up the work of parochial visitation;[26] and on 2 October he presided, with some discomfort, at a two hour ceremony marking the first general council, since the Reformation, of the Irish Association of the Knights of Malta, which was held at St Mary's Church, Haddington Road.[27]

Whatever the time or distress involved, he continued to make a steadfast effort to attend special occasions at local churches. He blessed the corner stones of new churches at Foxrock, Co Dublin and Rathmore, Co Kildare, blessed new extensions in Inchicore and Milltown, and opened a new church at Crumlin and a temporary place of worship for a new parish at Harold's Cross. At this last, crowds lined the roads to greet him and the trumpeters of a troop of Boy Scouts blew a fanfare.[28]

On 7 March 1935, he had joined with the Nuncio Apostolic, Paschal Robinson, at Dún Laoghaire to see off the National Holy Year Pilgrimage to Rome, which was composed of 1,600 pil-

grims, led by Cardinal MacRory. On a bitterly cold evening a
week later, he and the Nuncio were once more on Dún
Laoghaire pier, this time accompanied by President de Valera
and Sean T. Ó Ceallaigh, to welcome back the pilgrims. 'As the
cardinal stepped ashore, troops presented arms and the army
band struck up the Pope's Hymn and then the National
Anthem. The party drove into Dublin to Archbishop's House escorted by troops and outriders through mile after mile of cheering, flag-waving people.' Archbishop Byrne was host that night
to an excited but exhausted cardinal, who departed next day to an
even more dramatic welcome in the archdiocese of Armagh.[29]
Two days later, St Patrick's Day, as if to defy the grim economic
situation, President de Valera and his ministers drove in state
from Government Buildings to the Pro-Cathedral 'accompanied
by outriders in saffron and blue uniforms and escorted by Free
State cavalry'.[30]

A very different scene was played out in Belfast some
months later, as Catholics bore the brunt of sectarian violence.
Writing to Archbishop Byrne on 5 August 1935, Bishop
Mageean thanked him for his 'very generous cheque of £250 for
the Catholic victims of the Belfast outrages'. 'The number of
evicted families that we have been already able to check', the
bishop explained, 'is 434, embracing 1,903 individuals, and the
list is not yet complete. A still greater problem for us is the intimidation of the Catholic workers and the giving of their jobs to
others. This intimidation, on a most extensive and systematic
scale is still proceeding, and it would seem that their aim is to
exterminate the Catholics.'[31]

Key Catholic Action organisations
In that grim context, the hardships south of the border seemed
more bearable. Helping the people to cope materially and spiritually was part of the on-going work of some of the key Catholic
Action organisations. To the forefront, of course, in dealing with
economic needs was the St Vincent de Paul Society, to which the
archbishop contributed generously once again in November
1935.[32] Also prominent at various levels throughout the country, as has been noted, were the Catholic Truth Society and the
Catholic Young Men's Society. This last, through its national
council, at the beginning of 1934 petitioned the archbishop to
appoint a member of the clergy as director-general for the whole

Society. On 1 February, Dr Byrne appointed one of his vicars-general, Mgr Waters as director-general of the CYMS.[33] Under Waters' guidance new branches were formed, and by February 1935 branches were in the process of formation all over Ireland. The aims of the organisation were clarified and formulated: 'The CYMS existed to bring Catholic laymen in an organised body into the work of the Lay Apostolate, and to train them for Catholic Action, and also to promote the spiritual, intellectual, social and physical welfare of its members. It was not antagonistic to their fellow-countrymen of different religious views, but the Society would endeavour to counteract the activities of those who would question the authority of the Irish Hierarchy to guide the Catholic people in matters relating to Faith and morals.' 'The Society had no politics, and did not interfere in anyway with the views of its members in that respect; but no party questions were allowed to be discussed in the branches.'[34]

These three organisations had a special significance, as manifested in 1929 and in 1932, because they were active throughout the country. The impact of the various forces of Catholic Action was highlighted in the massive CTSI Congress at Kilkenny in late June 1935. Over the days of the Congress the average daily attendance at the various meetings and ceremonies was estimated at 35,000.[35] On 30 June, the final day of the Congress, 20,000 people, twice the population of Kilkenny city, gathered on the lawns of St Kieran's College for the final ceremonies. 'Eleven special trains brought thousands from Dublin, Belfast, Ballybrophy, Kildare, New Ross, Waterford, Wexford, Limerick, and towns along those routes. Hundreds walked in from villages and hamlets around Kilkenny.'[36] The Pontifical High Mass, celebrated by Dr O'Doherty, Bishop of Galway, was broadcast. Cardinal MacRory presided. The Archbishop of Dublin attended, and he and the Archbishop of Cashel and 16 bishops knelt on footstools. The event was given wide publicity with photographs in all the daily, weekly and provincial newspapers.[37] That Archbishop Byrne was present testified to the importance attached to the CTSI and to Catholic Action generally; and if, as suggested, he knelt throughout the long ceremony, this was further testimony to the importance of the occasion as well as to the strange nature of his illness.

THE LEGION OF MARY AND THE ARCHBISHOP

One Irish Catholic Action body seldom mentioned in Archbishop Byrne's records, the Legion of Mary, was active both at home and abroad well before 1935. It only received his formal approval in that year. The Legion's importance, and the archbishop's alleged hostility to it for so many years, merits particular consideration. Unfortunately, most of the information available to the historian comes from one source, the Legion.

The Criticism and the Context

Archbishop Byrne has frequently been criticised for his reluctance to support and formally recognise the Legion, and linked to that is the sweeping implication that he was generally hostile to lay organisations. The grounds for this view seem to be based entirely on his attitude to a clash that arose in the scout movement for girls. The disagreement occurred between the Catholic Girl Guides of Ireland, founded by Margaret Loftus and Brigid Ward, and an organisation founded by Catholic clergy. The archbishop tried vainly to make peace between them, and then set up a new organisation under a Fr Clarke. The two other bodies disbanded. The women, however, appealed to the Pope. They were highly praised for their work but instructed to obey the archbishop.[38] The papal reply reflected the ecclesial culture in which Catholic Action was expected to operate. 'Catholic Action', as indicated earlier, was confined to designated lay groups mandated by the local bishop. The mandate was essential. The lay groups were seen as tightly structured organisations serving as an arm of the hierarchy in lay life. This perception is crucial to an understanding of the clergy/lay relationship in Ireland during the first decades of Irish independence.[39] It is essential to an understanding of Archbishop Byrne's relationship with the Legion of Mary and its founder, Frank Duff.

Mr Duff had been active since 1913 in socio/religious activities, especially as a member of the St Vincent de Paul Society. Employed in the civil service, he and some fellow-employees picketed, on occasion, centres of proselytism; and, with the help of some women friends, he also sought to encourage women involved in prostitution to start a new way of life. As an aid to that end, he managed to open a house at 76 Harcourt Street, Dublin, where those women seeking to break away from prostitution could stay under the supervision of women appointed by Duff.

After this initiative was established, he then sought the approval of Mgr Fitzpatrick, the parish priest of the area. Some two years later, the secretary to the archbishop sent £100 from His Grace to the support of the work.[40]

Gradually people gathered around Frank Duff. He was a man of determined zeal and considerable charm, who was deeply religious, given to much prayer and daily attendance at Mass, but in no way overtly pious. His work commenced at parish level. Always he sought, but some times belatedly, the permission of the local parish priest for the work, and if this was not forthcoming the work was moved to another parish where it was welcome.

The enthusiasm of Duff and his followers led to their activities expanding quickly, and this made it desirable to formulate rules, aims and a constitution. This was done, and the resultant organisation looked to classical Roman structures for its names, legion and praesidia. It was destined to spread to a number of countries within a decade: a circumstance that added to Duff's conviction that the Legion was inspired and blessed by God. His conviction, in turn, helped to inspire, challenge, and fire the zeal of many young adults.

One of the areas where the Legion operated in its early years was on the north side of the city, a location which Duff called Bentley Place. It was close by the Pro-Cathedral and included Montgomery Street, Railway Street, Foley Street, Purdon Street, Elliot Place, and Faithful Place, the remnant of what was known as Nighttown, or the 'Monto', which featured in the writings of Joyce, Gogarty, and O'Casey.[41] It was a region where, for as long as could be remembered under British rule, the police had tolerated open brothels on a scale that was said to be unequalled anywhere in Europe, and where drink was available to all hours of the night. Frank Duff determined to make a change. For him sin was the greatest evil in the world; it put eternal souls at stake; therefore something would have to be done to combat it where, as in the Bentley Place area, it presented itself so arrogantly.

Although the trade had shrunk considerably with the evacuation of the British army and administration, Duff calculated that, among the ruins and tenements, there might still be 200 girls involved.[42] He, and a close follower, Josephine Plunkett, established contact with everybody in Bentley Place, girls, 'bullies' who controlled the girls and the behaviour of clients, workers in the brothels, drink-vendors, money lenders, visitors who came for drink or sex, and a whole assortment of hangers-on.[43]

Opposition to the Legion

Meantime, resistance to the Legion became evident among a number of parish priests. Its success was seen as likely to take from the membership of women's sodalities in parish churches, and there was resentment at the independence and growing influence of Frank Duff and his lay organisation. To legionaries it appeared that the Vincent de Paul Society was a long established lay organisation, which had come from abroad and had a saint as its founder and, as such, was accepted and appreciated, whereas the Legion had the hindrance of being founded by a local Dubliner who, besides, was vocal, independent, single-minded, and assertively confident that he had a divine calling to undertake the apostolate of the Legion. The resentment and suspicion of him was communicated to the archbishop's secretaries and to vicars-general such as the Revds Wall, Waters and Cronin, who had the ear of Dr Byrne.

Without consulting the parish priest

The attitude of Dr Byrne towards the Legion seems to have been adversely affected by an initiative taken by Duff in 1925. He and his close colleague, Josephine Plunkett, planned and worked to close down 'the Monto' or Bentley Place area. Serious discussions were conducted with the bosses of the brothels, who were known individually to Duff. Some responded to the pressure and closed down. More and more girls, as a result, made their way to Sancta Maria, the Legion's hostel. A residue, however, refused to budge, pointing to their debts and how hard it would be to live if they went out of business. By the beginning of 1925, Duff estimated that there were only 40 prostitutes in Bentley Place. He determined on a final assault. In February 1925, he enlisted the aid of three Jesuits, who were conducting the Lenten mission at the Pro-Cathedral. He was a frequenter of the Jesuit retreat houses at Milltown Park and Rathfarnham Castle, and knew many of the order. The three priests preaching at the Pro-Cathedral were Ernest Mackey, a well-known preacher and retreat director, Daniel Roche, less well-known, and Richard Devane who, as noticed earlier, was a more public figure with a strong social and moral conscience.

During the mission, the Jesuits launched a novena of prayer to the Sacred Heart in reparation for this great social evil, and in petition for its extirpation.[44] With the approval of the administrator of the Pro-Cathedral, Mgr Fitzpatrick, they joined Duff in meeting the remaining brothel owners and extracting from them promises to shut down their establishments. The owners agreed to close on the Tuesday following the conclusion of the Pro-Cathedral mission, after which the Legion planned to turn over the vacant houses to those in need of accommodation in the city.

On the day agreed, two brothels remained open. Duff and one of the Jesuit missioners approached the head of the Dublin Metropolitan Police, General W. R. E. Murphy, who agreed to shut down what remained of 'the Monto'. Shortly afterwards, the police arrived at night in a fleet of lorries, raided the premises and arrested 45 women, 12 pimps, some 50 customers, and the recalcitrant bosses.[45]

The occurrence was given much space in the newspapers the following day, though the reason for the action was not understood nor explained. A common view was that the purpose of the raid was to capture prominent civil war figures 'on the run', who were said to be sheltering there. That day, fifteen girls came to the hostel, in ones and twos, most of the women having been released into the custody of the Legion of Mary. Those who came to the Sancta Maria hostel were immediately given a retreat as a preliminary to being taken into residence. 'Thus, Bentley Place ended, and to mark its end Frank Duff went down there, drove a spike in a high wall, and hung on it a huge crucifix.'[46]

Criticism. The view of the Archbishop
The entire action did not go without criticism. It was commented that the operation would diffuse an evil that had hitherto been confined to one area, and Duff was criticised for involving priests like Frs Creedon and Toher in a movement that was undermining the clergy's responsibility for the care of souls.[47]

The archbishop, for his part, seems to have viewed the whole operation as unwise and excessive. He had served for years in the Pro-Cathedral and knew and respected the people of the parish. The priests had endeavoured to adapt to the reality of the situation, even to having an understanding with the proprietors of the red light area that if any customer or other person became gravely ill a priest would be called. He would stand at the door of the premises and attend to the sick person from there.[48] As archbishop, Edward Byrne, was the actual parish priest of the Pro-Cathedral parish, and he had not been consulted. The adverse reports against the Legion seemed confirmed. The action appeared extreme and high-handed, an indication of the Legion's exalted idea of itself and of its role, and of a cavalier attitude towards clergy and ecclesiastical authority. The archbishop conveyed his displeasure to Mgr Fitzpatrick for his participation in the venture.[49] Thereafter, he and a number of his colleagues in the diocese, kept Frank Duff and the Legion at a distance.

In self-defence

This became a serious issue for Duff in 1928. Previously, he had assumed that he had at least the archbishop's tacit approval. It came as a rude shock, therefore, in March 1928, when the superior of the Capuchins in Church Street informed him that he had absolutely reliable information that His Grace disapproved of the Legion. Duff, forthwith, endeavoured to arrange a meeting with Dr Byrne to clarify the situation. This failing, he sent a long rather aggrieved letter of eight foolscap pages to the archbishop on 24 November 1928.[50]

He commenced his communication by explaining that he had learned from a multitude of channels that for a long time past His Grace had regarded him with considerable disfavour. He was conscious of nothing to merit this, and he had made a number of attempts, without success, to meet His Grace and remove any misunderstanding there might be. Then, dealing with likely grounds for misunderstanding, he referred to a petition for a procession of the Blessed Sacrament, which the archbishop had refused. He explained that he had duly obtained the sanction of a vicar-general of the diocese before taking any action and he had been assisted in formulating the petition by Sir Joseph Glynn, president of the St Vincent de Paul Society. Once he had received His Grace's letter of disapproval, he had at once stopped all further proceedings. 'I can discern not the slightest degree of fault on my part', he declared, 'yet the episode has been treasured up and used against me ever since.' Next, he pointed out that it was alleged that the work at 76 Harcourt Street was carried on without authority. That was not so. Mgr Fitzpatrick gave very full sanctions and enthusiastic encouragement and he, Duff, had seen a letter from his Grace's secretary, about two years after the start of the venture, enclosing £100 in aid of the work.

After this start, Duff outlined the history of the Legion's work, and emphasised that he had heard from his friend Mathew Redmond Lalor that he had informed the archbishop about the activities of the Legion, and from this he, Duff, had assumed the archbishop approved of their work. 'Thus encouraged (as was believed), the association' had 'extended in a manner which appears to indicate that it is destined before long to exist in every quarter of the globe'. But always, before starting anywhere, parochial sanction had invariably been sought. He denied the charge that the Legion had taken over 'branches of the Ladies' Association of Charity of St Vincent de Paul', and stated bluntly that if formal sanction was not sought at times it was because 'all concerned were afraid to approach Your Grace' because reports everywhere current indicated that you had 'become most averse to me and to anything with which I was connected'.

On the breaking up of the Elliott Place (Bentley Place) area, which had been 'the subject of another charge of unwarranted action', Duff pointed out that full sanction for every step taken was obtained from the two administrators who officiated in the parish during that fateful month. He then dealt with the archbishop's alleged opposition to the Morning Star hostel for homeless men, and set about dealing with accusations of his undertaking the building without the archbishop's approval, and of applying to the Legion money promised to the Society of St Vincent de Paul. He denied any fault on his part, and claimed he was supported by the testimony of persons well-known as responsible and spiritual. He had consistently been condemned unheard. After fifteen years of unremitting labour in the diocese not one kind word had ever come his way from the archbishop.

Duff closed his lengthy case in forceful terms. The facts of the situation 'as they present themselves to me, do not seem to establish a case against me, in respect of all the above years of work, of the slightest indiscretion even, still less of anything grave. I feel that I have given ample grounds for the revision of an attitude towards me which is stinging to myself, destructive of my work, and being widely spoken of; and I humbly implore Your Grace to reconsider it.'

Esteem but not approval

Over a fortnight later, on 11 December, Duff responded warmly to a message from the archbishop, again through a third party:

> I thank Your Grace for the gracious message to me of which you have made Sir Joseph Glynn the bearer, and which means everything to me.
>
> In return, I beg to assure Your Grace that I will be in the future, as I have wished to be in the past, ever at your Grace's complete disposal.

On this letter in the archives, however, there is the brief and significant comment (by Byrne's secretary?): 'Reply to a message of personal esteem but not signifying approval of all his schemes.'[51]

Impatient indiscretions

From Frank Duff's long letter it is clear that he saw himself as without fault in his relations with the archbishop, and that all criticism of himself and the Legion was unfounded. In discussions with his friends he spoke frequently of 'persecution', of a campaign being waged against him by the diocese.[52] His long letter demonstrated his assertive independence, rather precipitous action, and a certain impatience with authority. He might not proceed against the will of a parish priest, but that did not stop him railing against the priest. At Legion meetings, besides, priests had a very subsidiary role. This fact, together with Duff's attitude and impatient comments, made its way back to the archbishop; and, not surprisingly in the prevailing ecclesiastical culture, Duff was viewed by at least some of His Grace's closest advisers as anti-clerical.[53]

Using contacts to expand

Meantime, Duff availed of his friendships and political contacts to further the work and influence of the Legion. When going to meet with Cardinal Bourne of Westminster he had a glowing letter of introduction from W. T. Cosgrave, President of the executive council of the Irish Free State. He was welcomed by the cardinal, and through him the Legion became known to Cardinal Verdier of Paris. The Archbishop of Glasgow also welcomed Duff and his organisation. In Ireland, he was strongly supported by Bishop Morrisroe of Achonry, and he found a powerful ally in Dr Joseph Mac Rory, Bishop of Down and Connor, whose diocese included the city of Belfast. In 1928, when Dr MacRory was appointed to Armagh as Primate of All Ireland, and subsequently was made cardinal, Frank Duff was greatly pleased; all the more so because of the strong rumour that the 'red hat' would go to Dublin, to Dr Byrne, which would have been, in Duff's view, 'a dreadful commentary on the part merit played in these appointments'.[54]

Feeling 'persecuted'

Despite Archbishop Byrne's 'gracious message' in December 1928, his first response the following year was to refuse a request. Duff had written asking permission to hold a one-day retreat in the Morning Star hostel for the 'derelict men' there. One of the conditions for the opening of the hostel had been that retreats not be held on the premises. About 25 February 1929, Duff received a reply, thanking him for his 'nice letter' but regretting that for various reasons the archbishop could not see his way to allow the requested retreat. There were retreats going on in most of the city churches, which should provide excellently for the needs of the men.[55] Duff replied at some length on that date making the case that the men in the Morning Star were a very mixed body of men, some of them had spent time in prison for serious crime, while others were 'most respectable types of men, whom pure misfortune had brought down'. The usual retreat in the churches would not meet their needs, and many would not attend. The possibility of sending them to the Jesuit retreat house at Rathfarnham had been explored, but the request had been turned down; hence, the need and importance of a retreat in the hostel itself. He concluded with a further appeal for an open expression of support from His Grace.[56]

The Legion had been associated with catering for women. Now, in enlisting male members of the Legion to run the Morning Star and even start retreats there, the Legion was moving more openly into the apostolate for men and encroaching further into the work conducted by the parish churches and the religious orders. Increased criticism seemed to find a ready welcome among some of the archbishop's advisers and secretaries.

In March 1929, Fr Creedon, who had been a moving spirit in the early years of the Legion, especially in the hostel in Harcourt Street, was moved from Francis Street, in the city, to Dalkey, a

suburb eight miles from the city centre. It was seen as a further
sign of 'persecution'. The refusal of the Jesuit retreat house in
Rathfarnham, which had a long association with retreats for
workingmen, heralded an even greater blow. Frank Duff, as
noticed earlier, had long frequented Jesuit retreat houses at
Rathfarnham and Milltown Park and had Jesuit friends; now
those houses were closed to Legion activities. Was this in response to a sense of disapproval on the part of the archdiocese?
It may have had some influence, but the main impetus, in the
case of the Jesuit houses, seems to have come from the General-
Superior in Rome. The expansion of the Legion Mary, and its
rather confined and rigid spirituality, was seen as a danger to
the international Jesuit sodalities of Our Lady for men and
women, and consequently Jesuits were instructed not to promote it. It was an unfortunate, short-sighted decision and instruction. The Legion continued to expand. The sodalities, at
least in Ireland, remained largely pious associations with little
direct impact on social ills or public morality.

If Mr Duff needed confirmation of his theory of 'persecution'
he would probably have found it in a letter of Mgr Francis J.
Wall to the archbishop on 15 April 1929. 'By the way, Mr
O'Reilly of the CTSI telephoned today to say that the 'Catholic
branch of Girls' Club' proves not to be that of 19 Rutland Square
but of the 'Legion of Mary', who assumed the title to the conster-
nation of the Rutland Square people. This means more dodging
of the 'clique' that runs the 'Legion of Mary'. However, Mr
O'Reilly tells me that Mr Duff has seen him and has withdrawn
his flag day. My answer to Mr O'R. was that I had no knowledge
the 'Legion of Mary' had any leave for such a collection (In fact, I
have no knowledge of their being sanctioned as a body). When I
see Mr. O'R. I will know more on '*latet anguis in herba*' (the lurk-
ing snake in the grass), if use were to be made of the members of
the Legion to do his collecting. They might then plead for further patronage on account of services rendered.'[57]

The Handbook issue

A plea for 'further patronage' came on 2 October 1929. It was occasioned by the very expansion of the Legion outside Ireland
and the question of a handbook. The expansion called for
greater cohesion and a basic uniformity. This was provided by a
handbook that laid down structures, the manner of conducting

meetings, prayers to be said, and rules to be followed. In 1926 the archbishop had sent a message of appreciation and esteem through Sir Joseph Glynn, adding that the handbook was being sympathetically examined with a view to formal approval. Duff was aware that His Grace thought it too philosophical and too long. It was then 28 pages, it later stretched to 290! He was optimistic, following the message, but time passed and there was no sign of formal approval. He decided to go ahead with the printing. The handbook could be used outside Dublin. By October 1929, there was still no word from Archbishop's House. Duff wrote to Dr Byrne that the Legion was now at work not only in Belfast, Cork, Waterford and Sligo, as well as in Dublin, but in London and four other cities in England and four cities in Scotland, and in each location he had met with and been supported by the archbishops and bishops of these areas. A grave obstacle to progress, however, was the absence of an *imprimatur* or mark of approval on the handbook, the draft of which Dr Byrne had under examination. The absence had led local priests to question whether the Legion was approved, and it could have 'fatal consequences' for the organisation's foreign development.

Moving on, he requested the archbishop to take the initiative at the forthcoming meeting of the bishops in bringing the Legion before them for their united endorsement. 'There seems little doubt', he concluded enthusiastically, 'that if endorsed by and supported by the Irish bishops, and then as a next step by His Holiness the Pope, the Legion of Mary will exist all over the world within the next decade and eventually form another great contribution from Ireland to Catholicity.'

To an admirer and friend it was prophetic language; to critics among the archbishop's colleagues, on the other hand, it must have seemed unreal, the excessive aspirations, even hubris, of an ambitious and difficult man.

No immediate approval of the Legion was forthcoming. The hiatus extended for a number of years more. In September 1933, Pope Pius XI gave 'a very special blessing' to the Legion, and the Papal Nuncio in Ireland, Pascal Robinson, showed himself a strong supporter. In the Dublin archdiocese, nevertheless, there was no movement towards formal approval until May 1934.

Towards a meeting of minds
On 29 May 1934, Duff and his close friends were taken aback by

a document drafted apparently by the vicars-general which suggested various variants on the sort of organisation propounded in the draft Legion handbook, gave very strong powers to priest spiritual directors, and proposed what Duff dismissed as 'a feminine form of the Catholic Young Men's Society'.[58]

Some time later, he and close supporters arranged a meeting with the vicars-general. In a letter, he gave his version of what ensued:

> We saw the Vicars and had our stormiest interview so far. Monsignor Waters again came to the men [referring, presumably to the entry of men into the Legion] and proposed certain changes which I point-blank refused to accept. He then made the usual assertion about my anti-clericalism. On this I vehemently protested and declared that if there was anything more of this kind I would refuse to continue the discussion. This produced an amazingly sobering effect. Eventually, after three hours, complete agreement was reached on all points. Monsignor Waters withdrawing his point at the end ...[59]

Approval Granted

All seemed favourably settled by 3 January 1935, when His Grace wrote to Frank Duff. The draft letter runs:

> My dear Mr Duff,
> I have received from Mgr Cronin and Mgr Waters an account of their conversations with you regarding the Constitution for the Legion of Mary. They have submitted to me the draft Constitution agreed upon by the Monsignori and yourself. I have examined them carefully and am now happy to convey to you my approval of them.
>
> I feel that the Legionaries, working in accordance with these Constitutions, and in the spirit of submission to ecclesiastical authority which they inculcate, will be abundantly blessed by God. The divine assistance is now assured to them by their devotion to Mary, their special Patroness.
>
> In conveying to you this formal approval of the Constitutions of the Legion of Mary I wish you and the Legionaries every blessing from God,
>   Yours Sincerely in Christ.'

P.S. In case you wish to have a copy of the Constitutions

signed by me you might send me a copy of the Constitutions signed by yourself. I could then send to you the copy I hold at present.

Frank Duff replied on 6 January expressing the joy of the whole Legion, and conveying on behalf of all Legionaries 'sincere thanks'. At the same time, he adroitly, if undiplomatically, sent His Grace's letter of approval to the press, in which it appeared under the heading: 'Legion of Mary Constitution. Draft Approval: Dublin Archbishop's Letter.'[60]

Thus, a long period of misunderstanding and distance seemed to have come to an end. In his remaining years, the archbishop would provide practical evidence of his support.

The Archbishop and the wider context
In the work and concerns of the archdiocese, the Legion was but one of more than 45 Catholic committees, guilds and associations[61] requiring attention, quite apart from a host of other possible issues.

Despite the complaints emanating from supporters of the Legion, and other criticisms regarding delays in correspondence and decisions from Archbishop's House, His Grace continued to hold a high place in the affections of his people. Nowhere, as might be expected, was this more evident than in his own episcopal parish. Once again, at the close of the men's retreat in the Pro-Cathedral, at which he presided, there were remarkable scenes of devotion and enthusiasm. 'The Pro-Cathedral', the *Irish Catholic Directory* reported, 'was crowded to the doors for the concluding devotions.' As His Grace left the presbytery at the end of the service, on the night of 7 April 1935, he was loudly cheered and 'a procession of several thousand men, and a number of women, escorted him as he was driven to his residence at Drumcondra. Hymns were played by the Workers' Union of Ireland band and the St Mary's pipe band, which accompanied the procession.'[62]

At the end of November, as earlier mentioned, crowds lined the roads to greet him at the establishment of a new parish at Harold's Cross. On the same day there was a further manifestation to cheer episcopal hearts – the city's largest theatre, the Theatre Royal, was thronged from floor to roof for the annual meeting of the Pioneer Total Abstinence Association, which now had more than 250,000 members.[63]

Christmas was busy but peaceful, with full churches and numerous confessions leading up to the feast; and the year closed with Edward Byrne still managing to carry on his role as archbishop, though with diminished energy and mobility.

CHAPTER THIRTEEN

1936-1938

*Communism. Catholic Action. The Spanish Civil War.
The Irish Constitution*

Death of Brian de Valera

Early in February 1936, there were widespread expressions of sympathy for President and Mrs de Valera on the tragic death of their youngest son, Brian, in a horse-riding accident in the Phoenix Park. On 10 February, Archbishop Byrne conveyed his deepest sympathy to the President and his wife, assuring them of his remembrance of their son in Holy Mass and in his prayers, and apologising for not calling in person as some eye-trouble kept him in the house. Moved by the archbishop's brief words, De Valera, four days later, assured him that he and his wife would never forget his kind message. They prayed God to reward him for his charity towards them.[1]

The Archbishop and Mass on Radio

During the year, events at home and abroad were brought closer to the people by the wider availability of radio broadcasts, following the installation of a high-powered station in Athlone. By 1937 there were 100,000 licensed radio sets. Archbishop Byrne was not at ease with the new medium. On 18 February 1936, he received a letter from the Director of Broadcasting wishing to know if there were any objections to his broadcasting on St Patrick's Day, in a special world programme, the sound of St Patrick's Bell now in the National Museum?[2] The archbishop's response is not extant, but later in the year he was certainly not in a receptive mood when requested to have High Mass broadcast. On 14 November, the Director announced that if His Grace had no objection they planned to broadcast High Mass on Christmas Day. He would approach the Fathers of Clarendon Street for permission to do so from their church. His Grace's reply is indicated by the comment written underneath the letter, 'I have every objection'. Presumably, he feared that Mass on the radio might lead to fewer people attending Mass in church.

CYMS and Communists

On the threat of communism, Dr Byrne was more reticent than most of his fellow prelates. His vicar-general, Mgr Waters, however, was in charge of the Catholic Young Men's Society (CYMS), which was very active against communists throughout Ireland. It had a vigorous intelligence network. Lists of communists in the Dublin area had been supplied to it from early in the 1930s;[3] and, on 25 January 1936, John Costelloe, the organising secretary of the CYMS, was able to inform J. J. Hyland, of the Oughterard Branch, Co Galway: 'You may rest assured that you will be placed in full possession of all the facts relating to communism affecting any part of Ireland'.[4] A week earlier, members of the CYMS had endeavoured to break up a communist meeting in Rathmines Town Hall, where guest speakers from the British Communist Party were expected. At the meeting, it was reported that men fought with 'chairs, pokers and sticks', while outside more young men carried banners with wording such as 'Dublin Rejects Communism'. The communists, in turn, mobilised some workers to eject anyone trying to disturb future meetings.[5]

Anger at events in Spain. Support for General Franco

Meantime, feelings were being inflamed by widely publicised accounts of churches being burned and priests and religious sisters being killed and tortured under the elected socialist government in Spain. When a revolt began against the government in July 1936, the sympathy felt for the revolutionaries found expression in the foundation of the Irish Christian Front within a month of the uprising. The new organisation was established by Catholic actionists within An Ríoghacht and the Knights of St Columbanus. It became immensely popular. Some of its meetings in Dublin, Cork and Waterford attracted very large crowds. Under the leadership of Paddy Belton TD, it seemed for a while that the ICF would become a populist, non-political means of unifying all Catholic Action bodies.[6]

The forces in Spain led by General Franco were spoken of in crusader terms, as defenders of religion and freedom, in the *Irish Independent* and the Catholic papers. The Spanish government was portrayed as atheistically communist, dependent on and supported by Soviet Russia. The Irish government, however, refused to condemn the leaders of the Spanish Republic, because they were the democratically elected rulers of the country. Ireland was divided on the matter, though a majority clearly supported the 'Catholic forces', as they were depicted. Archbishop Byrne strongly empathised with the Spanish bishops in their ordeal, and the Irish clergy seem to have supported Franco. When the *Irish Times'* correspondent in Spain, Lionel Fleming, favoured the republican side there was a sense of outrage, and virtually all Catholic educational advertising was withdrawn by the religious-run schools. The boycott hit the newspaper's finances so badly that the editor, Robert M. Smylie, was obliged to recall Fleming.[7]

The Bishops and the Communist threat in Ireland

The bishops' pastoral letters, which appeared on 23 February, warned against the communist movement worming its way into Ireland disguised as the 'United Ireland' movement, and stressed the importance of a 'truly Christian family life'. His Grace of Dublin emphasised that the home was the great force for promoting the love and service of God and that was why the enemies of God sought to destroy the bonds which maintain the family.[8]

The episcopal and extensive lay Catholic opposition to communism, and to the IRA in so far as it was linked to communism, created a climate in which known Communist/IRA activists, especially if occupying positions of influence, were viewed with suspicion and hostility. So it was with teacher, Frank Edwards, who was dismissed from his Christian Brothers' Waterford school, Mount Sion. His dismissal was strongly approved by the Bishop of Waterford, Jeremiah Kinane. Edwards appealed from the latter's decision to the archbishop of another jurisdiction, hoping that the Archbishop of Dublin would support him despite Dr Kinane's censure.

The superior of the Christian Brothers' School consulted the bishop before dismissing Mr Edwards. He informed his lordship 'that this teacher, despite the public warning – twice issued – of his parish priest and co-manager of the school, attended the Republican Congress and took an active part in its discussions. This fact was published in the press and is admitted by the teacher himself.' The principles and aims of the Republican Congress movement, Dr Kinane explained in a pastoral letter on the issue, were opposed to the teaching of the church; its principles were socialistic and communistic; it aimed at setting up a socialistic republic, evidently on the Russian model … One who belonged to a movement of this kind was unfit to be a teacher of Catholic children. The bishop offered Edwards the option of signing a statement, which would be made public, dissociating himself from the Republic Congress movement and promising not to join any similar organisation in the future, or losing his job. Edwards refused to sign and was dismissed.[9]

A year later, on 26 February 1936, Frank Edwards appealed to the Archbishop of Dublin. Referring to his dismissal, he declared that for his part he was reacting to conditions as he saw them, that he was sincerely Catholic and thought the work he was doing good. 'Anyway I have been dismissed', he continued. 'Since my dismissal I have been attending the university, reading for my BA degree, supporting myself by giving tuitions in Irish. This, however, is pretty difficult. So I am trying to get an appointment as a teacher. Accordingly, a friend of mine here saw the Minister for Education on my behalf, and I understand that if there is no objection on your part I could get an appointment in the city here.' He concluded:

> I beg to ask Your Grace whether you could be prepared to sanction my appointment. I am emboldened to write by the knowledge that I am a Catholic, that I would like to make a living in Ireland, that I should be happiest making my living as a teacher.10

The archbishop's reply, in the circumstances of the time, was predictable. A typed letter, from his secretary, informed Mr Edwards: 'His Grace wishes me to say that he is not prepared to accede to your request.' A further typed letter informed the Minister for Education of Frank Edward's reference to the minister, and that the archbishop had not acceded to the request.[11] The minister, Thomas Derrig, responding two days later, thanked his Grace for informing him of his decision, and assured him that when he was approached on this matter he made it quite clear that the appointment of any school teacher was in the first instance a question for the manager of the school concerned.[12]

Frank Edward's teaching career in Ireland seems to have come to an end at this point. A devoted admirer of the left-wing republican leader, Frank Ryan, he preserved his contacts with the Republican Congress movement and became a well-known communist and 'Friend of the Soviet Union'. In later life, he ran successful tours to Russia under the auspices of the Irish Communist Party, and was decorated for his services to the Soviet Union.

The Archbishop's health

The references to letters from the archbishop being typed and sent through his secretary, raises further questions about Dr Byrne's state of health. How well was he in 1936, less than five years before his death? As frequently with the archbishop, there are but faint clues. In February, in his letter to De Valera, he complained of 'eye-trouble' that kept him to the house. In November, a letter from the French embassy would regret that he was 'not well just now'. During the year, Bishop Wall stood in for him on many occasions. And Dr Byrne appealed to reasons of health for not accepting invitations that involved social occasions or travel not directly part of his diocesan functions. In many respects he had become quite reclusive. The editor of the *Belvederian* commented on this in an obituary article.

> As the years drew on, growing infirmities and, perhaps, the shadow of his lonely dignity, made the man whom we could remember as the most desired of companions, delightful guest and perfect host, retire into ever-deepening seclusion. He was cut off from us. His visits anywhere were very rare and it was some years since he had been to Belvedere. Yet, those whom urgent business or happy chance brought for a pleasing moment within his circle, can testify to the warm sincerity of his kindness, which lasted to the end ...[13]

On 1 January 1940, Mgr P. J. Walsh, the former secretary to the archbishop, would comment that His Grace was very feeble and particularly unsteady on his legs;[14] and again, a few days later, Walsh observed: 'For a man, not much over 67, he is very old in body. Mentally he has been better recently than he was five years ago.'[15]

Thus, in passing, one learns that around 1933-34, Archbishop Byrne had been sluggish or distrait mentally. There is no indication of when it began. One is tempted to think of 1933, after the intense exertions of the Eucharistic Congress. It is also not clear when it ended, or how persistent the condition was within each year – all the time, or with some days/weeks better than others? Certainly, during 1937, as De Valera was to testify, he was fully alert mentally, and this seems to have continued into 1940. Physically, however, in the second-half of the 1930s, there was an evident acceleration in the ageing process, reflected in his features, unsteady gait and growing feebleness as depicted in various photographs taken at church and other public functions.

Struggling on

Despite the progressive physical decline, and the fluctuations in his general health, Edward Byrne continued during these years to fulfill special functions related to the churches and convents of the diocese whenever he could. He presided as usual at the close of the men's month-long mission in the Pro-Cathedral, on 29 March, and received renewed energy from the acclaim of thousands of men, young and old. On 17 May he dedicated to St Thérèse of Lisieux a new chapel-of-ease which he blessed and opened at Mount Merrion. A month later he was present at a Missa Cantata to celebrate the golden jubilee of the Sacred Heart Home for Boys in Drumcondra;[16] and on 25 October he was present at High Mass and Benediction to mark the centenary of St Catherine's Dominican Convent, Blackrock.[17]

Defending the Rotary Club

During the year, he made a special effort to write in long hand in response to a query from the Nuncio, Paschal Robinson, 'about the body called the Rotary Club'. There seemed to be a question of it being censured by Rome. Byrne's response, dated merely 1936, is clearly legible. He described the club as composed almost exclusively of laymen. There had been a priest on its roll of membership but, of course, he resigned when the Holy See declared membership of this body to be inexpedient for priests. As far as he could discover there was nothing in the Rotary Club, as conducted in Dublin, to prevent Catholics from being members. It was not a danger either to faith or morals. As it was described to him, 'there is nothing anti-Catholic, irreligious or secret about it'. There were several Catholic members and some of them had been presidents of the body. He concluded staunchly:

> If there is any question of putting the Club under a ban, I am very strongly of opinion that such a course of action would do great harm in this city, and attach a stigma to many good

Catholic men who happen to be members of it and who do not deserve any censure.[18]

Thankfully, nothing came of the threatened censure. An element of exaggerated alarm was emanating from the Vatican in the final years of the pontificate of Pius XI.

The Legion of Mary again. Grounds for grievance
A letter from Frank Duff on 15 May made it clear that a most senior clergyman in the archdiocese was bitterly opposed to the Legion, and may have been the source of the hostility that the Legion experienced from clergy in the archdiocese. 'For a time past', he wrote,

> we have been painfully aware that some powerful influences were counterworking the Approval of 3 January 1935, and were proving only too successful in reducing it to nullity. I attach a copy of a letter addressed by me a month ago to the Right Revd Monsignor Cronin on this particular aspect of things.

The immediate occasion of that letter was the behaviour of Bishop Wall towards a member of the Legion, Miss Ethel Meagher, who planned to establish in the bishop's parish a club run by the Legion for maids or servant girls. On she seeking Dr Wall's permission, the latter stated that these clubs did no good. Miss Meagher replied that there were three Maids' clubs of the Legion doing very good work. After this, as she explained, and Duff underlined for the archbishop: 'He became very annoyed and said that they had started without the permission of the Archbishop, and that we had not got the Archbishop's permission to come to him. I said that I was sure that the Archbishop must have given his permission or the parish priests would not have allowed us to start the clubs in their parishes. He said that I was only saying that I was sure we had permission and that he knew that we had not, and that we had probably gone to the parish priests, as I had come to him, as if we had permission, and that the priests, thinking we had, had allowed us to start. He said that he knew better and that we had no permission. I said that the Archbishop had given his approval to the whole Legion. He said, yes, but that when we took up a special work, like a club, a special permission should be asked. I said that I did not know this. He said that there was no use talking further, that he would not have the clubs in his parish ... and he opened the door for me to go.'

Duff pointed out that according to the approved constitution of the Legion the practice had always been to get permission from the parish priest, and it was up to him, not the Legion, to contact the bishop if necessary. And it was not true that parish priests were deceptively spoken to and hoodwinked.

Bishop Wall, as auxiliary bishop to Dr Byrne, had taken over more and more responsibility as the archbishop became increasingly frail and had difficulty in walking. Consequently, Duff concluded his letter:

> If his Lordship has shown his mind to others in the manner he has to Miss Meagher, I fear that we need look no further for an explanation of the coldness which is being manifested towards the Legion by the parish priests of Dublin. I may be excused for saying that I think the latter is a loss to the diocese.[19]

The above account is, of course, that of but one party. Dr Wall's version is not available. Even if Miss Meagher's account were entirely accurate, it is difficult to see what the archbishop, in his weak state, could do in terms of censuring his auxiliary bishop. He endeavoured, however, to show forth his own support for the Legion in practical ways. When Duff and John Nagle went to Rome in April 1939, with a view to establishing the Legion there, Archbishop Byrne provided Duff with a letter of introduction to Cardinal Pizardo, head of the Holy Office, the central bureau of the Curia;[20] and some weeks later, on 22 May, when contacted by the Bishop of Roermond for his opinion of the Legion, then about to establish itself in Holland, Dr Byrne replied that it had his approval and was doing good work.[21]

Money for Spain

The suffering of the Spanish people led to the Irish Christian Front collecting funds to support hospital services in Spain, and Eoin O'Duffy, in a mixture of idealism and a search for a popular cause, formed an Irish Brigade to serve on Franco's side. On 20 November 1936, he and his followers left for Spain. Nearly a month later, on 16 December, Frank Ryan arrived in Spain with a unit of anti-fascist volunteers to join the government forces. Meantime, the Catholic hierarchy initiated a collection for Spain, the proceeds to go to the Cardinal Primate of Spain for distribution. The Archbishop of Dublin, as usual, was generous in his response. Writing to him on 30 November 1936, Cardinal MacRory commented: 'Your cheque is magnificent. You may be proud of your priests and people, especially when one remembers that here and there they have given a good deal to the Irish Christian Front. Your Grace's £6008.12.0 brings the amount already received to just over £40,000, and I have still to hear from two 'outliers', Galway and Limerick!' The cardinal added that he had not given any money to Paddy Belton and the Christian Front. It was up to the primate and the body of bishops to decide if they wished to give some of it to the Irish Christian Front for medical requirements.[22]

An unexpected contribution came from Berlin, from the Irish Legation, on 23 October. Charles Bewley, who had served in Rome but was Irish representative in Germany since 1933, enclosed, in a letter to the archbishop, a £25 subscription to the Bishops' Appeal for the relief of suffering Catholics in Spain, and observed: 'It is the duty of every Catholic to support to the best of his powers ... the battle of Christendom against the power of Communism.'[23]

International and local divisions

Two further letters to His Grace of Dublin reflected different views in international and local politics respectively.

In 1935, Mussolini had invaded Abyssinia (Ethiopia) without even a declaration of war. The League of Nations, including Ireland, branded Italy as an aggressor and imposed limited sanctions. The Italian war effort continued, nevertheless, and Addis Ababa was captured on 5 May 1936 with the help of air power and poison gas.[24]

Three days after the fall of Addis Ababa, a letter from the Italian consul in Dublin informed the archbishop that the Italian colony wished to have a *Te Deum* celebration in St Audoen's Church in thanksgiving for the Italian victory.

His Grace's refusal was put as diplomatically as possible. 'In view of the stand our government has taken with regard to the League of Nations, I greatly regret that at present I do not see my way to fall in with your request for a public *Te Deum* in St Audoen's Church. It might offer an opportunity to certain disaffected elements to make the *Te Deum* a political demonstration. It would make a difference were the Department of External

Affairs to certify that they had no objection to the religious function you wish to celebrate.'[25]

At the local level, fear of being associated with communism
had some bizarre consequences. On 10 August 1936, a typed
document, signed by a group of Fianna Fáil supporters, was
sent to the archbishop. It complained that Alderman Alfred
Byrne, Lord Mayor of Dublin, had placards posted outside the
churches which 'represented the (local) elections as a contest between the Lord Mayor and his friends and the friends of communism'. They wished to assure His Grace that they, and Fianna
Fáil, were not communists, that they were opposed to the foul
doctrine of communism, 'which has done, and is doing, such
havoc to the church in Mexico, in France, in Russia, and in
Spain.' They appealed to him to use his authority to prevent the
recurrence of such lies![26]

International developments

Internationally, the situation grew in tension during 1936, especially after Mussolini and Hitler joined together in what Mussolini
called 'the Axis'. In Britain and France, as a result, Fascism and
Nazism became the enemy rather than Soviet communism,
whereas in Italy and Germany communism remained the main
adversary. In Ireland in the final years of the 1930s, due largely
to the zeal and publicity generated by the various organs of
Catholic Action, communism continued to loom large and to be
blazoned as the insidious enemy of religion and liberty.

The closing weeks of 1936 were marked with drama in
England as King Edward VIII abdicated and George VI was appointed his successor. The dominion parliaments were required
to ratify the abdication of Edward and the appointment of his
successor. De Valera availed of the prevailing confusion in
Britain, and its concerns about the international situation, to
write the monarch and the Governor-General out of the existing
Irish constitution, while recognising the Crown for purposes of
diplomatic representation and international agreements.[27]

Incapacities and Leisure reading

It is noticeable during 1937 that many of the ceremonies that
Archbishop Byrne used to attend were transferred to Dr Wall.
These included meeting the Lord Mayor and members of the
Corporation in the Pro-Cathedral, on 28 March,[28] the ordination

of priests at Maynooth on 20 June, and presiding at the Mass for the opening of the academic year in October 1937. The Lord Mayor and Corporation officials sent 'their best wishes to His Grace the Archbishop', indicating that the latter was unable to attend for reasons of health. In June, His Grace was described as suffering from an attack of lumbago;[29] and in October he replied carefully to a 'charming invitation' to Mgr Michael Browne's ordination as Bishop of Galway, that unfortunately his health did not allow him 'to take long journeys at present'.[30]

Fortunately for the archbishop he remained an avid reader, and this continued during times of ill-health as during his more vigorous years. Among his 'Memorabilia'[31] are indications of his taste in reading into the 1930s. There are references to biographies of Gladstone, Chamberlain, Asquith, and James Broderick's life of St Peter Canisius, and articles on evolution, papal teaching, and on Freemasons and the 'Grand Orient' branch which were said to be active in the Spanish republican government. Among the quotations that Edward Byrne recorded from his reading was one attributed to Horace Walpole that had a chilling applicability to the 1930s: 'No great country was saved by a good man, because good men will not go to the lengths that may be necessary.'[32]

Keeping in touch

Despite accumulated ailments, the archbishop endeavoured, as usual, to fulfill as many ecclesial functions as he could. He began 1937 by receiving the representatives of the Irish Chapter of the Knights of the Sovereign Order of Malta on 1 January.[33] He was next active in public in March, presiding, as customary, at the close of the men's four-week retreat at the Pro-Cathedral; and three days later, on 17 March, at the Mass attended by the representatives of the state. His improved state of health continued into April, when he was present at the golden jubilee of the monastery of our Lady of Refuge in Gloucester Street.[34] He does not seem to have presided again until 16 September, when he opened and blessed the new chapel and training college for nuns at Carysfort Park, Blackrock; and six days later he dedicated the new church attached to the Mater Hospital. In October, he was laid up again, but on 3 November he insisted on attending the long ceremonies related to the exhumation and examination of the remains of John Andrew Houben, known in religion as Fr

Charles, a revered priest of the Passionist Congregation at Mount Argus, Harold's Cross, Dublin, as part of the process required by the Sacred Congregation of Rites in the cause of beatification.[35] What Dr Byrne's public attendances cost him is suggested in the press photograph, taken during 1937, on the occasion of the opening and blessing of a new chapel-of-ease at Portmarnock. His frail and aged appearance is palpable. He sought to be present as a support to his people, and they, for their part, deeply appreciated the effort he was making.

Suffering and reparation
His courage in the face of continuing set-backs, occasional physical humiliations, and an increasingly bleak future, was strengthened by his Christian belief in the relevance of intercession and 'reparation' – the capacity to atone for the evil done by others by one's prayer, penance, or suffering, or to win relief for others in difficulty by one's own prayer, penance or suffering. He exhorted his people in this shared belief, with respect to the seriously ill Pope Pius XI, in his Lenten pastoral letter in February 1937.

> During his prolonged and painful illness, borne with exquisite patience and characteristic fortitude, the Holy Father has offered his suffering particularly for Spain, Mexico, Russia and other countries where religion is now persecuted.
>
> It will be our privilege to join with the Supreme Pontiff in his prayer, by offering up our Lenten penance and prayer in reparation for the shocking outrages which are credibly reported to have happened in these unhappy countries.[36]

Instances of daily concerns
Of the daily work of the archbishop at this time, only the smallest indications remain and these tend to relate to somewhat exceptional letters from government officials or other figures of authority, or reports regarding communism, Spain, and the Irish Constitution.

Among the letters from the government was a circuitous one from Maurice Moynihan, De Valera's private secretary, to Thomas O'Donnell, Dr Byrne's secretary, reminding him that the office of Governor-General was abolished with the enactment of the Constitution Act, 1936, on 11 January 1937, and requesting that he would kindly bring this to His Grace's attention 'with a view to such actions as His Grace may direct to the post of chaplain to the Governor General'.[37] Shortly afterwards, on 22 January, Major General Michael Brennan, an old acquaintance of the archbishop, invited his Grace 'to formally bless the garrison church in Arbour Hill on some date suitable to yourself'.[38]

The archbishop was conscious most of all, during 1937, of the fears and alarms regarding Soviet communism which, more marked than in the previous year, had risen almost to frenzy. This heightened state had been augmented by the new papal encyclical on communism, *Divini Redemptoris*. The CYMS stepped up their vigilance activites throughout Ireland. The *News Bulletin* of the society's vigilance department advised members 'to deal effectively with agitators'. Swift and effective action was to be the norm in dealing with communist activity.[39]

Reports continued to arrive at Archbishop's House telling of organisations run by or infiltrated by communists. One, dated February 1937, suggested 'general predisposing conditions' towards communism in Ireland. These came to six: The after-effects of the civil war – a number of republicans joined Red associations; the growth of liberal/secular ideas – in publications, cinema, radio etc; the breakdown of traditional moral restraint – 'To those who lead an irregular life, communism furnishes a convenient code'; unemployment – which seems incurable under capitalism; depression in agriculture; and insufficient education in religion.[40]

The influential Vatican paper, *Osservatore Romano*, added to the fears of communism in Ireland. Basing its views on an article in the *Irish Catholic*, it reported that 250,000 Irish workers, who were members of trades unions affiliated to the Irish Trades Union Congress and to the Irish Labour Party, tacitly supported communism, and that Congress circulated an article in which the Catholic Church was described as the enemy of the workers. Mgr Michael Curran, rector of the Irish College, was sufficiently worried to bring the matter to the attention of William Norton TD, leader of the Labour Party, and to urge him to write to Cardinal Pacelli, the Cardinal Secretary of State, denying the allegations. To Curran, and doubtless to Edward Byrne, it was another instance of Rome misunderstanding the political/social situation in Ireland.

William Norton wrote to Cardinal Pacelli, the Secretary of

State, on 23 February 1937: 'As a Catholic and the accepted leader of the Irish Labour Party I desire most emphatically to repudiate both statements.' As to the further reference in *Osservatore* to 'Friends of the Soviet Union', he had no direct concern with them and he doubted that such organisations had any following in the country. The Labour Party took care to send a copy of their letter to Archbishop Byrne. Subsequently, in the face of accusations of communist infiltration of the party, Mr Norton published a pamphlet entitled *Cemeteries of Liberty* which claimed to be 'a clear and unequivocal statement of the Labour Party's attitude towards Communism and Fascism'. Nevertheless, criticism and suspicion continued,[43] and in this uncertain climate, the Irish hierarchy approached the Labour Party for a copy of its constitution. At their June meeting they established a committee to investigate the constitution and to furnish them with a statement. The four members of the committee were: Bishops Jeremiah Kinane, Waterford, Michael Browne, Galway, and Revds Patrick O'Neill and Cornelius Lucy destined to become respectively Bishops of Limerick and Cork. The committee made its report on 11 October 1937. They judged that the constitution contained a number of statements, of principle and of aim, which, according to the natural and current sense of the terms used, were opposed to Catholic teaching. In particular, these statements were opposed to the Catholic principles on private and individual ownership, and involved a denial of the essential liberty and natural rights of every individual in the state.[42]

The report presented and explained, over 6 typed pages, the sections of the Labour constitution in which they found fault. The hierarchy, however, decided to make no public use of the information.

Communism, Spain, the Irish Brigade

The Irish Brigade under Eoin O'Duffy returned home from Spain on 21 June 1937. They were given a reception at the Mansion House, which was presided over by the Right Rev Mgr Waters PP, VG, who said his sole purpose in taking the chair was to honour them as soldiers of the Cross.[43] In fact, as a body, they did not distinguish themselves as 'soldiers of the Cross'. They were poorly led and were divided among themselves.[44]

On 4 September, O'Duffy made a national appeal for funds for the men of the Irish brigade, who fought 'against the hordes of international communism concentrated in Spain' and were now out of work and in need. The archbishop contributed £21. More than two months later, on 23 November, O'Duffy wrote to the archbishop's secretary, Rev Dr P. Dunne, that he had heard that some members of the Brigade had been calling at Archbishop's House, and as he knew that his Grace in his charity and bigness of heart would not wish to turn them away, he was very concerned lest he should be imposed upon. The members of the Brigade, he explained, had been made aware that His Grace had contributed generously already, and except where Dr Dunne believed the case was very deserving he would respectfully suggest such callers should get nothing.[45]

Irish bishops and the Spanish hierarchy

At the same meeting at which the bishops received the report on the constitution of the Labour Party, their Lordships sent their reply to the appeal of the Spanish hierarchy, which had been addressed to the Catholic episcopate throughout the world. The reply was signed by Cardinal MacRory, as chairman of the bishops' conference, and Bishop J. Kinane, as secretary. Having praised the Spanish bishops and the impressive sincerity of their poignant appeal, the Irish document continued:

> We recognise, Venerable Brethren, the cruel injustice that has been done Catholics of Spain by the world Press at large – with some honourable exceptions – in its grossly tendentious presentation of the origin and development of the present tragic situation in your beloved country.
>
> The Irish people, however, had the true state of the case placed before them by the Catholic and national Press of Ireland, and the vast majority of them had never wavered in their sympathy for Catholic Spain, and for her sorely tried Hierarchy, clergy and religious.[46]

There was no reference here, and little reference in the greater part of writing in Ireland, to the Basque Catholics and their priests and why they were supporting the Spanish government, or to the barbarous attack on the Basque capital of Guernica by the forces associated with Franco, or, indeed, to the fact that six members of the Spanish hierarchy did not sign the 'Address to the Catholic Episcopate throughout the World'.[47]

The Archbishop and the Irish Constitution

On the home front, the most momentous event was the new constitution drawn up by De Valera, in which Edward Byrne had a role to play at a critical moment. De Valera sought advice on the constitution from a wide spectrum of people, most notably Fr McQuaid and some other Holy Ghost Fathers, and Fr Edward Cahill and some other Jesuits. In drafting the document he was influenced by aspects of Catholic social teaching, and he was particularly careful in indicating the standing of the Catholic Church. A number of his Catholic Action advisers pressed for formal recognition of the Catholic Church as the 'one true church', and strongly opposed referring to the Protestant Church as the 'Church of Ireland'. De Valera, conscious of Protestant feeling in the Six Counties and of his and Fianna Fáil's aspirations for a united Ireland, chose to ignore much of the Catholic advice on this part, Article 44, of the constitution.[48]

On this critical section, he worked out a formula, which he personally brought to the Papal Nuncio on 3 April 1937. The latter listened, and when De Valera said he would consult the Archbishop of Dublin, Paschal Robinson suggested that he should also consult Cardinal MacRory, who would be in Dublin the following day. De Valera and the cardinal were not on good terms. MacRory arrived with his own formula, which came down to a version of the 'one, true church', and he also declared himself strongly opposed to naming the Protestant Church the 'Church of Ireland'. This created a serious dilemma. How representative was His Eminence's point of view among the hierarchy? If it were widespread, De Valera's constitution would be faced with the joint opposition of church leaders and of Fine Gael, the main opposition party. Much depended on Archbishop Byrne. His stance proved critical. To De Valera's great relief, Dr Byrne proved supportive. He was sufficiently impressed by the wording of the preamble to the constitution that he felt it unnecessary to make any particular mention of the status of the Catholic Church in the general article on religion.[49]

Biographers of De Valera noted that he derived great encouragement from his meeting with the archbishop. The danger of unified episcopal opposition had receded.[50] Shortly after his visit to Dr Byrne, De Valera settled on the phrase 'recognises the special position' of the Catholic Church. He decided on a purely descriptive formulation with regard to the religions; and on the advice of the Church of Ireland Archbishop of Dublin, George A. F. Gregg, decided to give the churches the titles they themselves used, e.g. 'Holy, Catholic, Apostolic and Roman Church' in the case of the Catholic Church.

Cardinal MacRory brought his case to Rome without success. De Valera had appealed directly to the Vatican in support of his form of wording. Through Joseph Walshe, of External Affairs, the matter was negotiated with the Secretary of State, Cardinal Eugenio Pacelli, who grasped the delicacy of the Irish President's problem and was prepared to be neutral on the words proposed to him, namely that the Catholic Church was not recognised as the 'one true church' but rather as having 'a special position' as 'the guardian of the faith professed by the great majority of the Irish people', while other churches also received recognition.

The Constitution was published on 30 April 1937. Joseph Walshe delivered the document personally to Archbishop Byrne. The latter remained pleased with the Constitution, and subsequently commented wryly to De Valera: 'I have noticed that the Holy, Catholic, Apostolic and Roman Church still retains its special position.'

'The government', Dermot Keogh observed in *The Vatican, the Bishops and Irish Politics*, 'had good reason to be thankful to Byrne.'[55]

Byrne's response to the Constitution underlined his independence of mind. For reasons of disposition, or spiritual detachment, or health, or a combination of all three, he did not seek or welcome publicity as Cardinal MacRory seemed to do, but he remained very much his own person. Neither the official standing of De Valera nor the pressing personality of the cardinal seemed to sway his judgement.

The Constitution was approved by the Dáil on 14 June, and De Valera forthwith dissolved the Dáil and declared a snap general election. This involved a referendum on the constitution, and a political election. On 1 July 1937, the result of the referendum showed the passage of the constitution by 685,105 votes to 526,945, but the election result left Fianna Fáil without an overall majority. Its total of seats came to 69. The combination of other parties and independents also came to 69, which left the government dependent on the support of Independents.

The year 1937 closed with an impressive religious ceremony

to mark the inauguration of the new Constitution, *Bunreacht na hÉireann*. At 9.40 am the Taoiseach, Mr de Valera, with all the ministers of government, except the Tánaiste, Mr Sean T. O'Kelly, who was in Rome, drove in state from Government Buildings to the Pro-Cathedral in Marlborough Street, to assist at the Solemn Votive Mass of the Holy Ghost. They were accompanied by a cavalry escort in full-dress uniforms. They were received in the presbytery by the Archbishop of Dublin, Most Rev Dr Byrne; Very Rev M. E. Murphy, administrator of the Cathedral; and the parochial clergy. The congregation in the Pro-Cathedral included: Ministers, members of Dáil Éireann, representatives of the judiciary; Major General Brennan, Chief of Staff, with other leading army officers, and Colonel Bray, Commissioner of the Garda Síochána.'[52]

The new Constitution was welcomed in the Vatican and was generally well received. Even Cardinal MacRory proved ready to acknowledge, in his New Year message on 1 January 1938, that 'the new Constitution is a splendid charter, a broad and solid foundation on which to build up a nation that will be at once reverent and dutiful to God and just to all men.'[53]

Continuing in service

That year Archbishop Byrne reached his sixty-sixth birthday. He was alert in mind, and though physically feeble and older than his years, he had managed the previous August to travel abroad for a holiday.[54] It was to be his last opportunity to do so. In the New Year, he continued his pastoral work between lapses in health.

His Lenten letter, on 27 February 1938, focused on two sources of grave danger: the infiltration 'of communism within this island, and ... the gradual habituating themselves on the part of girls, many of whom have scarcely left school, to the frequent consumption of intoxicating drinks, the acquired taste for which must surely lead to disaster'.[55] On the national feast day, 17 March, he presided at a Mass attended by Mr de Valera and his ministers; and some days later, as was his practice, he made sure to attend the closing ceremonies of the men's retreat at the Pro-Cathedral. His reception that evening surpassed that of all other years, as if his people sensed they might not have him with them much longer. The *Irish Catholic Directory* reported the scene on the evening of 3 April 1938: 'An immense crowd gave

His Grace an enthusiastic ovation when he emerged from the presbytery after the ceremonies. The cheering lasted for several minutes, and the people pressed forward to receive the blessing of the archbishop, who was deeply moved by their affectionate greeting. He entered his car, and a procession, headed by the Workers' Union of Ireland Band, was formed to escort him to his house in Drumcondra. All along the route the same scenes of enthusiasm were witnessed, and at Archbishop's House there was renewed cheering.'[56] Almost six week later, on 15 May, again as was his custom, he issued a pastoral letter to be read in all the churches, in which he reminded the congregations that the next Eucharistic Congress was about to take place, this time in Budapest, and asking their prayers for its success.

Ecclesial/Political irony
Four days later, the unusual relationships in Irish politics continued to find expression in unsuspected places. The Papal Nuncio, Paschal Robinson, wrote to Shane Leslie on 19 May, thanking him for his efforts on behalf of Frank Ryan, who was in prison in Spain, and stating that the Prime Minister (Mr de Valera) was specially concerned about this matter and would be deeply grateful to him or to anyone else who could save Ryan's life. He added: 'Ryan was editor of the *Phoblacht*, the extreme republican paper here until De Valera suppressed it. He is a distinguished graduate of the National University and a very fine fellow in spite of his adherence to the "Reds".'[57]

Honouring the President
On 9 June, Mr de Valera informed Archbishop Byrne that, on the occasion of the entry upon office of Dr Douglas Hyde as President, arrangement had been made, with his approval, for the celebration of a solemn Votive Mass of the Holy Ghost in the Pro-Cathedral, at 10.00 am on Saturday 25 June. Then referring to other ceremonies in Dublin Castle, he remarked that if it were possible for the archbishop to attend, a formal invitation would be sent to him. He added a post-script in his own hand: 'It was my intention to call on Your Grace to explain, but I have been unable to do so.'

Whatever reluctance Dr Byrne may have felt about attending ceremonies likely to prove a considerable ordeal, he put it aside when he learned from Cardinal Mac Rory that Mr Sean T.

O'Kelly and Mr Little had called on him, on behalf of Mr de Valera, to ask him to be present at the inauguration as 'they seemed to fear that Your Grace would not attend'. His Eminence would be happy to attend if His Grace were not attending.[58]

Archbishop Byrne presided at the solemn Votive Mass in the Pro-Cathedral, which was attended by the Taoiseach and members of the government, members of the Oireachtas, churchmen and diplomats, the judiciary, army and civil servants. The President attended a special Church of Ireland service in St Patrick's Cathedral. Dr Byrne was also present at the inauguration of the President in Dublin Castle.

Death of a friend

At the end of June, a Carmelite friend from Edward's student days died. On 30 June 1938, the Carmelite prior, Fr Lawrence, thanked the archbishop for his very touching letter of sympathy and also for his enquiries during Father Bernard's illness. Fr Bernard 'was moved to tears when I told him of Your Grace's anxiety about his condition, and asked me to convey his sincere thanks to your Grace. He recalled to me your gracious visit to him during his student days at Venice, when Your Grace was returning from Rome after your ordination. I may safely presume to say that his joy at Your Grace's elevation to the archbishopric of this diocese was unrivalled'.[59] The words of appreciation were yet another testimony to the thoughtful qualities exhibited by Edward Byrne from his first days as a priest to his later years as archbishop.

A very painful situation and the public response

In October, the parish priest and congregation of each parish assured the archbishop of their prayers on the anniversary of his consecration. On 31 October, he thanked each parish priest and congregation for their thoughtfulness, but added that the consolation given him by the people of the diocese had been overwhelmed by a sorrow that had befallen him in the last few days, 'a sorrow greater than any sorrow that can fall to the lot of a bishop'. He explained: 'A terrible sacrilege has been committed in this diocese, which has not only brought grief, sudden and overwhelming to the priests of the diocese and to me, but will bring to our good Catholic people, now that it has to be made known, a feeling of horror such as they have probably never experienced in the past. The Blessed Sacrament contained in two ciboriums (*sic*) was stolen, together with the ciboriums, from one of our parish churches on the evening of Tuesday, 25 October. Owing to the praiseworthy exertions of the public authorities the ciboriums, greatly damaged, have been discovered, but of the Blessed Sacrament there is still no trace.' To someone with his deep Eucharistic faith the disrespect shown to the sacrament was particularly wounding.

He instructed each parish priest to hold a Eucharistic Hour of Reparation at a suitable time on the next Sunday 6 November, and to request his people 'to come, so that Our Divine Lord may at least have the comfort of knowing that our Dublin people are his friends, and that his sorrow in this sad hour is their sorrow also'.[60]

The public response was immediate and outstanding. 'Not since the Eucharistic Congress', the *Irish Catholic Directory* reported, 'has there been witnessed such a wonderful demonstration of piety by the people of Dublin. Many of the city churches were unable to accommodate the huge congregations, which overflowed into the streets.'[61] The response both consoled the archbishop and confirmed his deep esteem for his people.

The sombre international scene

On 28 August the German Catholic Bishops publicly complained of an intense campaign against the Catholic Church in Germany and outside its borders with a view to 'the introduction of a new Faith which has nothing in common with belief in the life to come'.[62]

A month later, at Munich, Chamberlain and Deladier met with Hitler and Mussolini and consented to the dismemberment of Czechoslovakia.

Two months later, again, came the news that one of the most outspoken critics of Soviet communism and Nazism was critically ill. Already on 29 November, the director of broadcasting in Irish radio wrote to Fr Tom O'Donnell, the archbishop's secretary, to propose broadcasting arrangements in the event of the death of His Holiness, Pope Pius XI. He suggested that broadcasting – except for the news – would cease when the news came, and that on the following evening a two hours programme comprising talks on the Holy Father's social teaching, the Pope of the Missions, and the Pope as a Man would be given, with recorded sacred music. He should like to have His Grace's general permission to allow the Jesuit Students from Miltown Park to chant, in a broadcast, the Office of the Dead as, owing to the circumstances, it would be impossible to arrange at very short notice.[63] The imminent prospect of the Pope's death and the increasing prospect of war in Europe cast a pall over the final weeks of 1938 and into the New Year.

CHAPTER FOURTEEN

1939-1940

Towards and Unexpected Terminus. Tributes. A Query

The New Year was to end in a world war. In Ireland an important foundation for the future had been laid the previous year by Anglo-Irish agreements on finance and trade, the recovery to Ireland of the 'Treaty ports', and by the emergence of a strong government following another snap general election, which gave Fianna Fáil 77 seats and a decisive overall majority.

January opened with IRA bomb attacks in England; and the month ended with the death on the continent of W. B. Yeats. The impending threat of international war resulted, on 9 February, in the Archbishop of Dublin receiving word from the Department of Education that the Ministry for Defence wished to set up a form of volunteer force in preparatory colleges for boys and in Training Colleges for men. It was hoped, as a consequence, to develop greater interest in physical education, pride in the National Defence Forces, and an improved spirit of citizenship.[1]

Mourning the Pope
The following day, 10 February, brought news of the death of Pope Pius XI, who had been pontiff since 1922. His death was deeply felt in Ireland. A period of national mourning was declared. The Irish flag was flown at half-mast over government buildings and on other public buildings in the capital and throughout the country. Theatres in Dublin were closed, dances postponed and cinemas shut down as a mark of respect. In Dáil Éireann deputies stood in respectful silence for a few moments before De Valera announced that he was suspending the sitting until after the funeral. He spoke briefly of this noble man and his work, while the leader of the opposition, William Cosgrave, remarked on the Pope's clarity of vision and exceptional courage and deemed him 'one of the greatest of the followers of St Peter'. Radio Éireann paid a tribute on 11 February, along the lines suggested the previous November.[2]

The week of mourning concluded with a solemn Office and Pontifical High Mass of Requiem in the Pro-Cathedral, at which Archbishop Byrne presided, and the Nuncio Apostolic, Paschal Robinson, was celebrant. It was described as most impressive, and a fitting conclusion to a week of mourning and prayer for the Pope. The attendance included President Douglas Hyde, members of the government and the Oireachtas, the diplomatic corps, the judiciary, the corporation, the army and the garda. Many shops remained closed during the forenoon, and thousands of people assembled in the vicinity of the Pro-Cathedral during the ceremony.[3]

Choosing and celebrating the successor
As soon as the week had passed, attention turned to the possible successor. After a very short conclave, the former Papal Secretary of State, Cardinal Eugenio Pacelli, was elected Pope on 2 March 1939, his 63rd birthday. He took the name Pius XII. The Irish government welcomed the result. They had had many favourable exchanges with Cardinal Pacelli since 1932, and especially in relation to the Constitution in 1937. Mr de Valera travelled to Rome to attend the coronation.[4] In Dublin's Pro-Cathedral on 12 March, the day of the papal coronation, Archbishop Byrne presided at a High Mass; following it the *Te Deum* was sung and Dr Paschal Robinson, Nuncio Apostolic, gave the solemn Benediction.[5] Five days later, on St Patrick's Day, Dr Byrne presided once again at High Mass in the Pro-Cathedral. It was attended by government ministers and officials, but there was no in-state drive to the church because of the absence of Mr de Valera in Rome.

A chaplain for the President
On 21 March, the archbishop's chaplain, Fr Richard Glennon, received a number of queries from Mr Dunphy, secretary to the President of Ireland, relating to the honours due to a Protestant president in a Catholic church and whether it would be proper, from the point of view of the Catholic Church that a Catholic aide-de-camp should be present in attendance on the president in a non-Catholic church? Glennon, on behalf of the archbishop, answered in detail on 29 March, having examined the requirements laid down by canon law and consulted a number of authors. Apart from the niceties of protocol and liturgy with relation to a

Catholic or Protestant president, it was made clear with respect to an aide-de-camp that the canon law disapproved of a Catholic aide-de-camp attending the president in a non-Catholic church, which meant, in practice, that the president should be provided with a Protestant aide-de-camp for such occasions.[6]

Continuing the public schedule

The following month brought an end to the civil war in Spain. On 24 April, as noted in the *Irish Catholic Directory*, Archbishop Byrne presided at a Solemn High Mass in thanksgiving for the victory of the Catholic cause in Spain. It was followed by the singing of the *Te Deum*. The large congregation included members of the Diplomatic Corps, people prominent in various Catholic organisations, and members of the Irish Brigade. At the conclusion of the service, messages were sent to Cardinal Goma Y Tomas, Primate of Spain, and General Franco, by a committee representative of 12 Catholic societies.[7]

Continuing his response to different situations, the archbishop, on 30 April, mindful of an appeal from the Pope for prayers for peace, had a letter read in all the churches encouraging a crusade of prayer through the month of May urging 'Our Heavenly Mother' to intercede for peace, and also urging parents and teachers to get the children to pray and be diligent in their attendance at the May devotions.[8]

Before the end of May, he was surprised to receive a letter and enclosure from Sean T. O'Kelly, writing from the Waldorf Astoria, New York. He had been at the installation of Dr Spellman as Archbishop of New York and dined with him. Archbishop Spellman claimed that the Eucharistic Congress in Dublin made a deeper impression than all previous Congresses. The profound piety of the people and the perfection of the organisation were unique. For the great success, Dr Byrne was responsible, O'Kelly observed. He enclosed a copy of the booklet of the ceremony with his warmest personal regards, and Dr Spellman's most sincere greetings and good wishes.[9] It was a further example of the warmth Edward Byrne evoked from people previously quite critical of him. Archbishop Byrne acknowledged briefly and gratefully the Tánaiste's kindness in thinking of him, and assured him that he deeply appreciated his goodness.[10]

Cinema censorship

During June there arrived a long down-to-earth communication requiring a degree of study and application that the archbishop was probably unable to give. Fr Richard Devane SJ, sent ten typed pages regarding cinema censorship, which he hoped His Grace would do him the favour of reading. The committee appointed by the government to enquire into the whole position of the cinema in Éire was due to draft its report soon. There was now a unique opportunity of doing much towards the controlling of the films to the best interests of the nation – especially as regards the moral cleansing of the cinema screen through extended censorship based on explicit, Christian-moral standards. Devane enclosed some articles that appeared in the *Irish Independent*, the terms of reference of the government's committee of inquiry, and the detailed self-imposed moral code formally and freely accepted by the film-producing companies of the USA. Whole sections of this code could, in Devane's view, be incorporated into the proposed new censorship code.[11] His Grace passed the material to Mgr Cronin for perusal.

Fr McQuaid's role in jeopardy

Another communication that must have occasioned some perplexity came from Fr John Charles McQuaid, who wrote fulsomely and, it would appear, from mixed motives. His provincial superior had told him that he was to be moved from his position of superior at Blackrock College in the near future. Fr McQuaid's concern was that only last year the archbishop had intervened to have him retained that he might represent him in the matter of the Children's Hospital. His provincial forbade him to speak of the matter, but he did not feel it wrong to speak to His Grace about the change. His superior acted without consultation and in very secret ways at times. He wrote to his superior yesterday saying that the archbishop should be informed as he was actively engaged in confidential negotiations on his behalf. In all this, he was acting out of loyalty to Dr Byrne, and he wished only to be loyal. He added: 'In whatever capacity it remains possible for me to work for Your Grace, I will most willingly continue to do all I can.'

He then went on to deal with the plans to amalgamate St Ultans and Harcourt Street Children's Hospitals, and added that Dr Collis was behind a new hospital in Crumlin for chronic rheumatic children, where children or adults might remain for up to three years. Such an institution in non-Catholic hands was the very negation of all that His Grace had worked for. When he received further information, Fr McQuaid concluded, he would ask the archbishop to be good enough to see him that he might report fully and in person.[12]

A final appearance
On 4 July celebrations were held in St Patrick's Home, Kilmainham, Dublin, to commemorate the centenary of the congregation of the Little Sisters of the Poor. The archbishop made a special effort to be present. He presided at the special Mass, and among those in attendance were the Taoiseach, the Tánaiste, and Mrs Clarke, Lord Mayor of Dublin. An *Evening Herald* photograph of the occasion reveals him stooped, assisted by a younger clergyman, and walking with difficulty and with the help of an umbrella. It was to be his final public appearance.[13]

Intimations of war
On 12 July, Archbishop's House received a formal reminder of international tensions and of the imminence of war. The secretary to the Ministry of Defence wrote to Fr O'Donnell regarding the training of primary teachers in air raid precautions, as had been discussed with His Grace on 19 April. To date some 1,200 teachers had received instruction. Now the training was being extended to each house of the Religious in the diocese. It would suffice if one member from each religious house undertook the training. The letter included a memorandum on air-raid precautions.[14]

Archival material
On the same date, the Irish Manuscripts Commission, which was publishing 'a calendar of the documents which belonged to the warden of the church of St Nicholas, Galway', wrote asking His Grace's permission that the Propaganda material relating to Ireland in the possession of the Archbishop of Dublin be transcribed by the Commission. There was no immediate reply from His Grace. The matter, perhaps, did not seem pressing, or the archbishop's attention was faltering, or his secretaries, between them, failed to respond. On 1 August, S. Brereton, secretary of the Commission, wrote to Fr Dunne, enclosing a copy of the letter of

12 July and stating that he would be grateful for a reply. The draft of the reply, written on Brereton's letter, and dated 12 August, observed that some of the documents in question were not in the Dublin archdiocese, and he (Fr Dunne) was transcribing those that were. 'It is the particular desire of the Archbishop', Dunne stated, 'that no reference be made in the publication to the existence of Propaganda transcripts in the Dublin archives.'[15] His Grace still sought, it would seem, to preserve as much independence as possible from the Roman bureaucracy.

The quiet munificence of Dr Byrne

On 27 August, Bishop Fogarty, of Killaloe, expressed surprise and gratitude on receiving a cheque of £50 towards his cathedral fund.[16] He subsequently made the donation public in Ennis, even though, as he confessed, he knew how Dr Byrne shrank from such notoriety and wished to keep his charity hidden.[17] In October, the archbishop made out a cheque for £1,000 towards a new church of Corpus Christi, Griffith Avenue;[18] and in November the Lord Mayor's secretary thanked him for his £100 contribution to the Mansion House Coal Fund to assist the poor over the winter.

A matter for compensation

Meantime, the demands of war impinged on the site of the proposed cathedral. The City Corporation decided to close Merrion Square while they were erecting air raid shelters there. His Grace's solicitors, Arthur O'Hagan and Son, stated 'that His Grace, the Archbishop, could not take the responsibility of refusing permission to have the square closed for the couple of months during which the work would be carried out with the possibility of a serious claim in case of an accident'. Persons in possession of keys were allowed to avail of the square. A Dr Peppard, who had paid £2.2.0 for the use of the square for a year, claimed a refund of the £2.2.0 because his nurse was refused admission to the Square. Up to this no other resident had made any claim. Subject to the approval of the Archbishop, his solicitors proposed to refund to anyone who claimed, £1.0.0 or one half of their subscription for the current year and to claim for these sums as part of the compensation to be paid by the Corporation in due course.[19]

As the year drew to a close, Dr Byrne met with an accident, but there was no immediate awareness of its gravity.

An Unfortunate Accident

On 1 January 1940, Mgr P. J. Walsh, parish priest in Glasthule, Co Dublin, and former secretary of the archbishop, informed Bishop Michael Fogarty, of Killaloe, that Dr Byrne, in endeavouring to get down a book from a shelf in his study, fell and remained lying unable to get up, or to ring for help. When he was found and the doctor summoned, it was thought that the pain in his leg was muscular.[20] Subsequently, it was discovered that he had a broken femur and would be in bed for four or five weeks. There was some anxiety, however, because of his frailty that pneumonia or other complications might develop. 'For a man, not much over 67', Walsh commented, he was 'very old in body', but 'mentally he had been better recently than he was five years ago'.[21]

At first, Dr Byrne seemed to be making steady progress. He was able to carry out some diocesan business[22] and he received many visitors, including the Nuncio Apostolic, Mgr Paschal Robinson,[23] and Bishop Fogarty.

Setback and decline

As time passed, however, the archbishop's condition worsened. On 26 January, Mgr Walsh provided Bishop Fogarty with the latest information. 'I don't know how exactly you found Dr Byrne when you called at Drumcondra. He varied then – one day down, very down, the next, rather alert and hopeful. I wish to post your Lordship up to date.' The archbishop's condition was not hopeful. He had been steadily worsening, was mentally dull and despondent and inclined to give up the fight. 'This morning, Fr Dunne told me that things are not improved since yesterday, *au contraire*. There is no immediate collapse expected, but the impression is that he is slowly slipping into the terminus.'[24]

The Terminus. The Death and Wake of Archbishop Edward Byrne

The impression proved accurate. On the morning of 9 February, His Grace, Most Rev Dr Edward J Byrne, Archbishop of Dublin and Primate of Ireland, died at Archbishop's House, Drumcondra.

On that date, the *Evening Herald* evoked not the frail, faltering figure of recent years, but the earlier primate – 'Tall and stately in appearance, and full of quiet dignity, he was eminently

gifted to command respect'; and the paper's contributors told of
the qualities that stood out in the people's memories, his humility,
wisdom, piety, and gentleness. One contributor, L. M. Honohan,
was moved to evoke such qualities in verse:

Unto his pastures drew
By counsel wise
And words that did not chide
...
Of stately figure he,
Of gentle mien,
Of piety profound
Of soul serene
...
Though great, yet humble
Always priestly he ...

Dr Collier, Bishop of Ossory, who was the panegyrist at the
month's mind on 11 March, endeavoured to provide as much information and insight as possible concerning the reticent archbishop. He told of his long devotion to the Eucharist and how in
his final days, when his self-effacement led him to say, 'I am
going, and I have done nothing', his friends reminded him of his
work for the poor and especially the praise given to God by the
Eucharistic Congress, and then a great peace descended and
stayed with him to the end.[25]

The remains of the archbishop were brought from
Archbishop's House to the Church of the Holy Cross, Clonliffe,
where they stayed for two days. Between 2.00 pm and 8.00 pm
thousands of people, especially the poor, flocked to the church
to pay their respects. On 12 February, the coffin was moved to
the Pro-Cathedral. The route from Clonliffe to the Pro-Cathedral
was lined with thousands of people. 'There were many touching
scenes', the *Evening Herald* commented on 12 February. 'At various points along the route people were kneeling in prayer, while
some overcome with grief, burst into tears as the horse-drawn
hearse approached.' Behind the hearse came Dr Byrne's three
secretaries, followed by the Taoiseach, Tánaiste, Ceann Comhairle,
chiefs of staff, the representatives of the Lord Mayor and other
officials. Business along the route was suspended. Flags flew at
half-mast. The roadway was a mass of kneeling people when
Marlborough Street was reached. The remains lay in state in the

Pro-Cathedral on 12 and 13 February from 2 to 9 pm. During the afternoon and evening thousands filed past the bier. So large were the crowds at times that the queues stretched from the church around the corner and up to O'Connell Street[26] as people waited patiently in piercing east winds to obtain a final glimpse of the calm face of their archbishop. 'For unaffected grief and solemnity', Dr Collier observed, 'the obsequies of our Archbishop will remain unique.'[27]

His last wishes, according to his secretary, were that no pomp or circumstance attend his passing from the world. This was adhered to as regards liturgy and prayers, and the funeral procession was left largely unannounced, yet the word spread and the city insisted on expressing its regard and reverence.

Funeral and burial
Shortly after 8 o'clock on the evening of 13 February, the coffin was closed and moved from the side altar to a catafalque in front of the high altar. Next day, entry to the solemn Office and re-quiem Mass was by ticket only. The funeral was scheduled for 11 am. People began to gather outside from 9 am, and by 11 o'clock the crowd had swollen to an estimated 5,000. Within the church Cardinal MacRory, the Nuncio Apostolic, four archbish-ops, nineteen bishops, two Cistercian abbots, and a large num-ber of priests were present for the solemn ceremonies; and also in attendance were the President of Éire, the Taoiseach, the Tánaiste, members of government, the diplomatic corps, mem-bers of the judiciary, representatives of many public bodies and the professions, as well as members of the Dáil and Seanad and high government officials.[28]

Following the final blessing, the body of Dr Edward Byrne was placed in the vaults of the Pro-Cathedral. His secretary, Patrick Dunne, was quoted on 13 February as stating: 'It was the wish of the Archbishop to have his remains lie in the vaults of the Pro-Cathedral until they could be placed in the crypt of the new cathedral in Merrion Square' – the great basilica in stone, which he envisaged, after the Emancipation Centenary in 1929, as the assertion of a Catholic people that the inferiority generated by the penal laws was gone forever.[29]

Tributes
Tributes to the dead archbishop and votes of sympathy poured

into Archbishop's House. The messages of sympathy came from all sorts of bodies and associations great and small. The tributes referred again and again to his care for the poor, his importance as a builder of churches and schools to meet the needs of expanding Dublin, his personal charm and approachability, and his shunning of publicity to the point of making no pronouncements except on necessary religious affairs.

'He was a silent archbishop', Dr Collier observed, and some were inclined to call his silence timidity, but 'nothing could be farther from truth and fact'. He was 'always kindly and human' with 'a wide understanding and tolerance of the shortcomings, follies and failings of others ... but where there was a question of any important point of church discipline, principle or right, he was inexorable. His judgement', however, was 'calm and sound', and he avoided 'hasty decisions'.[30] Speaking in Dublin Corporation, Alderman Tom Kelly TD, drew attention to the flag floating at half-mast on the tower of St Patrick's Church of Ireland Cathedral as typifying the respect and esteem in which the archbishop was held outside the Catholic Church. 'Dr Byrne avoided political affiliation', his panegyrist remarked, 'but he was keenly supportive of good order and tranquility within the state and internationally.' The *Irish Press* wrote of him: 'Clearly a great ecclesiastic rather than a man interested in public affairs, he held the respect of all creeds and classes despite very troubled times during the greater part of his episcopacy.'[31]

'Interested in public affairs'

Dr Byrne was not a political bishop, but it was not accurate to describe him as not 'interested in public affairs'. He had taken steps to avert the civil war, and Mr Cosgrave had ample evidence of his interest in public affairs, especially when it concerned the welfare of prisoners, or actions and policies conflicting with justice and morality. Historians have noted his correspondence and even friendship with the leader of Cumann na nGaedheal, which might suggest a distance or reserve in his relations with De Valera. This distance was there at first, but it dissipated after the Eucharistic Congress. De Valera, indeed, a man so careful in his use of words, sent the following 'confidential' letter to Bishop Wall, in response to the latter's message of appreciation at his presence at the funeral:

My dear Lord Bishop,

I received your letter. The members of the Government all looked upon it as a privilege that they were able by their presence at the funeral services to mark their esteem and affection for the late Archbishop. We all experienced his kindliness when he received us on several national occasions at the Pro-Cathedral: over and above this, on more than one occasion he showed his paternal interest in us and in our work. When difficulties about certain aspects of the Constitution arose, he was a most understanding counsellor and friend. I shall never cease to be grateful, and will always remember him for it.[32]

It is a testimony that bears out the observation in Dr Collier's address, that though Archbishop Byrne 'took no formal public part in political affairs, yet when called on for help or counsel, he was a sound and careful adviser, with a balanced mind and keen judgement, and many public men will gratefully acknowledge the help he gave in difficult and delicate negotiations. These things are not recorded in any written documents or archives, but they will live in the grateful memories of the men he helped.'[33]

A generous, humble, and 'Godly man'

A generous patron of worthy causes, Edward Byrne, as has been noted in previous pages, had a special regard for the work of the St Vincent de Paul Society. The president of the society spoke of him as more than a great church dignitary. 'He was a kindly father. He loved to attend the annual meetings of the Night Shelter ... His heart went out to those destitute men in need of a night's lodging in Dublin.' The speaker went on to praise his wonderful generosity to the poor and to tell of the boys and girls who had been educated 'in a good secondary school through His Grace's generosity'.

He was 'a Godly man, intensely religious and prayerful', the *Irish Catholic Directory* commented, with a deep faith, humility, and a strong sense of the responsibility of his office, and it was the combination of all these attributes, and the courage with which his malady was borne, that won the affection and admiration of people of all classes, and especially the poor and his much loved men's sodality.[34] Judge Comyn, at the Wicklow Circuit Court, captured something of the overall regard in his sweeping observation:

Of all the great prelates, both Gael and Norman, who have
cast lustre on this diocese, none was holier, more humble and
more loveable than the archbishop who is gone.[35]

For Professor Rudmore Brown, who wrote from Trinity
College Dublin, a 'great and good man has gone to his reward';
and the writer, Mary Macken, spoke of the loss to the people 'of
his great and saintly presence'.[36]

Last will and testament
On 11 December 1934, Dr Byrne had made his last will and testament. He had no immediate family with any claim on him. He
left virtually everything to his successor to dispose of. He appointed as executors and trustees, Mgr Cronin, and Rev Patrick
Dunne, one of his secretaries. He bequeathed to them all the furniture, chattels, motor car etc. in Archbishop's House to be held
in trust for the person 'who shall first succeed me as Roman
Catholic Archbishop of the Diocese of Dublin'. He directed his
executors, until the appointment of his successor, to provide out
of his estate 'for the support of and maintenance of my secretaries, chaplain, and servants in Archbishop's House'. He gave
his 'country residence known as Thorndale, Delgany, Co
Wicklow, and the lands held therewith and all furniture etc.' to
his trustees until his successor was appointed. If the said archbishop decided not to use the property, his trustees were to sell
it and the proceeds were to go to his residuary estate. All the
rest, residue and remainder of his property, were to be held in
trust to be applied to such charitable purposes as his successor
shall think fit. Finally, all funds and properties given to him for
charitable purposes to be used at his discretion, he decreed that
all should be applied to 'the erection, extension and structural
improvement of churches and schools in the diocese when and
required by the archbishop for the time being'.[37]

The successor

Hardly had the archbishop died than speculation about his successor became a frequent topic. It went on for several months. Mgr Boylan, professor of Hebrew at Maynooth, was favoured by many of the diocesan clergy, and he and his family expected that he would be appointed.[38] Frank Duff, with an eye to the treatment experienced by the Legion of Mary, is reputed to have written to Rome advising against the appointment of Bishop Francis Wall, who had temporary charge of the archdiocese as vicar capitular, or of Mgr James J. Dunne.[39] Eventually, Fr John Charles McQuaid CSSp, was announced as the successor to the see of Dublin.

Attitude of the clergy

Writing to Bishop Fogarty from Glasthule on 14 November 1940, Mgr Patrick Walsh conveyed the reaction of the Dublin clergy.

> Dr McQuaid's appointment was a surprise. His name was put forward – not by the bishops – some time ago. Then his and another name receded into the background. Boylan was definitely passed over some weeks ago. There is a suspicion among some of the clergy that there has been political meddling – a thing entirely to be deprecated.
>
> Dr Wall expressed well the attitude of the Dublin clergy: I have known Dr McQuaid for years – a neighbour here – but not intimately. I hope he will be an excellent bishop. We need in Dublin the best of bishops in our diocesan interest, and in the interests of the country. The clergy whom I have met generally feel that a slur has been put upon our body. They consider that the new archbishop is not of over-topping merit compared with some of our own priests; and they do not like the principle of appointing a Regular. Surprise, reverent acquiescence, loyal support for the nominee of the Holy See – these are the sentiments.[40]

Ten days later, Walsh wrote again. The clergy of Dublin had entrusted to him the task of presenting in Latin their address to the new archbishop. He enclosed his draft and asked Dr Fogarty to see if he had struck the right note. He then proceeded to give his own views on the new prelate quite apart from the draft:

Dr McQuaid is a man who, I think, will be very useful to your Episcopal body. He has been intimately associated with educational and social questions for years past. He is quiet, reticent, easy-mannered, and a far-seeing strategist who prepares his campaigns carefully beforehand. So that when the question of tactics arises, his adversaries have often found that he had them surrounded, their positions untenable. God grant he may turn out what we all earnestly wish

No Irish bishop, not even the cardinal, was consulted, and I think that even the nuncio's advice was not the deciding factor. Macaulay, the Irish representative at the Vatican, was *il diavolochi spinger* (devilish pusher).[41]

Political lobbying

Walsh's information was partly correct. William J. B. Macaulay, the Irish representative, had left a memorandum with the relevant Vatican personnel, perhaps Mgr Domenico Tardini, which pointed directly to McQuaid as the best choice for archbishop. He seems to have been told, however, that the nuncio was already interesting himself in finding the best man.[42] This suggests that the nuncio's recommendation was the most important, and may have resulted in a government representation to Paschal Robinson. Anecdotal evidence, however, suggests that, even before Dr Byrne's death, the nuncio favoured McQuaid's appointment. The biographer of John Charles McQuaid quotes the historian, Fr Seán Farragher, for the following story: 'Prior to Archbishop Byrne's death Paschal Robinson visited him to discuss, among other routine matters, the future stewardship of the diocese. After the meeting, Byrne told Fr Tom O'Donnell: "I am happy to know that my choice of successor has the support of the nuncio. And you will be happy too".'[43]

The nuncio had, of course, visited the ailing Dr Byrne, as mentioned earlier, and as to what was, or was not discussed, it is likely that Dr Byrne would have approved of McQuaid as a successor. The latter had the valuable qualities mentioned by Mgr P. G. Walsh, and he (Byrne) got on well with him, had trusted him and been impressed by his ability and his negotiating skills.

Dr Byrne's episcopate compared

There remains the image presented of Dr Byrne's episcopate as compared to that of Dr McQuaid.

John Cooney, biographer of John Charles McQuaid, remarks, on information attributed to Fr Denis Carroll CSSp, that Paschal Robinson 'was unhappy with the laxity that had crept into the Dublin diocese as a result of Byrne's prolonged illness, when the diocese had been run by his senior secretary, Fr Tom O'Donnell, and a group of powerful clergy, which included another of the archbishop's secretaries, Fr Patrick Dunne. This group would regularly settle diocesan business while playing billiards, and came to be known as "the billiards room cabinet".'[44]

A somewhat similar description of diocesan affairs, but without reference to the nuncio, appeared, perhaps for the first time in print, in the late John Feeney's short biography of Dr McQuaid, and is cited in Maurice Hartegan's much quoted PhD thesis on 'The Catholic Laity of Dublin, 1920-1940'. In short, compared to the highly efficient, autocratic administration of Dr McQuaid, the diocese under Dr Byrne is depicted as loosely organised, something of a shambles, and governed by a clique so casual as to make decisions concerning people and fellow priests while playing billiards. It is a colourful picture, illumined by the clever phrase 'the billiards room cabinet', but is it accurate?

The present author has found no evidence of 'laxity' calling for major reform. Neither, it seems, did the Papal Nuncio, Paschal Robinson. His reports to Rome for the critical years 1936-1940 make no reference to Byrne's health and administration.[45] Undoubtedly, Dr Byrne's ill-health greatly lessened his overall impact, but he was still sufficiently on top of events for De Valera to benefit from his advice little more than two years prior to his death; in his final illness he was still making important decisions; and the obituary in the *Times*, on 10 February 1940, affirmed that 'he retained until the last an active control over the ecclesiastical affairs of the archdiocese. His long relations with the archdiocese established relations of mutual confidence with the senior clergy and the existence of a well organised archiepiscopal curia was of great assistance to him throughout his long illness'.[46] Moreover, as Bishop Collier was at pains to emphasise, he enjoyed the loyalty and affection of his priests, young and old, who wished to do all they could to please him.

As regards 'the billiards room cabinet', one can readily understand Dr Byrne's secretaries making use of the billiard room in Archbishop's House, after all it was there for relaxation, and even discussing items of business from time to time as they

played, but it seems quite bizarre and almost incredible that
senior figures like Bishop Wall, Mgr Cronin and Mgr Waters
'would regularly join the secretaries and settle diocesan business while playing billiards'. We don't even know if they ever
played billiards during their years as priests. Again, there appears to be no substantive evidence that the Apostolic Nuncio
'was unhappy with the laxity that had crept into the Dublin diocese as a result of Byrne's prolonged illness'. The widespread
mourning of the people provides no indication of concern about
'laxity', and during Byrne's administration the faith and devotion
of the people was at a very high level.

Moreover, it cannot be ignored that, despite the inroads of
his illness from an early stage in his episcopate, he had embarked on the immensely successful Catholic Centenary celebrations, which so enthused him that he pressed Rome for the
Eucharistic Congress in Dublin, trusting Paul-like that he could
do all things in him who strengthened him. *In Deo Speravi* was
his motto. He was rewarded with an extraordinary manifestation of co-operation and goodwill that did much to heal the bitterness of the civil war. And again, despite his incapacities he
planned actively to meet the spiritual needs of an expanding
Dublin, and imparted a confidence and enthusiasm to his clergy
that led, in addition to new schools, to 'twenty-three new churches,
great and small, and six reconstructed buildings including the
Pro-Cathedral'. In addition, he had the vision of a great cathedral
and bought the site for it, leaving it to his successors to construct
it in better times. And despite his growing frailty and disability
in his final years, he, as noted in the *Times*, retained until the last,
with the aid of his well organised curia, an active control over
the ecclesiastical affairs of the archdiocese.

Human qualities
Finally, moving from the state of the diocese to a more personal,
human level, those who knew Edward Byrne best, as Dr Collier
recalled, spoke of him as 'a great gentleman, to whom the performance of gracious things came naturally', a lover of the arts,
literature and nature, who knew the name of every flower by the
wayside from Dublin to Wicklow. Above all, as bishop, he was
remembered as a friend and 'kindly father', a man with a com-
passionate heart to all his people, especially the poor, and he
was loved in return. Indeed, his very weakness may have been

his strength, drawing his people to him by his efforts to carry on with patience and cheerfulness, and by his deep unassuming spirituality.

By ordinary human reckoning, Edward Byrne is 'the forgotten archbishop', not deemed worthy of mention in a number of dictionaries of Irish biography.[47] Ironically, and a real measure of greatness as a Christian pastor, he would have been happy with such anonymity as a further link with the poor, who leave no mark in history's pages.

Notes

CHAPTER ONE

1. Dublin Diocesan Archives (DDA), Byrne papers. AB/7/a/1/48: 'Names of Ancestors and Relations of Most Rev E. J. Byrne DD, Archbishop of Dublin', as given by Mr William Costelloe, July 1923.
2. Edward–Edward junior, 9 May 1889. DDA. Blue folder. Letters from relatives and friends.
3. Bishop Collier's panegyric, original ms copy as distinct from shorter published version, p 5
4. DDA. Byrne papers. Schoolboy diary, 1885-1888
5. Words of James J. Macken, 61 Darthmouth Square, on 26 Aug 1920, in a letter of congratulation on Edward's elevation to bishop.
6. DDA. Letter of Sr Mac Loughlin, Convent of Mercy, Strabane, in which she observed: 'I never thought that one day I would kneel to kiss your hand instead of whacking it, but *tempore mutantur*.' In files of letters of congratulation on his appointment as bishop, file for 25 Aug 1920.
7. DDA. Diary for 25 Feb & 30 March 1885, 23 Sept 1886.
8. 'Belvedere in History' in J. Bowman ed, *Portraits. Belvedere College, Dublin, 1832-1982*; and letters of Fr Finlay-Fr Beckx, Belvedere archives, courtesy of Paul Andrews SJ, former rector; and see T. J. Morrissey, *Thomas A. Finlay SJ, 1848-1940* (Dublin 2004), pp 19-20.
9. The Intermediate Examinations were divided into Junior (under 15 years), Middle (under 17), Senior (under 18). Comment in *Freeman's Journal*, following his consecration as bishop in October 1920, in the course of 'an appreciation' by a contemporary; and DDA. Byrne papers. Blue folder, with letters from friends and relatives.
10. *The Belvederian*, 1940, vol xii, no 2, pp 28-29
11. See Gerry Walsh, *How' ya Doc? First Ninety Years of the Belvedere Newsboys' Club, 1918-2008* (Drogheda 2010).
12. These are referred to in letters to and from his mother, and the enjoyment of attending opera is indicated by a letter from his friend, Nick Murphy, 30 Oct 1887. DDA. Blue folder. Letters from relatives and friends.
13. DDA. Byrne papers. Blue folder with some 13 letters from relatives and friends.
14. DDA. Blue folder. Letters from relatives and friends.
15. Morrissey, Thomas J., *William J. Walsh, Archbishop of Dublin, 1841-1921* (Dublin 2000), pp 79-81.
16. DDA. Blue folder. Letters from relatives and friends.
17. Morrissey, T. J., *William J. Walsh* ..., pp.110-112; Tobias Kirby papers,

archives of Irish College Rome, and cf Emmet Larkin, *The Roman Catholic Church and the Plan of Campaign* (Cork 1978), pp 255-6.

18. R. F. Foster 'Parnell and his Neighbours' in K. Hannigan & W. Nolan eds., *Wicklow History and Society* (Dublin 1994), pp 900-902

19. Kirby papers in *Archivum Hibernicum*, 32, no 482, p 27, cit Morrissey, op cit, p 132

20. DDA. Blue folder iam cit.

21. Idem.

22. DDA. Byrne papers. His British passport description.

23. Irish College Rome Archives (ICRA). Fr John Hagan's papers, Hag 1/1923/538.

24. Rory Sweetman, 'Waving the green flag in the southern hemisphere: the Kellys and the Irish College Rome' in *The Irish College Rome and its World*, ed. Daire Keogh & Albert McDonnell (Dublin 2008), pp 209-11

25. ICRA. *Status Particularis Studiorum 1891-1908*, from July 1892-July 1895

26. Idem, *Distributio Praemiorum apud Pont. Collegium Urbanum de Propaganda Fide, 1875-1909*, for year 1894.

27. DDA. Box on 'Family and Student Days'. AB/7/a/1/17.

28. DDA. 'Family & Student Diary' Box. AB/7/a/1/2

29. Idem, AB/7/a/1/3

30. Idem, 1/5

31. DDA. 'Memorabilia' in 'Family & Student Days'. AB/7/a/1/1-12

32. DDA. 'Abp Byrne unsorted material'. It is not clear who was the recipient of the letter.

33. ICRA. Hag.1/1923/538. 1 Nov. 1894

34. DDA. 'Abp Byrne unsorted material'.

35. *Irish Catholic Directory* (ICD) 1896 (for 1895); 20 Jan 1895, pp 334-5.

36. Dermot Keogh. 'John Hagan and radical Irish nationalism, 1916-1930: a study in political Catholicism', in Keogh & McDonnell iam cit., pp 242-3

CHAPTER TWO

1. DDA. Byrne papers. 'Abp. Byrne unsorted material'

2. DDA. Byrne papers. Blue folder, the letters of Abp Walsh, mainly on appointments

3. Idem, blue folder. Letters of Abp Walsh.

4. DDA. '24 Aug 1920. Letters of congratulation from Rush, e.g. 'Rush is simply wild with excitement, and the whole town will be illuminated tonight.'

5. Idem, 'unsorted material'

6. DDA. Byrne papers. Dr Donnelly-Byrne, Nov 1900

7. ICRA. Logue-Murphy, 21 Nov 1901; in 'Murphy 1901, no 14'

8. Idem, Donnelly-Murphy, 26 Nov; 'Murphy, 1901, no 17'; and 29 Nov; 'Murphy, 1901, no 18'

9. Idem, Walsh-Murphy, 29 Nov; 'Murphy, 1901, no 19'. Italics mine.
10. Idem, Edward Byrne, St John's, Blackrock-Dr Murphy, 3 Dec 1901; 'Murphy 1901, no 21'.
11. Idem, Walsh-Murphy, 17 Dec 1901; 'Murphy 1901, no 23'.
12. DDA. 'Byrne unsorted material'
13. Duties of Vice-rector, courtesy Rev Albert McDonnell, rector Irish College Rome, 9 Feb 2010
14. DDA. Byrne papers. AB/7/1/ 41-49
15. Idem, Byrne papers. 'Unsorted material'
16. Idem, Donnelly-Byrne, 4 Jan 1903, in Blue folder with 'letters mainly of Abp Walsh'.
17. Idem, 'unsorted material'.
18. Idem
19. ICRA. Bp McRedmond-Byrne, 10 Sept 1903; 'Murphy 1903, no 51'
20. DDA. Blue folder, 'Letters mainly of Abp Walsh'.
21. ICRA. Byrne-Hagan. Hag 1/ 1920/363
22. DDA. File 'HXC 1920'. James Liston, Holy Cross College, Mosgiel-Fr Byrne, 16 May 1920.
23. ICRA. Donnelly-Murphy, 29 Jan 1904; 'Murphy 1904, no 11'.
24. DDA. Byrne papers. Blue folder. 'Letters mainly of Abp Walsh'
25. DDA. File 'ICR 1902'. Formal typed report for Academic Year 1902-3.
26. ICRA. Walsh-Murphy, 14 Feb 1904; 'Murphy 1904, no 19'
27. DDA. Blue folder, 'Letters mainly of Abp Walsh'.
28. DDA. Walsh-Byrne, 13 May 1904, Blue folder idem
29. ICRA. Hag 1/1923/538
30. ICD, 1906 (for 1905), November.
31. T. J. Morrissey, *William J. Walsh* ..., pp 242-3
32. Information courtesy of the late Mgr Michael Nolan.
33. D. McCarthy, *St Mary's Pro-Cathedral Dublin*, Irish Heritage Series (Dublin 1988).
34. DDA. File '28 Aug 1920'. Edward Martyn-Fr Byrne, 28 Aug 1920, on occasion of his appointment as bishop: 'There is no one worthier; you may derive confidence from that being the universal opinion.'
35. Idem, file for '27 Aug 1920'. Letter from G. Butler & Son, Monument House, Bachelor's Walk, congratulating the new bishop and assuring him that he would have his 'piano player' ready next week.
36. DDA. 'Unsorted material' and AB/7/a/1/7
37. DDA. 'Undated material c. 1920'. Letter of congratulations to the new bishop from Fr Clement, Capuchin, writing from Cork.
38. DDA. File '1-30 Sept', letter of congratulation to Bishop Byrne from Wm Brophy, Wigan, 7 Sept 1920.
39. Clr Michael Staines in tribute to Abp Byrne, in *Irish Press*, 14 Feb 1940
40. DDA. File '27 Aug 1920'. G. Butler & Son-Fr Byrne.
41. ICD,1910 (1909) June , p 479ff
42. DDA. Dillon-Mrs Byrne, 13 July 1909, in 'Abp Byrne Unsorted material'

43. ICD, 20 Jan 1910, pp 459-61.

CHAPTER THREE

1. ICD, 1912 (for 1911), p 532
2. ICRA. Byrne-Hagan, 23 March 1912. Hag 1/1912/25
3. ICD, 1914 (1913), p 533
4. ICD, 1914, 16-28 Oct 1913, pp 534-5
5. ICD, 25 Jan 1914, p 499, indicated that the needs of the children were such that in the three months up to 25 January, the Dublin Children's Distressed Fund, founded by the archbishop, had distributed: 'Boys clothing – 1,200 suits, 1,173 jerseys, 1,173 knickers, 1,598 shirts, and 2, 843 pairs of boots and stockings. Girls clothing – 2,329 dresses, 2,214 sets of underclothing, and 3,098 pairs of boots and stockings.'
6. DDA. Box AB/7/a/13; box 2 'Family and Student Matters'.
7. DDA. File '1-30 September 1920'. Letter of congratulation to the new bishop, on 30 Sept 1920, from Ebor (?) Hall, Clonbur, and enquiring: 'Have you done any fishing this season? Lough Corrib is just the same.'
8. ICD, 1915, 2 April 1914, p 508
9. ICD, May 1914, p.512
10. Idem, 29 July 1914, pp 527-8
11. Idem, 2 Aug 1914, p 528
12. Idem, 1916 (1915) and 15 Dec 1914, p 499
13. Idem, 1917, re Easter week 1916, p 509
14. 'A Record by Rev John Flanagan CC' in Roger McHugh's *Dublin 1916* (London 1916), p 190.
15. DDA. Letter of Sr Benedict O'Sullivan-Fr Byrne, 24 August 1920, on the occasion of his appointment as bishop.
16. ICD, 1917 (for 1916), p 510
17. Idem, May 1916, p 509
18. *Fifty Years A-Growing. Story of Independent Newspapers Ltd* (Dublin 1955), p 59
19. ICRA. Wm L. Farrell-Hagan, 2 June 1916; Hag 1/1916/69
20. Letter in T. J. Morrissey, *Bishop Edward Thomas O'Dwyer of Limerick, 1842-1917* (Dublin 2003), p 378
21. DDA. Byrne papers. 'Family & Student Days', in a brown-backed notebook filled with quotations ('Memorabilia') extending beyond family and student days, AB/7/a/1/1-2
22. ICD, 1918 (1917), pp 504-5. Foreign churchmen who contributed were Cardinals Farley, O'Connell, Gibbons, and Mgr Hartnett in North America, Bishop Verdon, Dunedin, New Zealand, and Archbishops Duhig, Mannix, Kelly, and Maitland in Australia.
23. T.J. Morrissey, *William J. Walsh* … pp 307-8
24. DDA. 'Undated Material c. 1920'. Fr P. J. Lynch, of diocese of Clogher, but resident in Dublin, in the course of a letter of congratulation to Fr Byrne on August 1920

25. Morrissey, op. cit., p 310

26. J. H. Bernard-Dr Davidson, Abp of Canterbury, April 1918, cit. D. W. Miller, *Church, State, and Nation in Ireland 1898-1921* (Dublin 1973), pp 407-9.

27. Dr Collier in ms of panegyric

28. DDA. Box on 'Diocese of Ossory'. Letter to Cardinal G. De Lai, 3 Feb 1918; and an account in English of decision at Bishops' meeting on 28 Oct 1918

29. DDA. Brown-backed hardcover notebook, AB/7, misplaced in Byrne papers under 'Family and Student Days'.

30. ICRA. Curran-Hagan, 27/4/1919; Hag 1/1919/87

31. DDA. Bp Collier's panegyric ms.

32. ICRA. E. R. Morrissey-Hagan, 1 May 1919; Hag 1/1919/94

33. Idem, Ryan-Hagan, 6 July 1919; Hag 1/1919/195

34. Idem, Curran-Hagan, 14 Sept; Hag 1/1919/537

35. ICRA. P. J. Lyons-Hagan, 5 May 1919; Hag 1/1919/97

36. Idem, Curran-Hagan, 14 Sept 1919; Hag 1/1919/537

37. ICD, 1920, for 8 & 20 Nov 1

38. T. J. Morrissey, *Bishop Edward Thomas O'Dwyer of Limerick, 1842-1917*, p 48

39. DDA. File '25 August 1920', congratulations to Bishop Byrne, from T. J. Maguire, Claremount Road, Sandymount, 'Your affectionate cousin'.

40. Armagh Diocesan Archives (ADA). Card Logue papers. Prot. N. 362/20

41. Morrissey, *William J. Walsh ...*, p 334

42. ICRA. Byrne-Hagan, 28 Aug 1920; Hag 1/1920/363

43. ICRA. Byrne-Curran, 2 Sept 1920. Curran papers (uncatalogued) box 1 (1914-1926) in folder 1914-1922.

44. DDA. File '25 Aug 1920'. John Waters-Ned Byrne

45. DDA. File '24 August 1920'. Fr Edward Masterson SJ, Milltown Park, to Bishop Byrne.

46. Idem, '25 August'. Dudlegh White-Fr Byrne.

47. Idem, Bishop D. Hallinan, Limerick, to Bishop Byrne

48. DDA. File '1-30 Sept 1920'. Michael Cardinal Logue, 2 Sept., to Bishop Byrne.

49. Idem, file '11-23 August 1920'. P. J. Walsh-Ned Byrne, 10 August.

50. Idem, file '1-30 Sept' Bishop Joseph Mac Rory-Bishop Byrne, 4 Sept

51. cf. T. J. Morrissey, *William J. Walsh, Archbishop of Dublin*, pp 339-40

52. DDA. 'Undated material c. 1920'. Fr P. J. Lynch, The Castle, Stillorgan, to Bishop Byrne on 26 August. Member of Clogher diocese.

CHAPTER FOUR

1. DDA. Box on 'Diocese of Ossory'. Bishop Brownrigg-Dr Byrne, Bishop of Spigaz, 18 April 1921

2. *Evening Herald*, 9 Feb 1940

3. Gabriel Daly OSA, 'Modernism' in J. A. Komanchak, M.Collins, D. A. Lane eds, *The New Dictionary of Theology* (Dublin 1987), pp 668-70

4. 'Lay Catholic Action' as envisaged by Pius X referred to works of charity undertaken by laity for the welfare of the Catholic Church. The works had to be subject to 'the advice and superior direction of ecclesiastical authority'. Pius X, *Il Formo Proposito* (1905), par 4, cit. M. Curtis, *The Splendid Cause*, p 6

5. Maurice Curtis, *The Splendid Cause. The Catholic Action Movement in Ireland in the 20th Century* (Dublin 2008), pp 54-5.

6. DDA. Published as a pamphlet, 1924; also in Curtis, op. cit., p 6

7. DDA. Box entitled 'Byrne appt as Abp', file containing congratulations from many sides.

8. DDA. 'Letters of Bishops'. Brownrigg-Byrne, 5 April 1922

9. This account is largely based on Maurice Hartigan's PhD thesis, St Patrick's College, Maynooth, 1992, 'The Catholic Laity of Dublin 1920-1940'

10. The spread of regular clergy has been estimated as follows by O'Hartegan, and probably includes religious brothers, as well as priests, in the case of some orders or congregations: Augustinians 13, Carmelites (discalced) 39, Capuchins 19, Dominicans 24, Franciscans 10, Holy Ghosts 38, Jesuits 83, Marists 12, Oblates 24, Vincentians 50.

11. 'The Souvenir 1928 of the Church of St Vincent de Paul, Marino', p 31. It gives the total number of churches built as 19. Bishop Collier in the manuscript of his panegyric at the 'month's mind' for Abp Byrne, 1940, mentions 23 new churches.

12. Curtis, op. cit., p 45

13. Hartigan, op. cit., pp 144-5

14. Idem, p 32, n 6

15. Idem, p 11

16. Idem, p 12

17. Fr John Rowe, p 85

18. In 1938 the question was raised as to how far rote learning was influencing everyday living, but nothing changed until the 1970s. Then a new curriculum was adopted for primary schools, but it is not evident that the new system has had a major impact on everyday living.

19. O'Hartegan, p 17

20. Idem, p 44

21. Registrar of Royal Hospital for Incurables-William Perrin, 6 Nov 1922, in DDA 'Hospitals-General, Byrne'.

CHAPTER FIVE

1. Italics mine

2. Italics in text

3. UCDA. De Valera papers, P 150/2903. Byrne-De Valera, 3 Jan 1922

4. DDA. Box Govt politics (1), file 'Lord Lieutenant': Byrne- McMahon, 29 Jan 1922, and same date FitzAlan-Byrne.
5. DDA. 'Bishops' Letters'. McHugh-Byrne, 18 Dec 1921
6. Killaloe Diocesan Archives (KDA), F. 9 A. 3: Ml Collins-Fogarty, 13 Jan 1922
7. ICRA. Hag 1/1922/27. Gilmartin-Hagan, 11 Jan 1922
8. UCDA. De Valera papers, P 150/ 1653: D. Fawsett-Ml Collins, 16 Jan 1922; Collins-Fawsett, 17 Jan 1922.
9. ICRA. Hag 1 /1922/56. O'Donnell-Hagan, 23 Jan 1922
10. ICRA. Hag 1/1922/ 77. Byrne-Hagan, 2 Feb 1922
11. Idem, Hag 1/ 1922/ 88. Hagan-Byrne, 7 Feb 1922
12. ICD, 1923 (1922), pp 551-2
13. ICRA. Hag 1/1922/ 194. O'Donnell-Hagan, 10 April 1922.
14. Idem, Hag 1/1922/ 197. Sean T.Ó Ceallaigh-Hagan, 11 April, 1922
15. Idem, Hag 1/1922/196. P. Dunne-Hagan, 11 April 1922
16. Mulhern-Hagan, 7 April 1922, cit. Patrick Murray, *Oracles of God. The Roman Catholic Church and Irish Politics, 1922-1937* (Dublin 2000), p 59.
17. DDA. 'Bishops' Letters'. Logue-Byrne, 5 April 1922
18. Idem, Harty-Byrne, 8 April 1922
19. George Seaver, *John Allen Fitzgerald Gregg, Archbishop of Dublin* (Dublin 1963), p 120. *Spes mea Dominus* = God is my hope.
20. T. P. Coogan, *De Valera* (London 1995), p 314
21. Seaver, *John Allen Fitzgerald Gregg* ..., p 120
22. Idem, p 121
23. DDA. 'Bishops' Letters'. Logue-Byrne, 15 April 1922
24. ICRA. Mulhern-Hagan, 7 April 1922, cit. P. Murray, *Oracles of God*, p 59
25. DDA. 'Diaries and Personalia", small diary for 1922
26. Idem, box on Govt politics (1). Opening address of the Abp at Peace Conference 1922
27. Idem, Notes of Abp Byrne
28. Wm O'Brien, *Forth the Banners Go* (Dublin 1969), pp 219-20
29. O'Brien, op. cit., p 220
30. Coogan, op. cit., p 315
31. ICRA. Hag 1/1922/230 (1). Byrne-Hagan, 1 May 1922
32. Idem
33. DDA. Small diary 1922.
34. DDA. Box 532. 'Govt Dept Education 1922-39'. Corcoran-Byrne, 13 & 16 May 1922
35. DDA. Govt politics (1). Byrne-Farren, 23 May 1922
36. Idem, Dept Education. O'hAodha-Byrne, 22 May 1922; Byrne-O'hAodha, 14 June 1922
37. ICRA. Hag 1/1922/ 303. Curran-Hagan, 14 June 1922
38. DDA. Govt politics (1). 'Office of President of Executive Council'. Cosgrave-Byrne, 22 June 1922

CHAPTER SIX

1. DDA. Box on Govt politics (1). 'Office of President' .... Oscar Traynor, 1 July 1922
2. DDA. Govt politics (1). J. F. Homan, 'Memorandum of Ambulance Work and Efforts for Peace 1922', p 5
3. National Archives Ireland (NAI). Dept of Taoiseach. S 1437; 1 July 1922
4. ICRA. Hag 1/1922/ 347. Curran-Hagan, 2 July 1922
5. DDA. Govt politics. 'Office of President...'. J. F. Homan, 'Memorandum etc'
6. DDA. Govt politics (1): J. Hancock- Ennis, 13 July 1922; Cosgrave-Byrne, 21 July
7. Idem, Byrne-Cosgrave, 23 July 1922
8. Murray, *Oracles of God ...*, pp 151-2
9. DDA. 'Letters of Bishops'. Brownrigg-Byrne, 12 July 1922
10. ICRA. Hag 1/1922/ 393. Hallinan-Hagan, July 1922
11. Idem, Hag 1/1922/ 375. Curran-Hagan, 19 July; Hag. 1/1922/381, idem, 20 July.
12. DDA. Govt politics (1) Plunkett-Byrne, 24 July 1922; copy of Abp's response, 25 July; Plunkett-Byrne, 25 July, 19 August, and response.
13. Idem, 'Dept of Justice'. O'Connor-Byrne, 21 August 1922
14. DDA. Govt politics (1). Dept of Justice folder. Byrne-Miss McSwiney, 24 Feb 1923
15. Photo by 'Hogan, Dublin' in unidentified newspaper cutting in DDA, folder on Pro-Cathedral
16. Dermot McCarthy, *St Mary's Pro-Cathedral* (Irish Heritage Series 60, Dublin 1988), p 23
17. DDA and Kildare & Leighlin Diocesan Archives. Foley-Byrne 22 Aug 1922
18. UCDA. De Valera papers. P. 150/ 2903. L. Ginnell TD-Archbishop of Dublin and editors of newspapers, 14 Sept 1922.
19. Cit. T. J. Morrissey, *A Man Called Hughes* (Dublin 1991), p 160.
20. Bryan in interview with author, 23 Jan 1985
21. DDA. Small diary 1922.
22. DDA. Box on Govt politics (1). Ó Ceallaigh-Byrne, 28 Aug 1922.
23. ICRA. Hag 1/1922/421-25, 426, 444: Mulcahy-Hagan, 2 Sept; Mulcahy-Rogers, 3 Sept; Hagan-Mulcahy, 4 Sept; Liam Mellows & Rory O'Connor-Hagan, 6 Sept (425); De Valera-Miss Ryan, 21 Sept (444).
24. ICRA. Hag 1/1922/ 181: Keohane-E. R. Morrissey, late Sept
25. DDA. Govt politics (1). Markham-Byrne, 10 Oct 1922
26. Italics mine
27. ICD, 1923 (1922), pp.603-13
28. DDA. Govt politics (1). C. O'Moore-Byrne, 11 Oct 1922
29. UCDA. De Valera papers. 'Pastoral' 150/1653
30. Idem

31. Idem
32. DDA. 'Letters of Religious'. Fr Gavin-Byrne, 3 Nov 1922
33. UCDA. MacSwiney papers. P 48a/194 (1). MacSwiney-Byrne, 5 Nov 1922
34. Idem, P 48a/194 (2). Byrne-MacSwiney, 8 Nov
35. NAI. S. 1369/9. Byrne-Cosgrave, 16 Nov 1922
36. DDA. Govt politics (1). Cosgrave-Byrne, 18 Nov 1922
37. Idem, Hagan- Byrne, 2 Dec 1922
38. ICRA. Hag 1/1922/ 515. Patrick O'Donnell-Hagan, 25 Nov 1922
39. UCDA. Patrick McGilligan papers. P 35c/158. Printed pamphlet, 'The Bishops' Pastoral. A Prisoner's Letter to His Grace the Archbishop'. The letter is by Pr. Ó Gallchobhair.
40. DDA. Govt politics (1). P. MacBride, Hon Sec London District Committee ...-Byrne, 17 Nov 1922
41. DDA. 'Bishops' Letters'. Logue-Byrne, 22 Nov 1922
42. Keogh, *Ireland and the Vatican: The Politics and Diplomacy of Church-State Relations 1922-1960* (Cork 1995), p 12
43. ICD, 1923 (1922), p 595
44. Idem, p 543
45. DDA. 'Office of President of Executive Council 1922'. Cosgrave-Byrne, 1 Dec 1922
46. DDA. 'Governor-General', 4 Dec 1922
47. Idem, 'Dept of Defence'. Byrne-Mulcahy 4 Dec. and copy of letter on 30 Dec
48. ICD, 1923 (1922). Pp 543-4
49. DDA. Govt.politics (1). Byrne-Cosgrave, 10 Dec 1922
50. D. Keogh, *The Vatican, the Bishops and Irish Politics, 1919-1930* (Cambridge UP 1986), p 98
51. ICRA. Hag 1/1922/555. CÁit Ó Ceallaigh-Hagan, 8 &12 Dec 1922
52. DDA. Govt politics (1). O'Higgins-Byrne, 20 Dec 1922
53. Idem, Mrs Childers-Byrne, 31 Dec 1922

CHAPTER SEVEN

1. DDA. Govt politics (2). Murphy-Byrne, 3, 12 Feb 1923
2. Idem, Govt politics (1). 'Dept Defence. General Correspondence 1922-39'. Mulcahy-Byrne, 6, 14 Feb 1923
3. Idem, Mulcahy-Byrne, 16 Feb 1923; and 'President of Exec Council', Cosgrave-Byrne, 19 April, re Murphy signing the undertaking.
4. Idem, 'Dept of Justice'. Byrne-Eithne Mac Swiney, 24 Feb 1923
5. Idem, 'Religious Congregations'. Byrne-Provincial of Passionists, 13 Feb 1923; Prov-Byrne, 14 Feb
6. ICD, 1924 (1923), pp 553-4
7. Idem
8. DDA. Govt politics (1). M. MacSwiney-De Valera, 10 Feb 1923; also to illegibly named recipient, 9 Feb 1923. Italics in text.
9. ICD,1924 (1923), 13 March 1923, p 562

10. Armagh Diocesan Archives (ADA). O'Fiaich Memorial Library, M. J. Curran-'My Lord Archbishop', 14 March 1923. Italics mine.
11. Keogh, *The Vatican, the Bishops, and Irish Politics 1919-1930*, p 113
12. Idem, p 262, fn 46
13. DDA. Govt politics (1). Duggan-Byrne, 15 March 1923
14. NAI. S.1437. Byrne-Cosgrave, 18 March 1923
15. DDA. Govt politics (1). 'Pres Exec Council'. Cosgrave-Byrne, 18 March
16. NAI. S. 1437. E. Duggan (Cosgrave's secretary)-Cosgrave, 20 March; Byrne-Cosgrave, 19 March 1923
17. UCDA. De Valera papers. P 150/1826. De Valera-Friends & Supporters, 19 May 1923
18. Idem, P. 150/1809. De Valera-Luzio, 30 April 1923
19. Idem, P. 150/1826. Notice/Letter, 19 May 1923
20. Keogh, *Ireland and the Vatican* ... p 27
21. ICRA. Hag 1/1923/528. Hagan-Mannix, 5 Oct 1923.
22. DDA. Govt politics (1). 'Office of President ...', Soden-Byrne, 13 April
23. Idem, Byrne-Mrs O'Kelly, no date
24. Idem, Byrne-Cosgrave
25. DDA. Govt politics, 1922-39 (2). A letter to Dr Byrne on 18 April had pointed out that the women had been on hunger strike for more than 22 days and had received the 'last sacrament'.
26. Idem, Govt politics (1). 'Office of President ...', Cosgrave-Byrne, 19 April. Italics mine.
27. Idem, Cosgrave-Byrne, 28 May 1923
28. Idem, 'Office of President ...', 1923
29. ICD, 1924 (1923), 17 June 1923, p 576
30. UCDA. Fitzgerald papers. p 80/1099 C1. Dr Charles O'Sullivan-B. McMahon Coffey, Cumann na nGaedheal, 10 July 1923
31. ICD, pp 577-8
32. ICRA. Hag 1/1923/321. Ml Cronin-Hagan, 19 June 1923
33. Idem, Hag 1/1923/533. P. Murphy, Roundwood, Wicklow, to Hagan, 8 October 1923, reported that he saw Seán T. after his release, 'he is looking well, the Chief is being treated well'.
34. ICD, 1924 (1923), 2 Sept 1923, pp 588-89
35. ICD, p. 590
36. DDA. 'Office of President ...', Cosgrave-Byrne, 26 Sept 1923
37. Idem, 'Governor General'. Healy-Byrne, 3 Oct 1923
38. Idem, 'Office of Pres', Cosgrave-Byrne, 28 Oct 1923
39. Idem, Govt politics (2). 'Office of President ...', Cosgrave-Byrne, Oct 1923
40. Idem, 21 Nov 1923. Also contains a typed document on the hunger-strikers
41. DDA. 'Governor General', Healy-Byrne, 22 Nov 1923
42. DDA. Govt politics (1). 'Office of President...,' Cosgrave-T. O'Donnell, 4 December.

43. DDA. Letter on Teacher Training, 21 June 1923, giving views of Bishops in response to a proposal from the Senate of NUI on 29 March.
44. DDA. Govt politics (2). 'Chaplains Correspondence, Feb-Oct 1923'; Byrne-O'Sullivan, 13 Feb 1923
45. Idem, Byrne-Mulcahy, July 1923
46. DDA. 'Bishops' Letters'. Byrne-Logue, 11 Dec 1923
47. Idem, Logue-Byrne, 17 Dec 1923
48. ICRA. Hag 1/1923/674 no date. 'The Pope refused to see them' in letter from Catholic Appeals Committee to Cardinal [Gasparri?] before their departure for Ireland
49. DDA. 'Bishops' Letters'. Byrne-Logue, 19 Dec 1923
50. ICD, 6 Nov, p 598
51. DDA. Govt politics (2) 1921-39. 'Dublin Corporation (1)', Mansion House Coal Fund: Irwin-Byrne, 22 Dec 1923
52. DDA. Govt politics (1). 'Dept Defence General Correspondence', 11 Dec 1923
53. ICD, 18 Nov 1923, p 600
54. Idem, 28 Nov, p 600
55. DDA. 'Religious Congregations'. Fahy-Byrne, 23 Dec 1923

CHAPTER EIGHT

1. DDA. Govt politics (2), 1922-39. 'Army Chaplains – health and vice issues, July 1923-Oct 1924
2. ICD, 26 Jan 1924, pp 553-4
3. Idem, pp 560-61
4. ICRA. Hag 1/1924/20. M. J. Curran-Hagan, 14 Jan 1924
5. DDA. 'Files General on Nuns and Brothers'
6. ICD, 22 March 1924, p 565
7. DDA. AB 7/ Lay 'Org-So' Box (1)
8. Interview with late Mgr Michael Nolan, 18 August 2008
9. DDA. Govt politics (1), file 'Dept of Finance', Letter of 14 Jan 1924; also re priests appointed to the committee, 10, 23 Jan 1936, and 1 Feb 1939
10. Idem, File on 'Governor General'
11. Idem, Govt politics (2). 'Garda Síochána, 1924-1940', letters 7, 12, 15 March 1924
12. DDA. No date on the document but enclosed with a letter for Mr Duggan, dated 4 March 1924
13. P. Murray, Oracles of God ..., fn, pp 113-14
14. NAI. S4127. Cosgrave-Downey, 21 Sept.1925
15. cit. Murray, op. cit., p 114
16. DDA. Abp Byrne-General McKeon, 14 May 1924
17. ICRA. Hag. 1/1924/36. Byrne-Hagan, 22 March 1924
18. Idem, Hag 1/1924/137. Curran-Hagan 23 March 1924
19. Idem, Hag 1/1924/217. O'Donnell-Hagan 12 May 1924
20. Idem, Hag 1/1924/ 287. 26 June 1924

21. Idem, Hag 1/1924/315. Curran-Hagan, 9 July 1924
22. ICD, 3 Feb 1924, p 555
23. Idem, 9 April, p 568
24. Idem, June 1924
25. Idem, July, p 586
26. ICD, 12 Nov, p 602
27. ICRA. Hag 1/1924/332. Seán T. Ó Ceallaigh-Hagan, 22 July 1924
28. DDA. Box Govt politics (2), File 1924-1939. Mrs Childers-Byrne, 27 Oct 1924
29. ICRA. Hag 1/1924/502
30. ICD, 18 Nov 1924, p 603
31. Idem, 30 Nov, p 609
32. Idem, p 549
33. Mary Purcell, *Matt Talbot and his times* (Dublin 1954), pp 234, 25-6
34. ICD, 25 Jan 1925, p 554
35. Idem, 31 Jan 1925
36. DDA. 'Bishops of Province of Armagh'. Bp Wm MacNulty-Byrne, 4 Feb 1924
37. DDA. Govt politics (1). Cosgrave-Byrne, 12 Feb 1925
38. Killaloe Diocesan Archives (KDA) F.4 F23. 'Letters of Significance', Cosgrave-Fogarty, 29 Jan 1925
39. Capitular appointments: Mgr James Dunne for dean; Fr Francis Wall PP for precentor; Mgr Patrick Walsh for chancellor
40. ICRA. Hag 1/1925/125. Byrne-Hagan, 8 March 1925
41. Idem, Hag 1/1925/425; based on file of the correspondence between Dempsey and the Archbishop, 14-17 Sept 1925
42. Kildare & Leighlin Archives, at Carlow College. PF/CBS/39. Byrne-Foley, 6 April 1925
43. Idem, PF/CBS/40. Byrne-Foley, Easter Monday
44. Idem, Foley-Byrne, 26 May 1925
45. Susan H. Wallace FSP, *Matt Talbot* (Boston 1940), p 83
46. Colm Kiernan ed, *Daniel Mannix and Ireland* (Dublin 1984), pp 190-91
47. ICRA. Hag 1/1925/ 298. Ó Ceallaigh-Hagan, 2 June 1925
48. Italics mine
49. Hagan-Prof Ml. J. Browne, 31 Oct 1925. Galway diocesan archives, cit P. Murray, *Oracles of God* ...,p 242, fn 444
50. DDA. Byrne-O'Donnell, Cardinal-Designate, 2 Dec 1925
51. ICD, (1926), 23 Dec 1925, p 560
52. DDA. File on 'Religious'. Fahy-Byrne, 4 Dec 1925

CHAPTER NINE

1. ICD, 1927 (1926), 14 Feb 1926
2. DDA. Govt politics (1) O'Higgins-Byrne, 5 Nov 1925 & 4 Jan 1926; and Private Secretary of Minister-Byrne, 14 Jan 1926, confirming the appointment of Cronin

3. Kieran Woodman, *Media Control in Ireland, 1923-1938* (Southern Illinois UP 1985), pp 40ff

4. DDA. Mgr Cronin's papers. Boylan-Byrne, 16 Oct 1929

5. Idem, undated 'note on the censorship of publications, for the use of his Grace, Archbishop'.

6. Idem, Dunne-Cronin, 19 Jan 1926.

7. Idem, 'Abp Walsh's Instructions on Censuring or Imprimatur for books', Abp's House, 30 Dec 1904

8. Idem, Fr P. Gannon-Cronin, 12 Jan 1928. Luigi Taparelli D'Azeglio SJ, 1793-1862, was one of the clearest political thinkers of the day. Editor of *La Civiltà Cattolica*, he was devoted to the church and yet ambitious for national unity. His dream was to see a union of Catholics and a liberation freed of anti-religious animus. See Walter V. Bangert, *A History of the Society of Jesus* (St Louis 1972), p 443

9. Armagh Diocesan Archives (ADA). MacRory papers, box 10, folder no 1. 'Rev Dr P. Coffey-Maynooth and Censorship–Dr Mac Caffrey, Maynooth', 7 March 1923

10. DDA. Mgr Cronin's papers. Memorandum sent under a covering letter to Dr P. Morrisroe, Bishop of Achonry, 11 Dec 1929. 'Dr Coffey's complaints about censorship', 11 Dec 1929, and attached letter from the Nuncio, 16 March 1931

11. DDA. Govt politics. 'Department of Education 1922-1929'. Pádraic Ó Brolacháin (Office of National Education)-Byrne, 17 Nov.- & 18 Dec 1926

12. ICD,1927 ('26), pp 573-4.

13. The Provisional Committee consisted of Michael J. Lennon, J. Durnin, SirJoseph Glynn, George Gavan Duffy BL, Patrick Waldron BL. Lennon was a district justice, Duffy was one of the signatories of the Treaty, Waldron was a prominent lawyer. Before long members included Mrs Berthon Waters, an economist, Eoin O'Keefe, owner of Duffy's Publishers and personal friend of Mr de Valera, as was Peadar O'Loghlan TD, Gabriel Fallon, a well-known writer and critic, and two senior civil servants, Maurice Moynihan and O. J. Redmond.

14. DDA. Mgr Cronin's papers. Article 1 of the Constitution.

15. cit. Curtis, *The Splendid Cause*, p 74, cf pp 73-76, and T. J. Morrissey, *A Man Called Hughes*, passim.

16. Curtis, pp 65-66. Decree 233.

17. Idem, p 67

18. DDA. 'Family and Student Days'. AB/7/a/1/1-12

19. Curtis, op. cit., pp 77-9

20. *The Leader*, 2 Nov 1929, pp 318-20, cit. Curtis, p 78

21. Souvenir programme of CYMS Federation Social Week, April 1924

22. Curtis, op. cit., pp 80-81

23. A.E. 'Twenty-Five Years of Nationality' in UCDA. Desmond Fitzgerald papers, P. 80/1094

24. DDA. Govt politics (2). 'President of Executive Council 1922-1939'. Cosgrave-Byrne, 16 Sept 1927
25. ADA. MacRory papers. T. O'Donnell-J. J. Walsh, 16 July 1928
26. DDA. Mac Rory-Byrne, 18 July 1928; and ADA. Mac Rory papers
27. Idem, Byrne-MacRory, 21 July 1928
28. DDA. Govt politics (2) 1922-39. 'Politics in General 1924-25, 1927'. Lemass-Byrne, 8 July 1927; Abp's Secretary-Lemass, 13 July 1927
29. DDA. Govt politics (1). 'Dept Justice'. Lemass-Dunne, 19 July 1927
30. UCDA. Patrick McGilligan's papers, P. 35b/112 (3) and P. 35b/112 (1).'The Church and the present position of the Saorstat. Abp Byrne's Pastoral', 16 July 1927
31. Italics mine
32. ICD, 1927, 1 July 1926, p 597
33. Idem, p 615
34. ICRA. Hag 1/1927/484. M. J. Curran-Hagan, 28 Sept 1927
35. ICD, 1928, 24 Oct 1927, p 613
36. Idem, pp 614-17
37. Idem, p 622
38. ADA. File on 'Irish Bishops'. John O'Donnell-Byrne, 30 Nov 1927
39. ICRA. Hag 1/1928/10. W. H. Grattan Flood, Co Wexford-Hagan, 8 Jan 1928
40. Idem, Hag 1/192785. S. T. Ó Ceallaigh-Hagan, 15 Feb 1927
41. Idem, Hag 1/1927/695. Dunne-Hagan, 27 Dec 1927
42. DDA. File on Religious. Ml Browne-Byrne, 16 Feb 1928
43. Italics in text
44. Italics mine
45. ICRA. Hag 1/1928/502 (1). E. R. Morrissey-Hagan, 29 Nov 1928
46. Idem, Hag 1/1928/584(1). P. Dunne-Hagan, 29 Dec 1928
47. *Black's Medical Dictionary* (London 1984), p 684.
48. Interview with the late Mgr Michael Nolan of Dublin Archdiocese, who kindly gave the author the benefit of his deep knowledge of the history of the archdiocese
49. DDA. 'Religious Congregations (Male)'. Fitzgerald-Byrne, 24 July 1928
50. Idem, Fr Sebastian-Byrne, 6 May & 26 May. Byrne had spoken frankly of the difficulty he experienced from superiors prior to Fr Sebastian
51. DDA. 'Religious Congregations'. Ml Browne-Byrne, 1 Aug 1928
52. DDA. Mac Rory-Byrne, 18 July 1928. ADA. Byrne-MacRory, 21 July 1928
53. Idem, File of 'Governor General'. Healy-Byrne, 9 Jan 1928
54. British Pathe newsreel, courtesy St Conleth's Catholic Heritage Association.

CHAPTER TEN

1. ICRA. Hag 1/1929/398. Seán T. Ó Ceallaigh-Hagan, 17 Nov 1929

2. Idem, Hag 1/1929/59. Fleming-Hagan, 5 Feb 1929
3. Idem, Hag 1/1929/76. Morrissey-Hagan, 15 Feb 1929
4. ICD, 1930, Lenten Pastoral 1929, pp 566-57
5. Gerry Keane, 'Centenary Celebrations of Catholic Emancipation Behind the Scenes', submitted in partial fulfilment of requirement for MA in Mater Dei Institute of Education, College of Dublin City University, 2004. Copy in DDA.
6. DDA. 'Irish Bishops. Minutes of Meetings, General Meeting, 21 June 1927', p 179, cit. G. Keane, op. cit., p 14.
7. ICD 1930 (1929 & Dec 1928), p 558
8. In addition, Mgr Wall and James Dunne, vicar-generals, were involved in the management of CTSI and kept a vigilant eye on events.
9. DDA. Govt politics (2). Garda Síochána, 1924-1940. O'Duffy-Byrne, 2 March 1924; Byrne-Duffy, 12 March
10. Already by 1924 there were 1,000 full time Pioneers and a further 1,000 temporary members. Gregory Allen, *The Garda Síochána: Policing Independent Ireland, 1922-82*, (Dublin 1992) pp 135-7
11. DDA. AB/7. Box 5. 'Lay Organisations: Emancipation Commemorative Committee 1928-1935', cit. G. Keane in op. cit., p 14
12. DDA. Idem. Commemorative Committee minutes, 25 May 1928
13. G. Keane, op. cit., p 16
14. *Irish News*, 18 June 1929: 'In O'Connell's Day. When will Northern Ireland see its new deliverer?' cit. Gillian McIntosh in 'Acts of National Communion: the Centenary Celebrations for Catholic Emancipation, the forerunner of the Eucharistic Congress' in Joost Augusteijn ed, *Ireland in the 1930s: New Perspectives* (Dublin 1999), p 85
15. cit. G. McIntosh, in ch. cit. in op. cit., p 86
16. NAI. 'Catholic Emancipation Centenary Celebrations 1929.' Taoiseach's Dept. S 5835. Sec. to Dept of Defence-Members of Exec Council, 8 March 1929
17. NAI. Idem. Cab 4/78 – item No 5
18. *Irish Independent*, 19 June 1929. cit. McIntosh, loc. cit., p 89
19. *Irish News*, 18 June 1929, cit. McIntosh
20. ICD, 1930 (1929), p 581
21. ICD gives the number as only a quarter of a million.
22. ICD, p 587
23. *Catholic Emancipation Centenary Record*, p 35
24. *Irish Independent*, 24 June 1929
25. ICD, 1930 (1929), p 587
26. *Catholic Emancipation Record*, p 39, cit. McIntosh, op. cit., pp 90-91
27. *Irish Independent*, 24 June 1929
28. DDA. Govt politics (1). 'The Dept of President of Exec Council 1924-1930', Cosgrave-Fr Dunne, 24 June 1929
29. ICD, idem, pp 591-2
30. D. Keogh, *The Vatican, the Bishops and Irish Politics 1939-1939*, p 153

31. D. Keogh, *Ireland and the Vatican. The Politics and Diplomacy of Church-State Relations, 1922-1960*, p 37

32. Idem, pp 53-54

33. Idem, p 65

34. NAI. 'Appointment of Papal Nuncio'. Taoiseach's Dept. S. 5954A

35. Idem, Cosgrave-Fogarty, 28 Nov 1929, cit. Keogh, op. cit., p 64

36. Keogh, Idem, p 65. Also see Gogarty-Hagan, ICRA. Hag 1/29 Nov/1929

37. Holograph letter, dated 15 May 1929. ICRA Hag 1/1929/219

38. Fogarty-Hagan, 29 Nov 1929. ICRA. Hag 1/1929/418

39. Keogh, *The Vatican, the Bishops and Irish Politics*, p 157

40. Keogh, *Ireland and the Vatican...*, p 54

41. Idem, p 57

42. NAI. Taoiseach's Dept. S. 5954A. Bewley-Walshe, 25 Nov 1929

43. DDA. Mageean-Byrne, 6 June 1929

44. Idem, MacRory-Byrne, 26 Nov 1929

45. Idem. A letter from John Condon OSA, 25 Nov 1929, to Abp Byrne observed that his not getting the red hat was 'a disappointment to the archdiocese, and a grievous disappointment to many of your friends'.

46. ICRA. Magennis-Hagan, 1 Jan 1930. Hag 1/1929/2. Also in Keogh, *Ireland and the Vatican*, p 69, which wrongly gives the date as 31 Dec 1929 and also has a misreading – 'surprised by how ill he looks' instead of 'how well he looks'.

47. ADA. Byrne-MacRory, 30 Dec 1929. The letter arrived in the Irish College on 9 Jan 1930 and only reached MacRory on 14 January, according to a note appended to the letter

48. ICD, 1931 (1930), p 56

49. cit. Keogh, *Ireland and the Vatican*, p 66

50. DDA. 'Holy See', box file. 'Nuncio'. Draft of letter, no date

51. Idem, Note on the draft letter

52. DDA. J. P. Walshe-Dunne, 5 Jan 1930

53. cit. UCDA. McGilligan papers. P 35b/113 (2)

54. ICRA. Deignan-Hagan, 26 Jan 1930. Hag 1/1930/16. Also Keogh, *Ireland and the Vatican ...*, p 74

55. Keogh, *The Vatican, the Bishops and Irish Politics*, p 157

56. Keogh, *Ireland and the Vatican ...*, p 75

57. Abp McQuaid to Sean Hughes SJ, secretary of the Catholic Headmasters' Association. Mentioned to the author by Hughes.

58. DDA. Box on 'Holy See'. File 'Nuncio'. Byrne-Nuncio, 14 May 1930

59. DDA. Govt politics (1). 'Dept of Justice'. J. Fitzgerald Kenny-Byrne, 17 Jan 1929

60. UCDA. Fitzgerald papers. P. 80/851 (C 20). 'Office of President-Minister for Defence'

61. DDA. Govt politics.(1) Cosgrave-Byrne, 20 Dec 1929

62. ICD, 1931(1930), pp 584-5

63. *Irish Independent*, 14 July 1930
64. DDA. 'New Cathedral, Merrion Square'. *Nunc Dimmitis* = In more modern usage, 'Now I can die in peace'.
65. ICD, 1931 (1930), pp 615-17
66. Idem, 23 Nov 1930, pp 646-49
67. Keogh, *Twentieth-Century Ireland: Nation and State*, (Dublin 1994), p 33
68. DDA. Govt politics. 'Dept of Education 1922-1939'. Joseph O'Neill-Byrne, 13 Oct 1930
69. Idem, J. M. O'Sullivan-Mgr Waters PP,VG, 12 Aug 1930
70. Idem, O'Sullivan-Byrne, 7 Oct 1930

CHAPTER ELEVEN

1. DDA. Box on 'Vicars General'. Francis Wall, Bishop of Thasos,-My Dear Dean, no name, 19 Aug.1931: 'His Grace ... gives us all the usual powers while he is on vacation at Delgany, just as if he were away from Ireland.'
2. DDA. Mgr Cronin papers. Cronin-Byrne, 29 Sept 1932: 'The writer is evidently an ill-conditioned fellow ... I should not care to see your Grace bothered about him ... Mgr Walsh or myself will deal with the matter.'
3. DDA. 'St Vincent de Paul Society'. Statement for 1931
4. DDA. Original fuller ms of Dr Collier's panegyric
5. DDA. 'Religious Congregations'. Fahy-Byrne, 1 Jan, 5 March 1931
6. NLIA. Shane Leslie diary, 11 April 1931, Ms 23, 382
7. ICD. 1932 (1931), pp 628-31
8. DDA. Govt politics (1). 'Office of President of Exec Council'
9. Emmet O'Connor, *Reds and the Green. Ireland, Russia and Communist Internationals, 1919-43* (Dublin 2004), pp 174-5
10. DDA. Govt politics (1). 'President of Exec Council'
11. Idem, Govt politics (2). 'Politics – General 1931'. Maud Gonne MacBride-Byrne, 10 June 1931
12. Idem, 'Lord Mayor of Dublin', 24, 25 June 1932
13. Among those who brought their problems to Armagh at times were: Rev J. C. McQuaid, Francis O'Reilly (CTSI), Paddy Belton during the Spanish Civil War, and Frank Fahy TD, with respect to Austrian refugees.
14. Frank Aiken-MacRory, 19 Oct 1931. ADA. MacRory papers, box 4, 'Government', folder no 11. Many of Aiken's former colleagues were in the IRA, and he was friendly with Sean Murray, a leading figure in the Irish Communist Party. See O'Connor, *The Red and the Green*, p 187
15. O'Connor, op. cit., ch 7 'Bolshevising Irish Communism, 1929-1931', esp pp 159-60
16. Idem, p 173
17. T. J. Morrissey, *William O'Brien, 1881-1968*, (Dublin 2007), pp 255-6, and chs 15 & 17 on fear of communism and its infiltration of the Labour Party.

18. ADA. MacRory papers. Byrne-MacRory, 3 April 1931. Italics in text
19. NAI. Dept Foreign Affairs, 2001/20/36. 'Irish Clergy Rome'. Bewley-Secretary (J. J. Walshe), 22 April 1931
20. NLIA. Letters to Hanna Sheehy Skeffington, Ms. 33,606 (21). Sr M. Columba-Sheehy Skeffington, 14 March 1932
21. Keogh, *The Vatican, the Bishops and Irish Politics*, p 182, including an interview with Prof T. D. Williams
22. NAI. Dept Foreign Affairs. 2001/20/36. 'Irish Clergy Rome', 14 April 1931
23. Idem, 13 March 1931
24. Idem, Bewley-Secretary (J. J. Walshe), 22 April 1931
25. ADA. MacRory papers. Byrne-MacRory, 12 March 1932. *Ecclesia de intentione non judicat* = 'The Church does not judge the intention', can only judge what is perceptible.
26. ICD, 1933, 5 June 1932, pp 590-96
27. ICD, 1934 (1933), pp 597-8
28. DDA. 'Eucharistic Congress'. MacRory-Byrne, 8 June 1932
29. Idem, Draft of letter, Byrne-MacRory, 9 June 1932. Italics mine
30. Idem, MacRory-Byrne, 16 June 1932
31. This account is based on the late Mgr Michael Nolan's research presented in an unpublished article 'A Tale of Two Gangways', which he kindly made available to the author on 29 June 2008
32. ICD, 1933 (1932), p 604. cf. pp 598-604
33. ICD, pp 604-13
34. Idem, pp 610-616
35. Idem, pp 633-37
36. J. A. Gaughan, ed, *Memoirs of Senator Joseph Connolly, 1885-1961. A founder of modern Ireland* (Dublin 1996), pp 287-9
37. ICD, p 654
38. Idem
39. DDA. 'Memorabilia'. AB/7/a/1/1-12
40. ICD 1934 ('33), p 595
41. Idem, p 584
42. Idem, pp 579-80
43. Idem, p 591
44. Idem, pp 597, 613
45. Photograph in Blackrock Annual, courtesy Fr Sean Farragher, Blackrock College
46. DDA. Govt politics. 'Dept Education 1922-'39, file 13'. O'Connell-Byrne, 9 March 1933
47. Idem, O'Connell-Byrne, 13 July
48. Idem, pp 597-99. 'Laymen', no mention of the considerable role of women!
49. Idem, p 607
50. Idem, p 595

CHAPTER TWELVE

1. F .O. C. Meenan, *St Vincent's Hospital 1834-1994. An Historical and Social Portrait* (Dublin 1995), pp 106-7
2. Idem
3. Idem, p 108
4. Tony Farmar, *Hollis Street 1894-1994. TheNational Maternity Hospital. A Centenary History* (Dublin 1995), pp 85-88
5. Idem.
6. DDA. 'Hospitals-General. Byrne'. 475. M ffrench Mullen (secretary)-Byrne, 10.Dec 1935
7. Idem. Draft of his Grace's statement to the deputation from St Ultan's Hospital, 20 Dec 1935
8. Idem. Byrne-City Manager, 13 Dec 1937
9. Idem. McQuaid-Byrne, 13 Dec 1937, re City Manager's suggestion about His Grace seeing the Lord Mayor
10. Idem. 21 Jan 1938
11. Idem. McQuaid-Byrne, 14 March 1939
12. Idem. McQuaid-Byrne, 16 Jan 1940 and McQuaid-Dunne, 18 Jan 1940
13. DDA. 'Hospitals-Hospitals' Commission, 1934 and 1935', No 474. Memo by Dr J. Stafford Johnson on a hospital system for a Catholic population that was 'two-thirds controlled by non-Catholics'. Also Byrne-Sir Joseph Glynn, 24 April 1934, on discrimination against the Mater Hospital. And see Henry Moore, of the board of the Mater, to Byrne, thanking him for his help in relation to the Sweeps' grant, and Byrne-Moore, 8 February, 'rejoicing that the Mater, in which I have so deep an interest, is coming well out of the Sweeps …'
14. DDA 'Hospitals-Hospitals' Commission 1934-35'. Rev Mother Superior General-Byrne, 9 July 1934
15. Idem. Byrne-Mother General, 2 May 1939
16. Idem. Dr Thomas O'Farrell-Dunne, 28 Oct 1939; and on 17 Nov 1939 when he quotes Arthur Cox
17. Idem. Mother General-Bishop (Wall), 27 April 1940
18. Idem. No 475. Mother Superior-Byrne 2 Dec 1927
19. J. Cooney, *John Charles McQuaid* (Dublin 1999), pp 86, 88-89
20. DDA. McQuaid Memorandum, AB8/A/VI/63, cit. Cooney, op. cit., pp 83-4
21. DDA. McQuaid-Byrne, 16 June 1934
22. D. O'Leary, *Vocationalism and Social Catholicism in Twentieth Century Ireland* (Dublin 2000), pp 51-2.
23. Cooney, op. cit., p 85
24. DDA. McQuaid-Byrne, 5 April 1934
25. DDA. 'Bishops of Province of Armagh'. Down and Connor, Feb 1934. Italics mine
26. DDA. Box on 'VG's Meetings
27. ICD, 2 Oct 1934
28. ICD, 1936 (1935)

29. Idem, p 600
30. Idem, p 601
31. DDA. Mageean- Byrne, 5 Aug 1935
32. ICD, 12 Nov 1935, p 637
33. ICD, 1935 (for 1934), p 577
34. Idem 1936 (1935), p 594
35. M. Curtis, *The Splendid Cause*, p 190
36. ICD, 30 June, p 617
37. Curtis, op. cit., pp 190-91
38. Hartigan, PhD thesis, Maynooth
39. Curtis, p 52
40. DDA. AB7/Lay Org Box. Duff-Byrne, 24 Nov 1928
41. Leon Ó Broin, *Frank Duff* (Dublin 1982), p 23
42. Idem
43. Idem, p 25
44. Frank Duff, *Miracles on Tap* (Dublin 1989), p 28, cit. Hartigan, PhD thesis, p 153
45. Hartigan, op. cit.; L. Ó Broin, op. cit., pp 25-6
46. Ó Broin, op. cit., p 26. Also consulted John Finnegan, *The Story of Monto*.
47. Ó Broin, p 27
48. Information courtesy of late Mgr Michael Nolan on 18/8/08
49. Idem
50. DDA. 'Legion of Mary'. Duff-Byrne, 28 Nov 1928
51. Idem, Duff-Byrne, 11 Dec 1928
52. Ó Broin, op. cit., p 33
53. Idem, p 38
54. Idem, p 35
55. DDA. 'Legion of Mary' file
56. Idem
57. Idem, Wall-Byrne, 15 April 1929
58. Duff-Celia Shaw, 29 May 1934, cit. Ó Broin, p 37
59. Ó Broin, cit. p 38, no date given
60. DDA. 'Legion of Mary', copies of letters 3 & 6 January 1935, and newspaper cuttings
61. See Curtis. Index to op. cit., pp 324ff
62. ICD,1936, 7 April 1935, p 603
63. Idem, Nov pp 638-9

CHAPTER THIRTEEN

1. DDA. Govt politics (2). 'Office of President'. Draft letter Byrne-De Valera, 10 Feb 1936; De Valera-Byrne, 14 Feb 1936
2. DDA. Govt politics (1). 'Dept Posts & Telegraphs', 17 Feb 1936
3. DDA. Seamus Hughes supplied a list from a confidential document in 1932, and a Patrick Cunningham provided further information on 27 Feb 1934

4. CYMS, Costelloe Correspondence, cit. Curtis, p 168
5. Curtis, pp 168-9
6. Idem
7. Cooney, op. cit., p 91
8. Idem, p 570
9. Idem, 6 Jan 1935, pp 578-581
10. DDA. 'Dept Education'. Edwards-Byrne, 26 Feb 1936
11. Idem, Byrne-Derrig, 3 March 1936
12. Idem, file 14. Derrig-Byrne, 5 March 1936
13. *The Belvederian* 1940, p 29
14. KDA. F.4 F.15. Walsh-Fogarty, 1 Jan 1940
15. Idem, 5 Jan 1940
16. ICD 1937 ('36), pp 586, 596, 601. *Missa Cantata*=a sung Mass
17. Idem, p 630
18. DDA. Byrne-Paschal Robinson, 1936. No other date
19. DDA. 'Legion of Mary'. Duff-Byrne, 15 May 1936, enclosing a copy of the letter of Miss Meagher to Miss Cruice (Cruise?) concerning her visit to Dr Wall on 11 May 1936
20. Hartigan, op. cit., pp 166-7
21. DDA. 'Legion of Mary'. Fr P. Teenwen for Bishop Lammens of Roermond-Byrne, 22 May 1939
22. DDA. Beige folder 'Spanish Civil War'. MacRory-Byrne, 30 Nov 1936
23. DDA. Govt politics (1). 'Dept of Foreign Affairs'. Chas Bewley-Byrne, 23 Oct 1936
24. A. W. Palmer, *A Dictionary of Modern History, 1789-1945* (Penguin 1964).
25. DDA. Govt politics (2). 'Foreign Embassies'. *Te Deum*=The beginning of a hymn in Latin sung on occasions of thanksgiving: *Te Deum laudamus* –'We praise thee, O God'
26. Idem. 'Politics in General, 1926-'39', 10 Aug 1936
27. See Oliver MacDonagh, *Ireland: The Union and its Aftermath* (London 1977), pp 130ff
28. ICD 1938 (37), p 594
29. DDA. Bp Keogh-Byrne, 29 June 1937
30. DDA. 'Bps of Province of Tuam'. Byrne-Browne, 2 Oct 1937
31. DDA. 'Memorabilia' AB/7/1/1/1-12
32. Idem
33. ICD 1938 (37), 1 Jan 1937, p 578
34. Idem, p 595
35. Idem, pp 634-5 and note
36. Idem, p 584
37. DDA. Govt politics (1). 'Office of President of Exec Council … 1936-'39'; Moynihan-O'Donnell, 12 Jan 1937
38. DDA. 'Dept Defence', Brennan-Byrne, 22 Jan 1937
39. Curtis, op. cit., pp.= 169-171
40. DDA. Govt politics (2) on communism, Feb 1937

41. T. J. Morrissey, *William O'Brien, 1881-1968*, pp 285-6
42. DDA. 'Communism & Labour Party', Report 11 Oct 1937
43. ICD 1938, 21 June, p 603
44. Ferghal McGarry, 'General O'Duffy, the National Corporate Party and th Irish Brigade' in Joost Augusteijn ed, *Ireland in the 1930s. New Perspectives*, pp 117, 140, 142
45. DDA. Govt politics. O'Duffy-Dunne, 23 Nov 1937
46. ICD,1938, 12 Oct 1937, pp 631-2. Also a printed copy in Bp Keane's papers, Limerick Diocesan Archives (LDA)
47. cf Bob Doyle, *Brigadista. An Irishman's fight against Fascism* (Dublin 2006), pp 221-27
48. Curtis, op. cit., pp 195ff
49. D. Keogh, *The Vatican, the Bishops and Irish Politics*, p 212
50. Lord Longford & T. O'Neill, *Éamon de Valera* (London 1970), pp 296-7. O'Neill & Ó Fiannachta, *De Valera*, vol 2 (Dublin 1970), p 335
51. D. Keogh, op. cit., pp 219-220
52. ICD 1939 (end of 1937 and 1938), 29 Dec 1937, p 613
53. Idem, p 614
54. DDA. Passport particulars
55. ICD, 1939 (1938), 27 Feb 1938, p 622
56. Idem, p 630
57. NLIA. Ms 22,3669. Shane Leslie papers. Robinson-Leslie, 19 May 1938
58. DDA. MacRory-Byrne, no date, but June 1938
59. DDA. 'Religious Congregations'. Fr Lawrence-Byrne, 30 June 1938
60. ICD, 1939, 6 Nov 1938, pp 660-61
61. Idem, pp 661-62
62. *Irish Independent*, 29 Aug 1938
63. DDA. Govt politics (1). 'Dept Posts & Telegraphs', 29 Nov 1938

CHAPTER FOURTEEN

1. DDA. 'Dept Education, file 16, 1922-'39'. P. Breathnach-Byrne, 9 Feb 1939
2. ICD 1940 ('39), p 630; and Keogh, *Ireland and the Vatican*, p 141
3. Idem, p 632
4. Keogh, *Ireland and the Vatican*, p 142
5. ICD, p 636
6. DDA. Govt politics (1). 'Uachtarán na hÉireann'. Dunphy-Glennon, 21 March 1939; Glennon-Dunphy, 29 March
7. ICD, 24 April, pp 639-40
8. Idem, pp 641-2
9. DDA. Govt politics (1) Sean T. O'Kelly-Byrne, 27 May 1939
10. Draft reply written on O'Kelly letter
11. DDA. Mgr Cronin papers. R. Devane-Byrne, 8 June 1939
12. DDA. 'Hospitals – General', blue folder. McQuaid-Byrne, 24 June 1939

13. Appeared in *Evening Herald*, 9 Feb 1940
14. DDA. 'Dept of Defence – general correspondence'. Sec of Dept-O'Donnell, 12 July 1939
15. DDA. Govt publications. 'Dept.Posts & Telegraphs'. Brereton-Dunne, 12 July, 1 August. Dunne-Brereton, 12 August 1939
16. DDA. Bp Fogarty-Byrne, 27 Aug 193
17. Idem, 20 Oct 1939. Italics mine
18. ICD, 1940, p 662
19. DDA. 'New Cathedral Merrion Sq', 22 Nov 1939. R.Ryan, O'Hagan & Son-Patrick Dunne
20. KDA. F.4 F.15. P. J. Walsh-Fogarty, 1 Jan 1940
21. Idem, Walsh-Fogarty, 5 Jan 1940
22. DDA. 'Dept Education, box file 14'. McQuaid-O'Donnell, 9 Jan 1940 and DDA. 'Religious' Reynolds-Byrne, 11 Jan 1940
23. DDA. 'Holy See' box. 'Nuncio file'. P. Robinson-O'Donnell, 12 Jan 1940
24. KDA. Loc. cit. Walsh-Fogarty, 26 Jan 1940
25. DDA. Original, unpublished text of Collier's panegyric, p 16
26. *Irish Independent*, 14 Feb 1940
27. Collier, p 7
28. ICD, 1941, pp 634-5
29. Dr Byrne's successor, Dr McQuaid, endeavoured to carry on his plans for the cathedral but ran into opposition from De Valera, who had other plans for Merrion Square, and also into shortage of funds in time of war and subsequent recession. See Cooney, *John Charles McQuaid*.
30. DDA. Original text of Collier's panegyric
31. *Irish Press*, 10 Feb.= 1940
32. DDA. 'Abp Byrne. Unsorted Material'. De Valera-Dr Wall, 19 Feb 1940
33. DDA. Original text of Dr Collier's address
34. ICD 1941, p 644
35. *Irish Press*, 14 Feb 1940
36. DDA. Obituary Letters, 12 Feb 1940
37. DDA. 'Abp Byrne. Unsorted Material'. File on his estate
38. Information courtesy of Fr Bill McKenna SJ, whose family were well acquainted with the Boylan family
39. Information courtesy Mgr Michael Nolan
40. KDA. Loc cit. Walsh-Fogarty, 14 Nov 1940
41. Idem, 24 Nov, 1940
42. Keogh, *Ireland and the Vatican*, pp 145-6
43. Fr Seán Farragher CSSp informed the present author that he clearly recalled hearing the story but could not now recall who told him. He thought that the original source was likely to have been Fr O'Donnell, the archbishop's secretary, who had been at school in Blackrock. Anecdotes flourished in relation to Dr McQuaid. Mr Matt Russell told me that his family had the story that when the dying Dr Byrne heard of Dr McQuaid's appointment he declared

'The Diocese is Saved". Another version has Dr McQuaid visiting the ailing archbishop who said to Dr Wall 'The diocese is saved'. All this months before Dr McQuaid's appointment, or before his name was mentioned as a strong candidate!

44. Cooney, p 114
45. I am indebted for this information about the nuncio's reports to Rome to Fr Marcel Chappin SJ, the archivist of the Secretariat of State, the Vatican.
46. DDA. Obituary cuttings. *The Times*, 10 Feb 1940
47. Archbishop Byrne finds no mention in the *Oxford Companion to Irish History*; none in *A Dictionary of Irish Biography*; and not even in *Dublin's Famous People*.

Index